Noah Webster

Dissertations on the English Language

Noah Webster

Dissertations on the English Language

ISBN/EAN: 9783337295974

Printed in Europe, USA, Canada, Australia, Japan

Cover: Foto ©Thomas Meinert / pixelio.de

More available books at **www.hansebooks.com**

DISSERTATIONS

ON THE

ENGLISH LANGUAGE :

WITH NOTES,

HISTORICAL AND CRITICAL.

To which is added,

BY WAY OF APPENDIX,

AN E S S A Y ON

A

REFORMED MODE OF SPELLING,

WITH

DR. *FRANKLIN's* ARGUMENTS ON THAT SUBJECT.

BY NOAH WEBSTER, JUN. ESQUIRE.

————PRIMA DISCENTIUM ELEMENTA, IN QUIBUS ET
IPSIS PARUM ELABORATUR.   *TACITUS.*

PRINTED AT *BOSTON*, FOR THE AUTHOR,
BY ISAIAH THOMAS AND COMPANY,
MDCCLXXXIX.

———

DEDICATIONS are uſually deſigned to flatter the Great, to acknowlege their ſervices, or court their favor and influence. But very different motives have led me to prefix the venerable name of FRANKLIN to this publication.

RESPECT for his Excellency's talents and exertions, as a great Philoſopher and a warm Patriot, I feel in common with all the lovers of ſcience and freedom; but my peculiar admiration of his character, ariſes from conſidering it as *great* in *common things.*

HIS

His Excellency has not labored to perplex himfelf and confound his countrymen with ingenious theories in ethics, and unintelligible fpeculations in theology and metaphyfics. He has not compiled volumes to prove or difprove the probability of univerfal falvation, or the eternal duration of future punifhments; content with a plain doctrine, taught by philofophy and common fenfe, and confirmed by chriftianity, that virtue and happinefs, vice and punifhment, are infeparably connected, and that "if we do well here, we fhall fare well hereafter." In the moft elevated ftations of life, his Excellency has never been above a conftant application to fome ufeful bufinefs; thus complying with that precept of the fourth command, "*fix days fhalt thou labor and do all thy work,*" which is as pofitive an injunction, and as binding upon all men, as the firft article, "*remember the Sabbath day, to keep it holy.*"

In

IN his philofophical refearches, he has been guided by experiment, and fought for *practical truths.* In the world, he has been induftrious to collect *facts,* (which compofe all our knowlege) and apply them to the moft ufeful purpofes of government, agriculture, commerce, manufactures, rural, domeftic and moral economy. In communicating his ideas he does not facrifice truth to embellifhment. His ftile is plain and elegantly neat; and his remarks are not fo general as to leave his ideas indefinite and obfcure. His pen follows his thoughts, and confequently leads the reader, without ftudy, into the fame train of thinking. In fhort, he writes for the child as well as the philofopher, and always writes well, becaufe he never takes pains to write.

VIOLENTLY attached to no political party, he labors to reconcile contending factions in government. Convinced, by the experience of a long life, that all men are liable to err, and acknowleging "that he has often found himfelf miftaken, and

 had

had occasion to change his opinions," he consents to measures which his judgement tells him are *theoretically wrong*, when the voices of a majority declare them to be *practically right*.

HE never attempts to usurp the divine prerogative of controling opinions; never charges another with ignorance, knavery and folly, nor endeavors to stab his reputation, for not subscribing a particular creed; much less does he ever assume a dictatorial authority, and sentence to final damnation, those who have the same chance of being right as himself, and whose conduct, whatever may be their opinions, is regulated by the rules of moral and social virtue.

FOR these reasons, as well as for the age, the eminent rank and public merits of this illustrious defender of American freedom, I revere a character equally known and respected in this and foreign countries.

HARTFORD, *May*, 1789.

PREFACE.

PREFACE.

YOUNG gentlemen who have gone through a courfe of academical ftudies, and received the ufual honors of a Univerfity, are apt to contract a fingular ftiffnefs in their converfation. They read Lowth's Introduction, or fome other grammatical treatife, believe what they read, without examining the grounds of the writer's opinion, and attempt to fhape their language by his rules. Thus they enter the world with fuch phrafes as, *a mean, averfe from, if he have, he has gotten,* and others which they deem *correct*; they pride themfelves, for fome time, in their fuperior learning and peculiarities; till further information, or the ridicule of the public, brings them to ufe the language of other people.

SUCH has been my progrefs, and that of many of my cotemporaries. After being fome years in that excellent fchool, the world, I recommenced my ftudies, endeavored, not merely to learn, but to underftand, the *a, b, c,* of the Englifh language, and in 1783 compiled and publifhed the Firft Part of my Grammatical Inftitute. The favorable reception of this, prompted me to extend my original plan, which led to a further inveftigation of the principles of language. After all my reading and obfervation for the courfe of ten years, I have been able to unlearn a confiderable part of what I learnt in early life; and at thirty years of age, can, with confidence, affirm, that our modern grammars have done much more hurt than good. The authors have labored to prove, what is obvioufly abfurd, viz. that our language is not made right; and in purfuance of this idea, have tried to make it over again, and perfuade the Englifh to fpeak by Latin rules, or by arbitrary rules of their own. Hence they have rejected many phrafes of pure Englifh, and fubftituted thofe which are neither Englifh nor fenfe. Writers and Grammarians have attempted for centuries to introduce a fubjunctive mode into Englifh, yet without effect;

effect ; the language requires none, diftinct from the indicative ; and therefore a fubjunctive form ftands in books only as a fingularity, and people in practice pay no regard to it. The people are right, and a critical inveftigation of the fubject, warrants me in faying, that common practice, even among the unlearned, is generally defenfible on the principles of analogy, and the ftructure of the language, and that very few of the alterations recommended by Lowth and his followers, can be vindicated on any better principle than fome Latin rule, or his own private opinion.

Some compilers have alfo attempted to introduce a *potential mode,* where they arrange thofe phrafes that have the *auxiliary* verbs, as they are called, *can, may,* &c. But all the helping verbs are principal verbs, and the verb following them is generally in the infinitive. *I can go, he may write, we fhall fee,* &c. are only a cuftomary ellipfis of *I can to go, he may to write, we fhall to fee* ; and are no more a potential mode than *I dare go, we faw him rife.*

In the indeclinable parts of fpeech, all authors were miftaken, till Mr. Horne Tooke explained them : Our conjuctions are moftly verbs in the imperative mode : Our adverbs and prepofitions are moftly verbs, nouns and adjectives, either feparate or combined ; and the proper definition of adverb and prepofition, is, " a word, or union of words, without the ordinary rules of government." *Becaufe* is a compound of the verb *be,* in the imperative, and the noun *caufe* ; *otherwife* is merely a corruption of *other ways* ; *wherefore* is a corruption of the Roman *qua-re,* with the addition of *for* ; *wifely* is nothing more than the two adjectives *wife like.* So that in many cafes, the want of a fpace between two words, or of the ufual rules of government, is the only circumftance that diftinguifhes them from ordinary nouns and verbs ; that is, the only thing that makes them *adverbs* or *prepofitions* ; fuch as, *becaufe, always, beyond, before, behind, forward, backward.* In fhort, had the Englifh never been acquainted with Greek and Latin, they
would

would never have thought of one half the diftinctions and rules which make up our Englifh grammars.

THE object of grammar, in a living language, is ufually mifunderftood. Men often fuppofe they muft learn their native language by grammar ; whereas they learn the language firft, and grammar afterwards. The principal bufinefs of a compiler of a grammar is, to feparate *local* or *partial* practice from the *general cuftom* of fpeaking ; and reject what is *local*, whether it exifts among the great or the fmall, the learned or ignorant, and recommend that which is univerfal, or general, or which conforms to the analogies of ftructure in a language. · Whether the words *means*, *pains*, *news*, ought to have been ufed originally in the fingular form ; or *fheep*, *deer*, *hofe*, in the plural ; or in other words, whether the language is well made, or might in fome inftances. be mended, are queftions of little confequence now ; it is our bufinefs to find what the Englifh language *is*, and not, how it *might have been made*. The moft difficult tafk now to be performed by the advocates of *pure Englifh*, is to reftrain the influence of men, learned in Greek and Latin, but ignorant of their own tongue ; who have laboured to reject much good Englifh, becaufe they have not underftood the original conftruction of the language. Should the following Differtations produce this effect, in the fmalleft degree, they may render effential fervice to our native tongue.

THESE Differtations derive their origin from acccidental circumftances, the hiftory of which is briefly this. The neceffity of fecuring the copy right of the Grammatical Inftitute in the different ftates, feconded by a defire of being acquainted with my own country, induced me to fufpend my profeffional purfuits, and vifit the Southern States. While I was waiting for the regular Seffions of the Legiflatures, in thofe ftates which had not paffed laws for protecting literary property, I amufed myfelf in writing remarks on the Englifh Language, without knowing to what purpofe they would be applied. They were begun in Baltimore in

the

the fummer of 1785; and at the perfuafion of a friend, and the confent of the Rev. Dr. Allifon, whofe politenefs deferves my grateful acknowlegements, they were read publicly to a fmall audience in the Prefbyterian Church. They were afterward read in about twenty of the large towns between Williamfburg in Virginia, and Portfmouth in New Hampfhire. Thefe public readings were attended with various fuccefs; the audiences were generally fmall, but always refpectable; and the readings were probably more ufeful to myfelf than to my hearers. I every where availed myfelf of the libraries and converfation of learned men, to correct my ideas, and collect new materials for a treatife, which is now prefented to the public.

THERE are few men who do not at times find themfelves at a lofs, refpecting the true pronunciation of certain words. Having no principles or rules, by which they can folve queftions of this kind, they imitate fome gentleman, whofe abilities and character entitle his opinions to refpect, but whofe pronunciation may be altogether accidental or capricious.

WITH refpect to many words, I have been in the fame uncertainty; and ufed formerly to change my pronunciation, in conformity to the practice of the laft man of fuperior learning whom I heard fpeak. My enquiries have been directed to inveftigate fome principles, which will remove all difficulties in pronunciation; the refult of which is a full fatisfaction in my own mind as to almoft every particular word. Whether the principles will prove equally fatisfactory to others, it is impoffible now to determin. Moft of the varieties in pronunciation are mentioned in the fecond and third Differtations; thofe which are not, the reader will be enabled to adjuft on the principles there unfolded.

IT will be obferved, that many of the remarks in this publication are not new. This will be no objection to the main defign; as fome remarks which are found in other philological treatifes, are neceffary to the general

plan

plan of this. A great part however of my opinions are new, and many of them directly oppofed to the rules laid down by former writers.

In the fingularity of fpelling certain words, I am authorized by Sidney, Clarendon, Middleton, Blackftone, Afh, or other eminent writers, whofe authority, being fupported by good principles and convenience, is deemed fuperior to that of Johnfon, whofe pedantry has corrupted the purity of our language, and whofe principles would in time deftroy all agreement between the fpelling and pronunciation of words. I once believed that a reformation of our othography would be unneceffary and impracticable. This opinion was hafty ; being the refult of a flight examination of the fubject. I now believe with Dr. Franklin that fuch a reformation is practicable and highly *neceffary*.

It has been my aim to fupport my opinions by numerous and refpectable authorities. In fome cafes, an author is quoted, but not the chapter or page. This was owing to neglect in firft tranfcribing paffages, which was often done, without any defign to ufe the quotations as authorities in the prefent work ; and the paffages could not afterwards be found without great trouble, and fometimes the author could not be a fecond time procured. In a very few inftances, a quotation has been taken at fecond hand on the credit of a faithful writer ; but never when I could obtain the original work. Many other ancient anthors would have been confulted, had it been practicable ; but the moft valuable of thefe are very fcarce, and many of them I have not heard of in America. It is to be lamented that old authors are neglected, and modern libraries compofed of abridgements, compilations, fhort effays, &c. which are calculated only for communicating fome general information and making fuperficial fcholars, to the prejudice of profound learning and true fcience.*

The

* ——" a fungous growth of Novels and pamphlets, the meaner productions of the French and Englifh preffes, in which it is to be feared (the reader) rarely finds any rational pleafure, and more rarely ftill, any folid improvement."——Harris. Hermes. 474.

The American ſtudent is often obliged, and too often diſpoſed, to drink at the ſtreams, inſtead of mounting to the ſources of information.

For the remarks on Engliſh Verſe in the fifth Diſſertation, I am much indebted to the celebrated author of M'Fingal, a gentleman who has " drank deep of the Pierian Spring," and who is equally diſtinguiſhed for wit, erudition, correct taſte, and profeſſional knowlege. ·

In explaining the principles of the language, I have aimed at perſpicuity, with a view to render the work uſeful to all claſſes of readers. The Notes at the end are deſigned to illuſtrate ſome points by authorities or arguments that could not be properly arranged in the text ; and to throw ſome light on ancient hiſtory. To the curious enquirer, theſe may be as entertaining as the Diſſertations themſelves. In two or three inſtances, I have found occaſion to change my opinion, ſince the publication of the Inſtitute ; but a future edition of that work will be conformed to the criticiſms in theſe Diſſertations.

To thoſe who aſk where a writer was born and educated, before they can aſcertain the value of his writings, I can only obſerve, it is expected this publication will fare like all others. Men every where ſuppoſe that their own ſtate or country has ſome excellence that does not belong to their neighbors ; and it is well, if they do not arrogate a ſuperiority in *every* reſpect. They think their own colleges the beſt ; their profeſſional men the moſt learned, and their citizens the moſt liberal and polite. I have been witneſs to numberleſs remarks and inſinuations of this kind in almoſt every ſtate in the union ; and after perſonal obſervation, can affirm that they generally proceed from groſs ignorance, or unpardonable prejudice. But it is very natural for men to think and ſay all theſe things of *home*, when they have little or no knowlege of any thing *abroad*.

Convinced that a writer is apt to overlook his own miſtakes, when they are very obvious to a reader, I have ſubmitted theſe Diſſertations to the criticiſm of good

judges

judges of the fubject, with full liberty of altering, amending and expunging any part of the work ; by which means feveral paffages have been omitted and others corrected. Still there may be faults in the book ; and as truth is the object of my enquiries, whenever the friendly critic fhall point out any errors, either in fact or opinion, it will be my pride and pleafure to acknowlege and correct them. Many years experience has taught me that the public, when well informed, ufually form a very juft opinion of a man and his writings, and I am perfectly difpofed to acquiefce in their decifion.

P. S. SEVERAL Effays, on more important fubjects, intended for an Appendix to this work, are neceffarily referved for a future volume.

CONTENTS.

CONTENTS.

A fketch

DISSERTATION V.

NOTES, HISTORICAL AND CRITICAL.

APPENDIX.

DIRECTIONS.

THE founds of the vowels, marked or referred to in the fecond and third Differtations, are according to the Key in the Firft Part of the Inftitute. Thus:

	a	e	i	o	u	y
Firft found,	late,	feet,	night,	note,	tune,	fky,
Second	hat,	let,	tin,		tun,	glory,
Third,		law,	fraud			
Fourth,		afk,	father,			
Fifth,		not,	what,			
Sixth,		prove,	room,			

The capitals, included in brackets [ ] in the text, are references to the Notes at the end.

DISSERTATIONS

ENGLISH LANGUAGE, &c.

DISSERTATION I.

I. Introduction.—II. History of the English Language.—III. Remarks.

INTRODUCTION.

REGULAR study of language has, in all civilized countries, formed a part of a liberal education. The Greeks, Romans, Italians and French succeſſively improved their native tongues, taught them in Academies at home, and rendered them entertaining and uſeful to the foreign ſtudent.

B

THE

THE English tongue, tho later in its progress towards perfection, has attained to a considerable degree of purity, strength and elegance, and been employed, by an active and scientific nation, to record almost all the events and discoveries of ancient and modern times.

THIS language is the inheritance which the Americans have received from their British parents. To cultivate and adorn it, is a task reserved for men who shall understand the connection between language and logic, and form an adequate idea of the influence which a uniformity of speech may have on national attachments.

IT will be readily admitted that the pleasures of reading and conversing, the advantage of accuracy in business, the necessity of clearness and precision in communicating ideas, require us to be able to speak and write our own tongue with ease and correctness. But there are more important reasons, why the language of this country should be reduced to such fixed principles, as may give its pronunciation and construction all the certainty and uniformity which any living tongue is capable of receiving.

THE

THE United States were settled by emi-
grants from different parts of Europe.
But their descendants mostly speak the
same tongue ; and the intercourse among
the learned of the different States, which
the revolution has begun, and an American Court will perpetuate, must gradually
destroy the differences of dialect which our
anceftors brought from their native countries. This approximation of dialects will
be certain ; but without the operation of
other caufes than an intercourse at Court,
it will be flow and partial. The body of
the people, governed by habit, will still
retain their respective peculiarities of
fpeaking ; and for want of fchools and
proper books, fall into many inaccuracies,
which, incorporating with the language of
the state where they live, may imperceptibly corrupt the national language. Nothing but the establifhment of fchools and
fome uniformity in the ufe of books, can
annihilate differences in fpeaking and preferve the purity of the American tongue.
A famenefs of pronunciation is of confiderable confequence in a political view ; for
provincial accents are difagreeable to ftrangers and fometimes have an unhappy effect upon the focial affections. All men
have local attachments, which lead them

to believe their own practice to be the least exceptionable. Pride and prejudice incline men to treat the practice of their neighbors with some degree of contempt. Thus small differences in pronunciation at first excite ridicule—a habit of laughing at the singularities of strangers is followed by disrespect—and without respect friendship is a name, and social intercourse a mere ceremony.

These remarks hold equally true, with respect to individuals, to small societies and to large communities. Small causes, such as a nick-name, or a vulgar tone in speaking, have actually created a dissocial spirit between the inhabitants of the different states, which is often discoverable in private business and public deliberations. Our political harmony is therefore concerned in a uniformity of language.

As an independent nation, our honor requires us to have a system of our own, in language as well as government. Great Britain, whose children we are, and whose language we speak, should no longer be *our* standard; for the taste of her writers is already corrupted, and her language on the decline. But if it were not so, she is

at

at too great a diftance to be our model, and to inftruct us in the principles of our own tongue.

It muft be confidered further, that the Englifh is the common root or ftock from which our national language will be derived. All others will gradually wafte away—and within a century and a half, North America will be peopled with a hundred millions of men, *all fpeaking the fame language.* Place this idea in comparifon with the prefent and poffible future bounds of the language in Europe—confider the Eaftern Continent as inhabited by nations, whofe knowlege and intercourfe are embarraffed by differences of language; then anticipate the period when the people of one quarter of the world, will be able to affociate and converfe together like children of the fame family.* Compare this profpect, which is not vifionary, with the ftate of the Englifh language in Europe, almoft confined to an Ifland and to a few millions of people; then let

reafon

---

* Even fuppofing that a number of republics, kingdoms or empires, fhould within a century arife and divide this vaft territory; ftill the fubjects of all will fpeak the fame language, and the confequence of this uniformity will be an intimacy of focial intercourfe hitherto unknown, and a boundlefs diffufion of knowlege.

reafon and reputation decide, how far A-
merica fhould be dependent on a tranfat-
lantic nation, for her ftandard and improvements in language.

LET me add, that whatever predilection
the Americans. may have for their native
European tongues, and particularly the
Britifh defcendants for the Englifh, yet
feveral circumftances render a future feparation of the American tongue from the
Englifh, neceffary and unavoidable. The
vicinity of the European nations, with the
uninterrupted communication in peace,
and the changes of dominion in war, are
gradually affimilating their refpective languages. The Englifh with others is fuffering continual alterations. America,
placed at a diftance from thofe nations,
will feel, in a much lefs degree, the influence of the affimilating caufes ; at the
fame time, numerous local caufes, fuch as
a new country, new affociations of people,
new combinations of ideas in arts and fcience, and fome intercourfe with tribes
wholly unknown in Europe, will introduce
new words into the American tongue.
Thefe caufes will produce, in a courfe of
time, a language in North America, as different from the future language of England,

land, as the modern Dutch, Danish and Swedish are from the German, or from one another : Like remote branches of a tree fpringing from the fame ftock ; or rays of light, fhot from the fame center, and diverging from each other, in proportion to their diftance from the point of feparation.

WHETHER the inhabitants of America can be brought to a perfect uniformity in the pronunciation of words, it is not eafy to predict ; but it is certain that no attempt of the kind has been made, and an experiment, begun and purfued on the right principles, is the only way to decide the queftion. Schools in Great Britain have gone far towards demolifhing local dialects—commerce has alfo had its influence—and in America thefe caufes, operating more generally, muft have a proportional effect.

IN many parts of America, people at prefent attempt to copy the Englifh phrafes and pronunciation—an attempt that is favored by their habits, their prepoffeffions and the intercourfe between the two countries. This attempt has, within the period of a few years, produced a multitude

tude of changes in thefe particulars, efpecially among the leading claffes of people. Thefe changes make a difference between the language of the higher and common ranks ; and indeed between the *fame* ranks in *different* ftates ; as the rage for copying the Englifh, does not prevail equally in every part of North America.

But befides the reafons already affigned to prove this imitation abfurd, there is a difficulty attending it, which will defeat the end propofed by its advocates ; which is, that the Englifh themfelves have no ftandard of pronunciation, nor can they ever have one on the plan they propofe. The Authors, who have attempted to give us a ftandard, make the practice of the court and ftage in London the fole criterion of propriety in fpeaking. An attempt to eftablifh a ftandard on this foundation is both *unjuft* and *idle*. It is unjuft, becaufe it is abridging the nation of its rights: The *general practice* of a nation is the rule of propriety, and this practice fhould at leaft be confulted in fo important a matter, as that of making laws for fpeaking. While all men are upon a footing and no fingularities are accounted vulgar or ridiculous, every man enjoys perfect liberty.

But

But when a particular set of men, in exalted stations, undertake to say, " we are the standards of propriety and elegance, and if all men do not conform to our practice, they shall be accounted vulgar and ignorant," they take a very great liberty with the rules of the language and the rights of civility.

But an attempt to fix a standard on the practice of any particular class of people is highly absurd : As a friend of mine once observed, it is like fixing a light house on a floating island. It is an attempt to *fix* that which is in itself *variable* ; at least it must be variable so long as it is supposed that a local practice has no standard but a *local practice* ; that is, no standard but *itself*. While this doctrine is believed, it will be impossible for a nation to follow as fast as the standard changes—for if the gentlemen at court constitute a standard, they are above it themselves, and their practice must shift with their passions and their whims.

But this is not all. If the practice of a few men in the capital is to be the standard, a knowlege of this must be communicated to the whole nation. Who shall

do

do this ? An able compiler perhaps attempts to give this practice in a dictionary; but it is probable that the pronunciation, even at court, or on the stage, is not uniform. The compiler therefore muft follow his particular friends and patrons; in which cafe he is fure to be oppofed and the authority of his ftandard called in queftion; or he muft give two pronunciations as the ftandard, which leaves the ftudent in the fame uncertainty as it found him. Both thefe events have actually taken place in England, with refpect to the moft approved ftandards; and of courfe no one is univerfally followed.

Besides, if language muft vary, like fafhions, at the caprice of a court, we muft have our ftandard dictionaries republifhed, with the fafhionable pronunciation, at leaft once in five years; otherwife a gentleman in the country will become intolerably vulgar, by not being in a fituation to adopt the fafhion of the day. The *new* editions of them will fuperfede the *old*, and we fhall have our pronunciation to re-learn, with the polite alterations, which are generally corruptions.

Such are the confequences of attempting to make a *local* practice the *ftandard* of
language

language in a *nation*. The attempt muſt keep the language in perpetual fluctuation, and the learner in uncertainty.

IF a ſtandard therefore cannot be fixed on local and variable cuſtom, on what ſhall it be fixed ? If the moſt eminent ſpeakers are not to direct our practice, where ſhall we look for a guide ? The anſwer is extremely eaſy ; the *rules of the language itſelf*, and the *general practice of the nation*, conſtitute propriety in ſpeaking. If we examine the ſtructure of any language, we ſhall find a certain principle of analogy running through the whole. We ſhall find in Engliſh that ſimilar combinations of letters have uſually the ſame pronunciation ; and that words, having the ſame terminating ſyllable, generally have the accent at the ſame diſtance from that termination. Theſe principles of analogy were not the reſult of deſign—they muſt have been the effect of accident, or that tendency which all men feel towards uniformity.* But the

* THIS diſpoſition is taken notice of by Dr. Blair, Lect. 8. Where he obſerves, "that tho the formation of abſtract or general conceptions is ſuppoſed to be a difficult operation of the mind, yet ſuch conceptions muſt have entered into the firſt formation of languages"—" this invention of abſtract terms requires no great exertion of metaphyſical capacity"---

the principles, when eftablifhed, are pro-
ductive of great convenience, and become
an authority fuperior to the arbitrary deci-
fions of any man or clafs of men. There
is one exception only to this remark : When
a deviation from analogy has become the
univerfal practice of a nation, it then takes
place of all rules and becomes the ftandard
of propriety.

THE two points therefore, which I conceive to be the bafis of a ftandard in fpeaking, are thefe; *univerfal undifputed practice*,
and the *principle of analogy*. *Univerfal
practice* is generally, perhaps always, a
rule of propriety ; and in difputed points,
where people differ in opinion and practice, *analogy* fhould always decide the controverfy.

THESE are authorities to which all men
will fubmit—they are fuperior to the o-
pinions

pacity"---" Men are *naturally* inclined to call all thofe objects which refemble each other by one common name---
We may daily obferve this practifed by children, in their
firft attempts towards acquiring language."

I CANNOT, with this great critic, call the procefs by which
fimilar objects acquire the *fame* name, an act of *abftraction*,
or the name an *abftract term*. Logical diftinctions may lead
us aftray. There is in the mind an *inftinctive difpofition*, or
principle of affociation, which will account for all common
names and the analogies in language.

pinions and caprices of the great, and to the negligence and ignorance of the multitude. The authority of individuals is always liable to be called in queftion——but the unanimous confent of a nation, and a fixed principle interwoven with the very conftruction of a language, coeval and co-extenfive with it, are like the common laws of a land, or the immutable rules of morality, the propriety of which every man, however refractory, is forced to acknowlege, and to which moft men will readily fubmit. Fafhion is ufually the child of caprice and the being of a day; principles of propriety are founded in the very nature of things, and remain unmoved and unchanged, amidft all the fluctuations of human affairs and the revolutions of time.

It muft be confeffed that languages are changing, from age to age, in proportion to improvements in fcience. Words, as Horace obferves, are like leaves of trees; the old ones are dropping off and new ones growing. Thefe changes are the neceffary confequence of changes in cuftoms, the introduction of new arts, and new ideas in the fciences. Still the body of a language and its general rules remain for ages the fame, and the new words ufually conform

to

to thefe rules ; otherwife they ftand as exceptions, which are not to overthrow the
principle of analogy already eftablifhed.

BUT when a language has arrived at a
certain ftage of improvement, it muft be
ftationary or become retrograde ; for improvements in fcience either ceafe, or become flow and too inconfiderable to affect
materially the tone of a language. This
ftage of improvement is the period when a
nation abounds with writers of the firft
clafs, both for abilities and tafte. This
period in England commenced with the
age of Queen Elizabeth and ended with
the reign of George II. It would have
been fortunate for the language, had the
ftile of writing and the pronunciation of
words been fixed, as they ftood in the reign
of Queen Ann and her fucceffor. Few
improvements have been made fince that
time ; but innumerable corruptions in
pronunciation have been introduced by
Garrick, and in ftile, by Johnfon, Gibbon
and their imitators.*   THE

*THE progrefs of corruption in language is defcribed with
precifion, and philofophical reafons affigned with great
judgement, by that celebrated French writer, Condillac, in his
Origin of Human Knowledge.   Part 2.

   " IT is nearly the fame here as in phyfics, where motion,
the fource of life, becomes the principle of deftruction.
                                        When

THE great Sidney wrote in a pure ftile ; yet the beft models of purity and elegance, are the works of Sir William Temple, Dr. Middleton,

When a language abounds with original writers in every kind, the more a perfon is endowed with abilities, the more difficult he thinks it will be to furpafs them. A mere equality would not fatisfy his ambition ; like them he wants the pre-eminence. He therefore tries a new road. But as every ftile analagous to the chara&ter of the language and to his own, has been already ufed by preceding writers, he has nothing left but to deviate from analogy. Thus in order to be an original, he is obliged to contribute to the ruin of a language, which, a century fooner, he would have helped to improve.

" THO fuch writers may be criticized, their fuperior abilities muft ftill command fuccefs. The eafe theie is in copying their defe&ts, foon perfuades men of indifferent capacities, that they fhall acquire the fame degree of reputation. Then begins the reign of ftrained and fubtle conceits, of affe&ted antithefes, of fpecious paradoxes, of frivolous and far-fetched expreffions, of new-fangled words, and in fhort, of the jargon of perfons, whofe underftandings have been debauched by bad metaphyfics. The public applauds ; foolifh and ridiculous writings, the beings of a day, are furprifingly multiplied ; a vicious tafte infe&ts the arts and fciences, which is followed by a vifible decreafe of men of abilities."

ONE would think that Condillac had defigned here to give a defcription of the prefent tafte of the Englifh writers, and a ftate of their literature.

THE foregoing fentiments feem to have been borrowed from Velleius Paterculus. Hift. Rom. L. 1. Cap. 17.

THE fame paffage is copied by Sig. Carlo Denina, Profeffor of Eloquence and Belles Lettres in the Univerfity of Turin,

Middleton, Lord Bolingbroke, Mr. Addifon and Dean Swift.   But a little inferior
to thefe, are the writings of Mr. Pope, Sir
Richard Steele, Dr. Arbuthnot, with fome
of their cotemporaries.   Sir William Blackftone has given the law ftile all the elegance and precifion of which it is capable.
Dr. Price and Dr. Prieftley write with purity, and Sir William Jones feems to have
copied the eafe, fimplicity and elegance of
Middleton and Addifon.

But how few of the modern writers
have purfued the fame manner of writing?
Johnfon's ftile is a mixture of Latin and
Englifh ; an intolerable compofition of
Latinity, affected fmoothnefs, fcholaftic accuracy and roundnefs of periods.   The benefits derived from his morality and his erudition, will hardly counterbalance the mif-
chief done by his manner of writing.   The
names of a Robertfon, a Hume, a Home
and a Blair, almoft filence criticifm ; but
I muft repeat what a very learned Scotch
gentleman once acknowleged to me,
                              " that

in his " Revolutions of Literature," page 47 ; and if I miftake not, the fentiments are adopted by Lord Kaims, in his
Sketches of the Hiftory of Man.

Similar reafons may be affigned for the prevalence of an
affected and vitious pronunciation.

" that the Scotch writers are not models of
the pure English ftile." Their ftile is
generally ftiff, fometimes very awkward,
and not always correct.* Robertfon labors his ftile and fometimes introduces a
word merely for the fake of rounding a
period. Hume has borrowed French idioms without number; in other refpects
he has given an excellent model of hiftorical ftile. Lord Kaims' manner is ftiff;
and Dr Blair, whofe ftile is lefs exceptionable in thefe particulars, has however introduced, into his writings, feveral foreign
idioms and ungrammatical phrafes. The
Scotch writers now ftand almoft the firft
for erudition; but perhaps no man can
write a foreign language with genuin purity.

GIBBON's harmony of profe is calculated
to delight our ears; but it is difficult to
comprehend his meaning and the chain of
his

---

* DR. Witherfpoon is an exception. His ftile is eafy,
fimple and elegant. I confider Dr. Franklin and Dr.
Witherfpoon as the two beft writers in America. The
words they ufe, and their arrangement, appear to flow fpon-
taneoufly from their manner of thinking. The vaft fuperiority of their ftiles over thofe of Gibbon and Gillies, is owing to this circumftance, that the two American writers
have beftowed their labor upon *ideas*, and the Englifh hiftorians upon *words*.

C

his ideas, as faft as we naturally read ; and almoft impoffible to recollect them, at any fubfequent period. Perfpicuity, the firft requifite in ftile, is fometimes facrificed to melody ; the mind of a reader is conftantly dazzled by a glare of ornament, or charmed from the fubject by the mufic of the language. As he is one of the *firft*, it is hoped he may be the *laft*, to attempt the gratification of our *ears*, at the expenfe of our *underftanding*.

Such however is the tafte of the age ; fimplicity of ftile is neglected for ornament, and fenfe is facrificed to found.*

ALTHO

---

* THE fame tafte prevailed in Rome, under the Emperors, when genius was proftituted to the mean purpofes of flattery. "It muft be acknowleged indeed, that after the diffolution of the Roman republic, this art began to be perverted by being too much admired. Men grew exceffively fond of the numerous ftile, and readily facrificed the ftrength and energy of their difcourfe to the harmony of their language. Pliny the younger often complains of this contemptible affectation : And Quintilian fpeaks of certain profe writers in his time, who boafted that their compofitions were fo ftrictly numerous, that their hearers might even beat time to their meafures. And it fhould feem that even in Tully's time, this matter was carried to excefs ; fince even then the orators dealt fo much in numbers, that it was made a queftion, wherein they differed from the Poets."——Mafon's Effay on the Power and Harmony of Profaic Numbers. Introduction, page 4.

THIS was an abufe of the art. Melody fhould be ftudied ; but not principally.

ALTHO ſtile, or the choice of words and manner of arranging them, may be neceſſarily liable to change, yet it does not follow that pronunciation and orthography cannot be rendered in a great meaſure permanent. An orthography, in which there would be a perfect correſpondence between the ſpelling and pronunciation, would go very far towards effecting this deſireable object. The Greek language ſuffered little or no change in theſe particulars, for about a thouſand years; and the Roman was in a great degree fixed for ſeveral centuries.

RAPID changes of language proceed from violent cauſes; but theſe cauſes cannot be ſuppoſed to exiſt in North America. It is contrary to all rational calculation, that the United States will ever be conquered by any one nation, ſpeaking a different language from that of the country. Removed from the danger of corruption by conqueſt, our language can change only with the ſlow operation of the cauſes before-mentioned and the progreſs of arts and ſciences, unleſs the folly of imitating our parent country ſhould continue to govern us, and lead us into endleſs innovation. This folly however will loſe its influence gradually, as our particular habits of re-

ſpect

fpect for that country fhall wear away, and
our *amor patriæ* acquire ftrength and infpire us with a fuitable refpect for our own
national character.

WE have therefore the faireft opportunity of eftablifhing a national language,
and of giving it uniformity and perfpicuity, in North America, that ever prefented
itfelf to mankind.   Now is the time to begin the plan.   The minds of the Americans are roufed by the events of a revolution ; the neceffity of organizing the political body and of forming conftitutions of
government that fhall fecure freedom and
property, has called all the faculties of the
mind into exertion; and the danger of
lofing the benefits of independence, has
difpofed every man to embrace any fcheme
that fhall tend, in its future operation, to
reconcile the people of America to each
other, and weaken the prejudices which
oppofe a cordial union.

MY defign, in thefe differtations, is critical-
ly to inveftigate the rules of pronunciation
in our language ; to examin the paft .and
prefent practice of the Englifh, both in the
pronunciation of words and conftruction
of fentences ; to exhibit the principal differences

ferences between the practice in England and America, and the differences in the feveral parts of America, with a view to reconcile them on the principles of *univerfal practice* and *analogy*. I have no fyftem of my own to offer; my fole defign is to explain what I fuppofe to be authorities, fuperior to all private opinions, and to examin local dialects by thofe authorities.

Most writers upon this fubject have fplit upon one rock : They lay down certain rules, arbitrary perhaps or drawn from the principles of other languages, and then condemn all Englifh phrafes which do not coincide with thofe rules. They feem not to confider that grammar is formed on language, and not language on grammar. Inftead of examining to find what the Englifh language *is*, they endeavor to fhow what it *ought to be* according to their rules. It is for this reafon that fome of the criticifms of the moft celebrated philologers are fo far from being juft, that they tend to overthrow the rules, and corrupt the true idiom, of the Englifh tongue. Several examples of this will appear in the courfe of thefe Differtations.

To learn the Englifh language in its purity, it is neceffary to examin and com-

C 3

pare

pare the beſt authors from Chaucer to the preſent time. In executing the following work, the moſt approved compilations have been conſulted, and the opinions of the learned authors conſidered as reſpectable, not as deciſive, authorities. The language itſelf has been examined with great induſtry, with a view to diſcover and defend its principles on the beſt grounds, *analogies in ſtruɛture*, and *immemorial uſage*. I have had recourſe to the works of authors who wrote prior to Chaucer, and have even borrowed ſome light upon this ſubject, from the early ages of Gothic ignorance. Believing, with the author of " Diverſions of Purley," that the peculiar ſtructure of our language is Saxon, and that its principles can be diſcovered only in its Teutonic original, it has been my buſineſs, as far as the materials in my poſſeſſion would permit, to compare the Engliſh with the other branches of the ſame ſtock, particularly the German and the Daniſh. Theſe reſearches have thrown light upon the meaning and conſtruction of particular phraſes, and enabled me to vindicate ſome expreſſions in the language which are often uſed, but generally condemned by grammarians.

My

My knowlege of the practice of speaking in different parts of America, is derived from perfonal obfervation. My knowlege of the paft and prefent ftate of the language in England, is taken from the writers who have treated exprefsly of the fubject.* The authorities neceffary to prove particular points will be quoted, as occafion fhall require.

The tafk of examining words cannot be agreeable to a writer, nor can his criticifms be very entertaining to the reader. Yet this tafk I have impofed upon myfelf; for I believe it the only method to correct common miftakes. A general rule may be fufficient for a claffical fcholar, who makes it his bufinefs to apply the rule to all cafes : But moft readers muft have their particular errors laid before their eyes, or they will not difcover them.

To offer to correct the miftakes of others, is alfo a *hazardous* tafk, and commonly expofes a man to abufe and ill will. To avoid this I can only fay, that my motives for the undertaking were not local nor perfonal; my enquiries are for truth, and my criticifms, it is hoped, will be marked with candor.

BUT

---

* WALLIS, Johnfon, Kenrick, Sheridan, with a multitude of inferior compilers.

BUT before I proceed to explain the principles of pronunciation, it is neceſſary to give a ſketch of the hiſtory of our language from the earlieſt times, and endeavor to diſcover from what ſources it is derived.

HISTORY *of the* ENGLISH LANGUAGE.

THE firſt correct accounts we have of Britain were given by Julius Ceſar, who invaded and conquered the ſouthern parts of the iſland, about fifty four years before the Chriſtian era.* Tacitus, in his *Life of Julius Agricola*, has deſcribed the natives of the iſland, and given it as his opinion, that they came from Gaul (now France.) The inhabitants of Caledonia, now Scotland, in the color of their hair and ſize of their limbs, reſembled the Germans. Some appearances in the people of the more

ſouthern

* HE found the inhabitants of the maritime towns ſome-what civilized,* and in their manners reſembling the Gauls, with whom they had ſome commercial intercourſe. It is probable that the Britons came originally from the continent, from which their iſland is ſeparated by a ſtrait of no great extent.

* "Ex his omnibus, long eſunt humaniſſimi, qui Cantium incolunt : Quæ regio eſt maritima omnis ; *neque multum* a Gallica differunt conſuetudine."——Ceſar De Bello Gallico, Lib. 5.

ſouthern parts of the iſland, and their poſition with reſpect to Spain, indicated *their* deſcent from the ancient Iberi.   But thoſe who inhabited the ſhores, oppoſite to France, reſembled the Gauls, in their religious ceremonies, their courage, and particularly in their language : " Sermo haud multum diverſus."*

IT is an uncontroverted point, that the primitive language of Britain was the ſame as that of Gaul.† This language was denominated the *Celtic*, from the *Celtæ*, or *Keltæ*, a famous tribe of people that inhabited Gaul.   Many writers ſuppoſe the Celtic to have been the primitive elementary language, from which moſt, or all the preſent languages of Europe, and ſome of the languages of Aſia and Africa, are derived.   Some authors go ſo far as to aſſert that the Greek and Roman may be traced to the ſame ſource.   To prove this opinion well founded, they endeavor to diſcover an affinity between theſe languages, by analizing words in each, and tracing them to the ſame elements or monoſyllabic

* TACITUS. Jul. Agric. Vit 11.

† " ERAT autem priſca iſthæc Gallis et Britannis communis lingua, ultra omnium hiſtoriarum memoriam antiquæ." ——Wallis Gram.

bic roots.   In this they have fucceeded fo
far as to difcover a great number of words,
which, with fmall dialectical variations,
are common to the Greek and Latin
and to moft of the living languages of
Europe.   Perhaps thefe radicals, common
to all languages of which we have any
knowlege, were fufficient to form a fimple language, adequate to the purpofes of
fpeech among rude nations. [A]

But as the firft inhabitants of the earth
had, for many ages, no method of fixing
founds, or very imperfect methods, their
language muft have been liable to confiderable mutations, even when they lived and
converfed together. But after they had
feparated from each other, by extending
their fettlements into diftant regions, and
an intercourfe between the colonies had
ceafed, their languages muft have in a great
meafure loft their affinity to each other.
The radical words, common to all, muft
have affumed dialectical diftinctions, and
new objects and inventions, peculiar to the
different tribes, muft have originated new
terms among each, to which the others
were ftrangers. Different nations would
advance, by very different degrees of rapidity, to a ftate of civilization, and as

words

words multiply with ideas, one language would become more copious than another, as well as more regular and polifhed. In the courfe of many centuries, thefe caufes would obfcure the common radicals, and make fuch acceffions of new words to each dialect, as to form them all into diftinct languages. An uncivilized people have occafion for few words; perhaps five or fix hundred would anfwer all their purpofes. And if we fhould thoroughly examin any of the prefent languages of the world, we fhould probably find that the roots of the moft copious do not amount to more than that number. The Greek, it is faid, may be traced to about three or four hundred radical words. Thefe roots or elementary words are ufually monofyllables, and moftly names of fenfible objects. By applying thefe names figuratively, favages make them anfwer the purpofe of expreffing other ideas, and by combining them in an almoft infinite variety of ways, civilized nations form copious and elegant languages.

Thus it happens that in the exifting languages of Europe, there are many words evidently the fame; the orthography and pronunciation do not exactly coincide in all

the

the countries where they are ufed ; yet the refemblance is obvious in *thefe* particulars; and with refpect to their *meaning*, there is fuch an affinity, as to demonftrate that the nations, in whofe languages they are found, all fprung from the fame parents.

THE primitive language of Europe probably retained its original form and purity in the Weft, much later than on the borders of Afia ;* for the Gauls and Britons had made lefs advances in knowlege, than the eaftern nations, and had probably ⋅ fuffered fewer fhocks from war and conqueft. The Greeks firft formed an elegant language out of the barbarous dialects ⋅fpoken on the borders of the Egean Sea. The Romans afterwards did the fame in Italy, and gradually changed the languages of the countries which they conquered, by introducing their own. It was the policy of the Roman ftate to make *fubjects*, rather than *flaves*, of their conquered nations ; and the introduction of their own tongue among them was confidered as a neceffary ftep towards removing prejudices, facilitating an intercourfe with their provinces, and

reconciling

---

* THIS is faid upon the hypothefis, that the ancient Celtic or Britifh had a common origin with the Hebrew, Phenician and Greek. For proofs of this, fee the notes at the end.

reconciling diftant nations to the Roman government.

Julius Cesar found the Gauls and Britons at peace, united by a fimilarity of manners and language, and by a famenefs of intereft. His conqueft of their countries made fome inroads upon their language. But altho the Romans had poffeffion of thefe countries more than four hundred years, during which time Roman garrifons were ftationed in Gaul and Britain, the young men of both countries were drafted into the Roman fervice, and many Britifh youth went to Rome for an education, ftill the native Celtic language remained without material alteration. It is obvious indeed that many of the higher claffes of people were acquainted with Latin, and there are traces of that language ftill found among the Welfh, the defcendants of the ancient Britons. But the body of the people, either for want of opportunity to learn the Latin, or thro an inveterate hatred of their conquerors, continued wedded to their native tongue. This would have ftill been the language of France and England, had it not fuffered more violent fhocks, than by the Roman conquefts.

But

But in the fifth century, the southern parts of Europe began to be alarmed by the invasion of the Goths, Vandals, Huns and other fierce barbarians from the North. For three centuries, all the fertile provinces of the Roman empire were ravaged by these hardy invaders, the most of whom settled in the countries which they conquered.

These nations, mixing with the natives of the country where they settled, changed or corrupted the primitive language. From the jargon of Celtic and Roman, blended with the language of the Franks, Normans, Burgundians, &c. sprung the modern French. From the mixture of Latin, with the language of the Huns, Lombards, &c. sprung the present Italian. From a similar composition of Latin, with the language of the Visigoths and other northern tribes, and some remains of the Moorish language, left in Spain by the Saracens, are formed the modern Spanish and Portuguese.

In the general desolation, occasioned by these conquests, the island of Britain did not escape. The Saxons, a tribe of northern nations, which inhabited the country

try

try now called Denmark, or the fhores of the Baltic, now within the Empire of Germany, invaded Britain, foon after the Roman legions had been called home to defend the Empire againft other tribes of barbarians. It is faid the Saxons were at firft invited to affift the Britons againft the inroads of the Picts or Scots, and that having defeated the invaders, they were tempted, by the fertility of the foil, to remain in the ifland, and afterwards took poffeffion of it for themfelves.

But whatever was the firft caufe of their leaving their native country, it is certain, that numerous bodies of adventurers, at different times, went over and feated themfelves in the ifland. They did not ceafe till they had poffeffed themfelves of all the fertile and cultivated parts of England. The univerfality of the conqueft is demonftrated by the total change of language; there being no more affinity between the Saxon or Englifh, and the ancient Britifh, than between any two languages of Europe.

The Britifh however was not loft. The brave inhabitants, who furvived the liberty of their country, and could not brook

the

the idea of living with their conquerors, retired to the countries within the mountains on the weſt of the iſland, now called *Wales* and *Cornwall*, where they maintained their independence for many centuries, and where their language is ſtill preſerved. The Welſh and the Corniſh therefore are the pureſt remains of the primitive Celtic language.

To theſe we may add the Armoric, or language of the Bas Breton, on the coaſt of France ; the inhabitants of which are genuin deſcendants of the old Britons. The time and occaſion of this ſettlement in France are not certain. Perhaps a body of Britons were driven thither by the Saxon conqueſt of England ; or what is more probable, as it is a tradition among the people, the Armoricans are the poſterity of ſome Britiſh ſoldiers, who had been in the Roman army when it was called to Italy to defend the empire, and on their return, being informed that the Saxons had taken poſſeſſion of their native country, ſeated themſelves on the oppoſite coaſt of France.*

BUT

---

* TEMPLE's Introd. to Hiſt. of England.

BUT whatever was the cauſe of the ſettlement, the language of the people is the
old Britiſh or Celtic ; for altho they muſt
have been ſeparated from their countrymen about twelve or fourteen hundred
years, yet there is ſuch an affinity ſtill between the Welſh and the Armoric, that
the Welſh ſoldiers, who paſſed thro Brittany in a late war,* could converſe famil-
iarly with the inhabitants.   If any other
proof than this were neceſſary to convince
the reader, we might mention the name of
this province, *Brittany*, and produce a long
catalogue of Armoric words, collated with
the Welſh and Corniſh.

ONE would think that the Iriſh, by reaſon
of their vicinity to England, would have
ſpoken the ſame language ; yet it is found
that the old Iriſh tongue has very little affinity with the Welſh.   Sir William Temple aſſerts† that the Erſe, or Caledonian
language, and the old Iriſh, which are radically the ſame, and ſpoken alſo on the Iſle
of Man, have no affinity with any other
language now ſpoken.   But the celebrated
Lluyd

* AT the conqueſt of Beliſle.   See the Preface to Mallet's North. Antiq. page 23.

† WORKS, Vol. 3. Introd. to Hiſt. Eng.

D

Lluyd and others, who have been more critical in their inveſtigations of this ſub‑ject, maintain that the Iriſh has a real af‑finity with the Cambrian or Britiſh. They further ſhow that many names of places in S. Britain, the meaning of which is loſt in the Welſh, can be explained only by words now extant in the Iriſh and Erſe. This is a ſufficient proof of a common origin.*

But on this point hiſtorians are divided in opinion. Some ſuppoſe that the north of

* Indeed a good reaſon may be given for the apparent difference in the ſeveral branches of the old Celtic. In this language, words are declined by changing the initial letters, or by prefixing an article with an apoſtrophe. By theſe means, words are ſo altered, that a ſuperficial obſerver may confound the radical letters, with thoſe which are added for the ſake of expreſſing different relations. Thus the Brit‑iſh word *pen* ſignifies, a head ; *pen gûr*, a man's head ; *i ben*, his head ; *i phen*, her head ; *y'm mhen*, my head. This by the way is no contemptible evidence that the Britiſh was derived from the Phenician or Hebrew, in the latter of which, words are declined by prefixes, as well as ſuffixes.

For the difference between the Iriſh and Britiſh, Lluyd aſſigns other reaſons. The anceſtors of the Iriſh and High‑land Scots, who were called Guydelians, might have been the original Celts, who firſt inhabited Britain ; and the Cymri or Welſh, another race, or a branch of the Celtic Cimbri, might, either by colonization or conqueſt, take poſ‑ſeſſion of Britain, and introduce a very different dialect of the ſame radical language. The Iriſh language might be ſomewhat changed by Cantabrian words, imported by the Scots from Spain ; and the Cymraeg or Britiſh might ſuffer conſiderable changes during 400 years ſubjection to the Ro‑mans. See Pref. to Mallet's North, Antiq. page 42.

of Ireland was firſt peopled by emigrations from Scotland, and the famenefs of their language renders this opinion probable. But whence do the Scots derive their origin ? The moſt probable account of the fettlement of Scotland is, that it was peopled from Norway or fome other northern country, by a tribe of thofe nations that went under the general denomination of *Scythians* ; for *Scot* and *Scythian* are from the fame root.

THERE are writers, however, who contend that Ireland muſt have been fettled from Spain, for there are many Spaniſh words found in the language of the country. But the number of thefe is too inconfiderable to render the argument conclufive.

WITHIN a few years, an attempt has been made to trace the origin of the Iriſh nation, to the Carthaginians. The author of a fmall work, entitled " An Eſſay on the Antiquities of Ireland," has examined, in a play of Plautus, the Punic fpeech which has the marks of being the genuin language of Carthage, and has collated it with the ancient Iriſh. In this fpeech there is a furprifing affinity between the languages. [B]

But without running into a field of conjecture, it is fufficient for my purpofe to obferve, that the Irifh, the Erfe, and the language fpoken on the Ifle of Man, are indifputably the fame, and muft have been very ancient : That the Welfh, the Corn-ifh, and the Armoric are now a diftinct language, and unqueftionably the remains of the Celtic, or that language which was common to Gaul and Britain, when they were invaded by Julius Cefar. The Irifh and the Britifh may be as diftinct as the Hebrew and the Britifh, and yet a critical etymologift may difcover in both, common radicals enough to convince him that both are the offspring of the fame parent.

Hitherto our refearches have thrown but little light upon the prefent Englifh language. For the fubftance of this we muft look to the Saxon branch of the Teu-tonic.*

THE

---

* "Erat autem illa Anglo-Saxonum lingua antiquæ Teu-tonicæ propago, (nifi antiquæ Gothicæ feu Geticæ potius dixeris, unde forfan ipfa Teutonica duxerit originem) ut et Francica illa in Galliam advecta, et hodierna Germanica, Belgica, Danica, Suevica, Boruffica, aliæque affines lin-guæ."——Wallis.

THE Teutones and Goths or Getæ were the nations that inhabited the north of Europe. They were in a rude ftate and had no hiftorical records by which their defcent could be afcertained. They however had a clafs of men under the denomination of *Scalds* or *Bards*, whofe bufinefs it was to recount in verfe the illuftrious actions of their heroes, and to preferve their traditions. Thefe *Scalds* all agree that their anceftors came from the eaft ;* and it is well known alfo that Herodotus mentions the *Germans* as a Perfian people.† It is probable that they extended their fettlements gradually, or were driven from Afia by the Roman invafions under Pompey, during the reign of Mithridates, and under the conduct of Odin, their hero and lawgiver, eftablifhed themfelves on the fhores of the Baltic.

FROM thefe nations proceeded thofe fierce and numerous warriors, who, under different leaders invaded and fubdued all the fouthern parts of Europe ; changed the government, the manners and the language

of

* MALLET's North. Antiq.

* " Αλλοι δὲ Περσαι εισι οιδὲ, Πανθελαιόι, Δερουσιαιοι, Γερμανιοι."——Herodotus in Clio. ed. 1570, page 24.

D 3

of the primitive inhabitants, and gave them
their prefent complexion. The Saxons,
who inhabited the northern parts of Germany, or Denmark, were the tribe that
conquered England, and introduced a language and a form of government, the principles of which are ftill exiftent among
their defcendants, both in England and A-
merica. This happened in the fifth and
fixth centuries.

OUR language is therefore derived from
the fame ftock as the German, the Dutch,
the Danifh, the Swedifh, and the Swifs.
Of all thefe branches, the German is perhaps the principal, and that which has fuffered the leaft by the violence of conqueft
or the changes of time. Between this and
the pure Englifh, there is a clofe affinity,
as may be obferved by any perfon indifferently well acquainted with both.

FROM the eftablifhment of the Saxons
in England, to the Norman conqueft, the
language of the country fuffered but little
variation. The invafions of the Danes and
their government of the kingdom, during
a fhort period, could not but affect the
language, yet not materially, as the ifland
fuffered a change of mafters, rather than

of

of people or laws ; and indeed the Danes themfelves fpoke a dialect of the Saxon language.

But the conqueft by William, the Norman, in 1066, introduced important changes into the language, as well as the government of the Englifh nation. William was followed by multitudes of his countrymen; thefe formed his court, and filled the rich livings, temporal and ecclefiaftical, which were forfeited or left vacant by the death of their former poffeffors who were flain in the battle of Haftings. The language of the conquerors, which was a mixture of Latin and Norman, immediately became fafhionable at Court, and was ufed in all legiflative and judicial proceedings. It continued to be the polite and law language of the nation about three centuries ; when, in the thirty fixth year of Edward III.* an act of parliament was paffed, ordaining that in future all pleas in courts fhould be made in Englifh and recorded in Latin. In the preamble to this act, the reafon affigned for making it is, " that the people of the realm did not underftand French.†

THIS

* 1362.

† In this act of Edward III. there is an exprefs refervation in favor of particular law-phrafes or technical terms, which,

THIS proves that the Norman French was spoken only by the nobility, who were mostly of Norman extraction, and by the higher orders of men in office, at court, or in the cities. The body of the people, descendants of the Saxons, still retained their primitive tongue.* During this period, when French was the polite, and Saxon the vulgar language of the English, the Latin was also understood by the learned, who were mostly the regular and secular clergy. On the revival of literature in Europe, Latin was studied with classical correctness, and the number and excellence of the Greek and Roman authors, with the elegance of the languages, have recommended them to the attention of succeeding generations. The records of parliament and of judicial proceedings were kept in Latin,

which, by long use, had acquired peculiar force and propriety, and whose place could not be well supplied by English words or phrases. Hence the number of French words still used in law proceedings.

* WE have the testimony of Robert, Earl of Gloucester (who wrote under Henry III. and Edward I.) to this purpose. Page 364.

"Vor bote a man couth French, me tolth of hym well lute,
"Ac lowe men holdeth to Englyfs and to her kunde speeche yute."

For but a man knoweth French, men told of him well little, and lowe men holdeth to English and to their native tongue.——That is, unless a man could speak French he was little esteemed.

Latin, from the thirty fixth of Edward III.
to the fourth of George II.* when, by act
of parliament, the *Englifh* was ordered to
be the language of the *Englifh* laws and
public records.   Of thefe three languages,
the Saxon, the Norman French and the
Latin, our prefent Englifh is compofed.

THE incorporation of the Roman and
other foreign tongues with the Englifh,
took place principally under the firft Norman kings.   It was attended with fome
difficulty, and Chaucer has been cenfured
by his cotemporaries for introducing cart-
loads of French words into his writings.†

LANGUAGE is the effect of neceffity,
and when a nation has a language which
is competent to all their purpofes of communicating ideas, they will not embrace
new words and phrafes.   This is the reafon why the yeomanry of the Englifh nation have never adopted the improvements
of

* 1731.

† " Ex hac malefano novetatis pruritu, Belgæ Gallicas
voces paffim civitate fua donando patrii fermonis puritatem
nuper non leviter inquinârunt, et Chaucerus Poeta, peffimo
exemplo, *integris vocum plauftris ex eadem Gallia in noftram
linguam inveclis,* eam, nimis antea a Normannorum victoriæ
adulteratam, omni fere nâtiva gratia et nitore fpoliavit."——
Skinner Etymol. L, A, Pref,

of the Englifh tongue. The Saxon was competent to moft of the purpofes of an agricultural people ; and the clafs of men who have not advanced beyond that ftate, which in fact makes the body of the na-tion, at leaft in America, feldom ufe any words except thofe of Saxon original.

BUT as men proceed in the progrefs of fociety, their ideas multiply, and new words are neceffary to exprefs them. They muft therefore either invent words, or combine thofe before ufed into compounds, or bor-row words of fuitable import from a for-eign language. The latter method was principally purfued by the Englifh. The learned of the nation fpoke and wrote Lat-in, which had been the language of a po-lite and improved nation, and confequent-ly abounds with terms in the various arts and fciences. When the Englifh found their native tongue deficient, they had re-courfe to the Roman or Greek, where they were immediately fupplied with words, ex-preffive of their new ideas, and eafily con-forming to the genius of the Englifh lan-guage.

THE Englifh retained its Saxon appear-ance till the twelfth century.[C] From this
period

period to Chaucer, who wrote in the reign of Edward III. about the year 1360 or 70, the changes were flow and gradual. Chaucer was a man of a very liberal education; well verfed in the Greek and Roman authors; and his mind had been improved by his travels. His genius and acquirements led him to ftray from the common ftile of writing, and enrich his verfe with the elegance of the *Provençal* language, at that time the moft polifhed in Europe.* His abilities, his reputation and his influence at court, enabled him, in oppofition to his adverfaries, to introduce many beauties and much energy into our language.[D]

FROM Chaucer to Addifon our language was progreffively refined, and enriched with a variety of words, adequate to all its ufes among a people highly improved. The French language has furnifhed us with military terms; the Dutch with fea phrafes; the Greek and Roman with words proper to form and polifh the poetical, hiftorical and rhetorical ftiles, and with terms in mathematics, philofophy and phyfic; the modern

* RAIMOND IV. of Aragon, count of Provence, rendered his Court a temple of the mufes, and to this reforted the lovers of the Belles Lettres from every part of Europe. About the year 1300, a tafte for the Provençal language and poetry was imbibed in Italy, and foon after in England.— Denina, Chap. 4.

ern Italian has fupplied us with terms in mufic, painting and fculpture; and in the Saxon, the ground-work of the whole, the yeomanry find all the words for which they have any ufe in domeftic life or in the agricultural and moft fimple mechanical employments.

In this progrefs, the language has not only been enriched with a copious fupply of words, but the accent of words has generally been eftablifhed in fuch a manner as to render pronunciation melodious. The fpoken language is alfo foftened, by an omiffion of the harfh and guttural founds which originally belonged to the language, and which are ftill retained by the Germans, Scotch and Dutch. At the fame time, it is not, like the French, enervated by a lofs of confonants. It holds a mean between the harfhnefs of the German, and the feeblenefs of the French. It has more fmoothnefs and fluency than the northern languages, and lefs mufic in its vocal founds, than the Spanifh and Italian. As the Englifh have attempted every branch of fcience, and generally proceeded farther in their improvements than other nations, fo their language is proportionably copious and expreffive.

REMARKS.

REMARKS.

HAVING given this general hiftory and the prefent ftate of the language, I proceed to fome remarks that naturally refult from the fubject.

1. The primitive language of the Eng-lifh nation was the Saxon, and the words derived from that, now conftitute the ground-work of modern Englifh. Hence all the rules of inflection, and moft of the rules of conftruction, are Saxon. The plu-ral terminations of nouns, the variations of the pronouns, the endings which mark the comparifon of adjectives, and the in-flections of the verbs, are wholly of Teu-tonic origin. For this reafon, the rules of grammatical conftruction and the pro-priety of particular phrafes, can be afcer-tained only by the ancient Saxon, and the modern Englifh writings. The Greek and Roman languages were conftructed on dif-ferent principles, which circumftance has not been fufficiently attended to, by thofe who have attempted to compile Englifh Grammars. The confequence is, that falfe principles have been introduced and taught as the rules of the Englifh language,

guage, by which means very eminent writers have been led into miſtakes.

2. IT has been remarked that the common people, deſcendants of the Saxons,
uſe principally words derived from the native language of their anceſtors, with few
derivatives from the foreign tongues, for
which they have no occaſion. This fact
ſuggeſts the impropriety of writing ſermons, or other diſcourſes deſigned for general uſe, in the elevated Engliſh ſtile. To
adapt a ſtile to common capacities, the
language ſhould conſiſt, as much as poſſible, of Saxon words, or of Latin and French
derivatives which are introduced into familiar diſcourſe. The modern taſte for introducing uncommon words into writings,
for rounding periods, and riſing into what
is falſely called the elegant and ſublime ſtile,
has had an unhappy effect in rendering
language obſcure or unintelligible.*

3. THE

* A REMARKABLE example of this kind of ſtile, we have
in Elphinſtone's principles of the Engliſh Language. The
author has taken great pains to be obſcure, and has ſucceeded
to admiration.

OF this kind of ſtile, the reader may ſee a ſpecimen in the
following paſſage, taken from Young's ſpirit of Athens.
Page 6.

"SURELY,

3. THE number and perfection of the languages from which the Engliſh is collected, muſt account for its copiouſneſs and the multitude of ſynonimous words with which it abounds.

A PRIMITIVE unmixed language rarely contains two words of the ſame ſignification. On the contrary, rude nations often uſe one word to expreſs ſeveral ideas, which have ſome reſemblance or analogy to each other, in the conſtitution of things.

FROM

"SURELY, in every mind, there is an emulation of virtuous ſuperiority, which, however fortune or the meaner paſſions may hebitate its powers, ſtill, at every example of ſucceſs in the particular object of its predilection, glows into a momentary flame, which from frequent reſuſcitation may acquire a ſtability and ſtrength ſufficient to reach at the attainment of what, at firſt, was regarded ſolely as matter of admiration ; the idea of imitation which hath thus enraptured the fancy, may in times of perilous criſis ſomewhat elevate the mind and influence the conduct ; and if ſuch ever may be the effect, what other lecture can ballance the utility of that, which thus animates the man, and urges him to noble and diſintereſted ſervices in a good, great and public cauſe."

THE author could hardly have invented an arrangement, better calculated to obſcure his meaning.

IT is ſaid of Moliere, that before he would ſuffer a new play of his to be acted, he read it to an old woman, and judged, by the effect it had upon her, what reception it would meet with on the ſtage. It is a pity, ſome modern writers do not copy the example.

FROM the poverty of a language proceed repetitions of the fame word, to exprefs an idea with particular force, or in the
fuperlative degree.   Hence the Hebraifms,
as they are called, of the Bible ; to *rejoice*
with *joy*; to *fear* with great *fear*.   This
mode of fpeaking is frequent among all
nations whofe languages are imperfect.

BUT the Englifh, on the other hand, a-
bounds with fynonimous terms, fo that a
repetition of *words* is generally unneceffary,
even when there is a neceffity of repeat-
ing the *idea* in the fame fentence.

THIS copioufnefs, while it affords great
advantages to a judicious writer, may alfo
be abufed, and become the caufe of a pro-
lix verbofe ftile.   Inftances of this fault
occur in almoft every author ; it is one
of the greateft, as well as moft frequent
faults in writing, and yet has fcarcely been
cenfured by critics.*

THERE are indeed but few inftances in
which two or three words exprefs *precifely*
the

* DR. Blair has made a few excellent remarks on this
fault, under the article *Precifion*, Lecture 10.   I do not remember to have feen any other criticifms upon this fubject.

the fame idea; but there are many inftances of words conveying *nearly* the fame fenfe, which are thrown together by carelefs writers without the leaft occafion. Take for example a paffage of Mr. Addifon's Cato:

> " So the *pure, limpid* ftream, when *foul* with *ftains*
> Of rufhing torrents and defcending rains,
> *Works* itfelf *clear* and as it runs *refines*,
> Till by degrees the floating mirror fhines."

Pure and *limpid* are here too nearly fynonimous to be applied to the fame object. The fame objection lies to the ufe of " *foul* with *ftains*." Between *working clear* and *refining*, there is perhaps no difference in idea : And the arrangement in the fecond line is objectionable, for the confequence is placed before the caufe ; *rufhing torrents* being the confequence of *defcending rains*. Such an affemblage of fynonimous words clogs and enfeebles the expreffion, and fatigues the mind of the reader. Writers · of an inferior clafs are particularly fond of crouding together epithets. If they would defcribe a man they hate, he is a *low, vile, mean, defpicable, contemptible* fellow. If they would defcribe a man of an amiable character, he is the moft *kind, humane, loving, tender, affectionate* being imaginable.

E   Epithets,

Epithets, fo liberally beſtowed, confuſe our ideas and leave the mind without any diſtinct knowlege of the character. [E]

To a copiouſneſs of language, on the other hand, may be aſcribed the decline of action in ſpeaking, and the want of animation. When nations have but few words to expreſs their ideas, they have recourſe to figures, to ſignificant tones, looks and geſtures, to ſupply the defect. Hence the figurative language of the Orientals of antiquity ; hence the imagery of the Caledonian Bard ;* the bold metaphorical language of the American natives, and the expreſſive tones and geſticulations that attend their ſpeaking.

To this cauſe alſo muſt we aſcribe the muſic of the Greek language, and the action which accompanied the rehearſals on the ſtage. What was the effect of neceſſity at firſt, became afterwards a matter of art. This was the origin of the pantomime. Modern operas are alſo an imitation of the ancient muſical rehearſals of the theater.†

BUT

* OSSIAN.

† SEE Blair, Lecture 6, and Condillac, in his Eſſay on the Origin of Human Knowlege. The *dancing* of David, and others,

BUT as languages become rich and fur-
nish words for communicating every idea,
action muft naturally ceafe. Men will not
give themfelves the pain of exerting their
limbs and body to make themfelves underftood, when a bare opening of their lips
will anfwer the purpofe. This may be
affigned as one principal caufe of the decline of eloquence in modern ages, particularly among the Englifh.

To the fame caufe, in part, may we afcribe the difference in the French and Englifh manner of fpeaking. It is a common
obfervation, that the French ufe more action and are more animated in converfation, than the Englifh. The caufe ufually
affigned, is, the natural vivacity of the
French nation ; which appears to me not
fatisfactory ; for the Germans, who refemble

others, mentioned in the Old Teftament, was a folemn exercife, in which action was joined with words to exprefs i-
deas.

IT is faid to have been a difpute between Cicero and
Rofcius, whether the former could exprefs an idea by a
greater variety of *words*, or the latter by a greater variety of
gefture.——"Satis conftat, contendere cum (Ciceronem)
cum ipfo hiftrione (Rofcio) folitum, utrum ille fæpius ean-
dem fententiam variis geftibus efficeret, an ipfe per eloquen-
tiæ copiam fermone diverfo pronunciaret."——Macrob.
Saturn. 2, 10.

ble the French, in some degree, in their manner of speaking, are neverthelefs a more grave people than the Englifh.

I suspect that the difference may in part be thus accounted for. The French, tho by no means a barren language, wants words to exprefs many ideas, for which the Englifh is provided. For example, the Englifh has two forms for the future tenfe of verbs; *fhall* and *will*; each of which has a diftinct meaning. *Shall* exprefles event in the firft perfon, and promife, command or threatning in the fecond and third. *Will*, in the firft perfon, promifes; in the fecond and third, foretells. The French has no fuch diftinction. The phrafe *je lui payerai*, the only form of the future, cannot convey fuch diftinct meanings, as *promife* and *event*, unlefs accompanied with fome expreffive tone or gefture. A Frenchman therefore, to exprefs the force of the Englifh, *I will pay*, muft fupply the want of a diftinct word by action, or have recourfe to a circumlocution. The fame remark holds with refpect to *would* and *fhould*, which, in a variety of combinations, retain diftinct fignifications.

The French has properly but one word, *plume*, for the three Englifh words, *feather*,

pen

pen and *quill.* Its verbs have not such a variety of combinations to express the precise time of an action as the English. *J'e-cris* is the only phrase for the English, *I write* and *I am writing*, which have distinct uses ; and I do not know whether there is any phrase used in French which will exactly correspond with the English phrases answering to the inceptive verb of the Romans, *I am going to write*, or, *am about writing.**

THIS solution of a difficulty, which has occurred to many people, in comparing the manners

---

* I CANNOT think the French *devenir* prefixed to a verb answers exactly to both these English forms. The deficiency of the French in this respect, may be observed in the following passage :

"S'IL est vrai que vous *aimiez* la justice, & que vous *alliez* en Créte pour apprendre les loix du bon roi Minos, n'-endurcissez point votre cœur contre mes soupirs & contre mes larmes."——Telemaque, Liv. 4.

IF we translate the passage thus : " If it is true that you *love* justice and *go* to Crete," &c. we lose the force of the verb *alliez* ; for the sense is evidently, *are going, are now on your journey.* " If it is true that you *love* justice and *are going* to Crete," &c.

IN French the verbs *aimiez* and *alliez* are both in the same tense, and have the same form of construction ; in English the verbs should be in the same tense, but have different forms of construction. In French the force of *alliez* is collected from the sense of the passage ; but in English, it is expressed by a particular construction.

manners of the Englifh and French, may
not be the true one; but it appears rational. Other caufes alfo have a material
influence upon eloquence, particularly the
form of government and the ftate of fociety. In thefe refpects England and France
may not be fo favorable to the cultivation
of oratory, as were the republics of Greece
and Rome. But if a free government is
the beft foil for the growth of eloquence,
why fhould it flourifh in France rather
than in England, which is faid to be the
fact with refpect to pulpit eloquence ? The
genius of the nation may have its effect ;
but it is prefumed, the ftate of the language may be confidered as an auxiliary
caufe, if not a principal.

FROM the foregoing hiftory of the language, we learn the caufes of its incorrect
orthography. The Saxon characters, fome
of which were Roman, both in fhape and
power, while others were peculiar to the
language, continued in ufe till the four-
teenth century. Thefe were afterwards laid
afide for the Old Englifh characters, as they
are ufually called ; which were introduced
with the art of printing from Germany,*
and

* On the firft invention of printing, letters were cut in
wood and fixed. They were afterwards engraved upon
metal,

and continued in ufe, till within a century. But both the Saxon and German letters were much inferior to the Roman in the fimplicity and elegance of their form ; for which reafon moft of the European nations have rejected their primitive characters and adopted the Roman.*

In changing the characters of an alphabet, as well as in expreffing the founds of one language by letters of an other, fome difficulty will often arife from the want of a perfect correfpondence between the true founds of letters in both. Altho there is, and muft be, a great uniformity in the articulate founds of all men, yet there are alfo differences peculiar to each nation, which others have not proper characters to exprefs.

Thus the Romans, when they would exprefs the found of the Greek θ and of χ, for want of fuitable characters, wrote

th

metal, ftill fixed. The third ftage of improvement was the cafting of moveable types. It is probable that this was a work of labor and expenfe ; and it muft have been a long time, before they caft more than one kind of character. Hence the German character was ufed in England.

* The Germans and Dutch are exceptions : They ufe their old characters in their own language : but they ufe the Latin character and language in works of fcience.

th and *ch*. We conclude from this circumftance, that the Greek found of the
former was that of *t* followed by an afpirate, and the latter, that of *k* with an afpirate. Yet it is very probable that the
founds were guttural in Greek, and not
exactly reprefented by the Latin combinations *th* and *ch*.

THUS two Saxon characters are reprefented in modern Englifh, by the Latin
combination *th*, as in *think, thou*. Thefe
Saxon characters were fingle letters and
had diftinct powers. We preferve the diftinction of founds to this day, but are fubject to the inconvenience of having no
mark by which the eye can difcern that
diftinction.

ON the other hand, *fh* was ufually written by the Saxons *fc*, as *fceaft*, fhaft ; *fceam*,
fhame ; *fceal*, fhall. What was the pronunciation of *fc* cannot be determined ;
but it is evident that each letter had a diftinct found. It is moft probable that before *a*, *o*, and *u*, *fc* were pronounced *fk*, or
c might have had the force of *ch* in *choofe*.
It is very clear that *c* had this found before *e* and *i* ; for the Saxon words in which
ch now precede *e* or *i*, were formerly fpelt
with

with *c* only; as *child* from the Saxon *cild*; *chill* from *cele*; *chink* from *cinnon*, to gape; *chick* from *cicen*. If therefore *c* before *e* and *i* had the force of *ch*, *fceaft* muſt have been pronounced *fcheaft*, which would eaſily be ſoftened down and contracted into *fhaft*.

But whatever was the ſound of *fc* in the Saxon, the ſound derived from it is now ſimple, and has no ſingle character to repreſent it in our language; for the proper ſounds of *f* and *h* combined, do not form the ſound which we invariably annex to *fh*. By not retaining the primitive Saxon *c* after *f*, we have probably loſt the pronunciation and introduced an irregularity.

It is not certain however that a change of the alphabet was prior to the change of pronunciation; for the latter might have produced the former. But the effect is certain; we have a ſimple ſound without a proper character, which is always an imperfection.*

We have therefore in Engliſh the two ſounds of *th*, the aſpirate in *think*, and the vocal in *this*, both of which are ſimple conſonant

---

* This may be ſupplied by uniting the two characters *f* and *h* in one, and naming the combination *Efh*.

fonant founds, peculiar to the language, and derived from two *fingle* characters. Each ought ftill to be reprefented by a diftinct fingle letter. *Sh*, on the other hand, exprefs a fimple found, derived from *two* feparate Saxon confonants, which muft have been originally pronounced as two letters. Thefe irregularities muft have been partly owing to a change of alphabet.*

OTHER irregularities have been occafioned by an injudicious application of the letters of one alphabet to the founds of another language,

THE Roman *c* fome writers fuppofe was hard, like *k*, before all the vowels and diphthongs. It certainly was fo before all except *e* and *i* ; where, there is reafon to fuppofe, it had the found of *ch* or *ts*. It is very evident that it had not the found of *f*, which we now annex to it in *civil, cellar*. When the Roman alphabet, therefore, took place of the primitive Englifh characters, the Greek *k* fhould have been always written

before

---

* THE Germans, who invented printing, had not proper types for the two Saxon or Englifh characters ; they therefore made ufe of *th* as a fubftitute for both, which defect we have not yet fupplied.

before *a, o, u,* as in *cat, cord, cup* ; and *f* before *e* and *i*. Or *c* fhould have been called *ke*, limited to one found, and always ufed inftead of *k*. If our anceftors had retained the Roman pronunciation of *c* before *e* and *i*, they would probably have fpelt *cera, civilis, chera, chivilis,** *ch* having its Englifh found of *tfh*, as in *charm*. But if they pronounced thefe words as we do, they fhould have fubftituted *f, fera, fivilis*. In fhort, they fhould have limited every charaćter to one found ; in which cafe, one of the three letters, *c, k, f,* would have been entirely omitted as ufelefs. This would have delivered us from a large clafs of difficulties.

WHETHER the *ph* and *ch*, in Greek derivatives, were originally introduced into Englifh, becaufe our anceftors preferved the afpirate ; or whether the *h* was retained merely to fhow the etymology of words, it is not eafy to decide. The probability is, that thefe letters were never afpirated in Englifh, but that *ph* has ever been pronounced *f*, and *ch* generally *k*; as in *Philip, chorus*. It is probable however that the Romans, from whom the Englifh borrowed their charaćters, preferved the afpirate ;

for

* Or *tfera, tfivilis.*

for they very fcrupuloufly retained the *h*
after *p* and *c*; and they attempted to copy
exactly the Greek pronunciation.* They
borrowed all words in *ph*, *ch* and *th* from
the Greeks. We have preferved the characters, but have moftly loft the afpirate;
ph has invariably the found of *f*; *ch*, in
Greek derivatives, generally that of *k*; and
th has become the reprefentative of two
fimple confonants. With this change of
pronunciation, the orthography fhould
have changed; *philofophy* fhould now be
written *filofofy*; and *chorus*, *korus*; *th* might
become a fingle character and be called
Eth. [F]

But it was the fate of our language to
be fhaken by violent revolutions, and aban-
doned to accident or the caprice of un-
fkillful heads. The operation of imperceptible

* "Eundem olim *(ph)* fonum habuiffe ac *f* infcriptiones
veteres confirmant, in quibus alterum pro altero promifcue
adhiberi cernimus : ut *phidelis*" (pro fidelis.)——Middleton de Lat. Liter. Pron. Dif.

Our letter *f* has fome degree of afpiration in its found;
but had its orginal Roman found been precifely that of the
Greek Φ *phi*, it is probable that *f* would have been wholly ufed in derivatives where the *phi* occurred. I fufpect
that *ph* in Latin muft have been originally more ftrongly
afpirated than *f*; but the tranfition from the found of the
one to that of the other was eafy, and the diftinction was gradually loft.

ceptible caufes, common to all languages, in all ages, has alfo been gradually changing the fpelling and pronunciation.

In Chaucer's time, the infinitive mode and plural number of verbs, in the prefent tenfe, ended often in *en*; as *loven*, for *to love* or *they love*. But *loveth* was fometimes ufed in the plural, and *n* began to be omitted in the infinitive. The French termination *effe*, as in *Goddeffe*, *richeffe*, was ufed, and the final *e* was often pronounced. The plural number of nouns ufually ended in *es*, as *houndes*; and in the fame manner terminated the genitive cafe. Nouns now ending in *y*, ended then in *ie*, as *florie*; *y* was ftill prefixed to participles, as *ybent*; and *y* was often ufed where we now write *g*, as *yeve* for *give*.

From that period the orthography was ftill varying, at leaft in fome particulars, till the beginning of the prefent century. The group of eminent writers who were cotemporary with Swift, gave great ftability to the fpelling; yet fome good authorities differ from them in feveral points. Johnfon, who has been ufually followed by fucceeding compilers of dictionaries, preferves the *u* in *honour*, *favour*, and fimilar
words;

words ; as alfo the final *k* in *publick*, &c;
Afh, followed by many writers, very properly reftores thefe words to the Roman fpelling, by omitting the *u* and *k*. Excepting
thefe particulars, the orthography of our
language is nearly fixed.

THE pronunciation has been neglected
till a few years ago ; when Sheridan and
Kenrick, with feveral compilers of lefs note,
attempted to give us a ftandard. Unluck-
ily they have all made the attempt on
falfe principles ; and will, if followed,
multiply the anomalies, which already
deform the language and embarrafs the
learner.*

THE language, is compofed of a variety of materials, and it requires fome
labor to adjuft the parts and reduce them
to order.

To accomplifh this purpofe, we muft
fearch for fuch principles of analogy as
ftill exift in its conftruction, and make
them the pillars of a regular fyftem. Where
fuch principles cannot be found, let us
examin

* WE may except Kenrick, who has paid fome regard to
principles, in marking the pronunciation.

examin the opinions of the learned, and
the practice of the nations which fpeak
the pure Englifh, that we may determine
by the weight of authority, the *common law*
of language, thofe queftions which do not
come within any eftablifhed rules.

DISSERTATION

DISSERTATION II.

*Of the English Alphabet.—Rules of Pronun-
ciation.—Differences of Pronunciation and
controverted Points examined.*

Of the ENGLISH ALPHABET.

ROM a general hiſtory of
the Engliſh language, and
ſome remarks upon that
ſubject, I proceed to examin its elements, or the powers of the letters which
compoſe our alphabet.

THERE are in Engliſh, twenty five characters or letters which are the repreſenta-
tives of certain ſounds, either ſimple or
combined ; a, b, c, d, e, f, g, i, j, k, l, m,
n, o, p, q, r, ſ, t, u, v, w, x, y, z. The
Engliſh have alſo the character *h*, which

marks an aſpiration or ſtrong breathing, but has very little ſound of its own. [G]

LETTERS, according to the ſounds they repreſent, or the purpoſes they ſerve, are very naturally divided into three kinds; *vowels*, *dipthongs*, and *conſonants*.

IN order to obtain clear ideas of our alphabet, let us attend to the following definitions :

1. A VOCAL ſound, formed by opening the mouth, and by a ſingle poſition of the organs of ſpeech, is a ſimple ſound or vowel. Moſt of the vowels in Engliſh are capable of being prolonged at pleaſure, without varying the poſition of the organs.

2. No more than one ſimple ſound can be formed by one aperture of the mouth, and one poſition of the organs of ſpeech. The only difference that can be made with the ſame poſition of the organs, is, to prolong and ſhorten the ſame ſound.

3. Two ſimple ſounds, cloſely united in pronunciation, or following each other ſo rapidly that the diſtinction is ſcarcely perceptible, form a dipthong. In pronoun-

cing

cing a dipthong, two pofitions of the parts of the mouth are required.

4. THOSE letters which are not marks of articulate founds, but reprefent indiftinct founds, formed by fome contact of the parts of the mouth, or by compreffing thofe parts, check all found, are denominated confonants.

By the firft definition we afcertain the number of vowels in Englifh. In pronouncing each of the letters a, a, a, e, o, o, u, we obferve but one pofition or aperture of the mouth ; the founds are therefore fimple, and the letters are called *vowels*. The fix firft founds are capable of being prolonged at pleafure.

By the fecond definition, we determine which founds are the fame in quality, and different only in the time of being pronounced. Thus *i* in *fit* has the fame quality of found as *ee* in *feet*, for both are pronounced with the fame difpofition of the organs ; but the firft is the fhorteft articulation of the found, and the laft, a long or grave articulation. The other vowels have alfo their fhort or abrupt founds ; *a* in *late*

has

has its short found in *let* ; *a* in *cart* has its short found in *carry* ; *a* in *fall* has its short found in *folly* ; *oo* in *fool* its short found in *full*. O is sometimes shortened in common parlance, as in *colt* ; but the distinction between *o* in *coal* and *colt*, seems to be accidental or caused by the final consonant, and not sufficiently settled or important to require a separate consideration.

By the third definition we are enabled to ascertain the dipthongs in our language. The letters *i*, *u* and *y* are usually classed among the vowels ; but the first or long found of each requires, in pronunciation, two positions of the organs of speech, or rather a transition from the position necessary to form one simple found, to the position necessary to form another simple found. We begin the found of *i* nearly with the same aperture of the glottis, as we do the broad *a* or *aw* : The aperture however is not quite so great : We rapidly close the mouth to the position where we pronounce *ee*, and there stop the found. This letter is therefore a dipthong. *Y* has no property but what belongs to *i*.

U ALSO is not strictly a vowel ; nor is it, as it is commonly represented, composed

of

of *e* and *oo*. We do not begin the found
in the pofition neceffary to found *ee*, as is
obvious in the words *falute, falubrious, revolution* ; but with a greater aperture of the
mouth and with a pofition perfectly eafy
and natural. From that pofition we pafs
to the pofition with which we pronounce
oo, and there clofe the found.

It muft however be obferved that when
thefe letters, *i, u,* are followed by a confonant, the two founds of the dipthong are
not clearly diftinguifhable. We do not,
in *fight*, hear the found of *ee* ; nor the found
of *oo* in *cube*. The confonant compreffes
the organs and clofes the found of the
word fo fuddenly, that the ear can diftinguifh but a fimple vocal found : And notwithftanding thefe letters are dipthongs,
when confidered by themfelves, yet in combination with confonants, they are often
marks of fimple founds or vowels.

The fhort found of *i* and *y*, is merely
fhort *ee*.   The found of *u* in *tun*, is a feparate vowel, which has no affinity to any
other found in the language.

The found of *oi* or *oy* is dipthongal,
compofed of the third or broad *a*, and *ee*.
The

The found of *ou* or *ow* is alfo dipthongal, compounded of third *a* and *oo*. The found however does not require quite fo great an aperture of the mouth as broad *a*; the pofition is more natural, and the articulation requires lefs exertion.

THE union of *a* and *w* in *law*, has been very erroneoufly confidered a dipthong. Whatever might have been the ancient pronunciation of thefe letters (and it is probable that good reafons operated to produce their union) they now exhibit but one fimple vocal found. The fame may be obferved of *ee, oo, au, ai, ea, ei, ie, eo, oa,* and perhaps fome other combinations, each of which actually exhibits the found of one letter only, which found is as fimple as that of *a* or *o*.*

UNDER the head of dipthongs we may perhaps range *wa, we, wo, wi,* &c. *W* has nearly the fhort found of *oo*; for *will, dwell* are pronounced as if written *ooill, dooell.* It is a controverted point, whether *w* fhould be claffed with the vowels or confonants. I fhall only obferve, that it is pronounced by opening the mouth, without a contact

of

---

* Dr. Sheridan has coined a word for thefe combinations; he calls them *digraphs,* that is, *double written.*

of the parts; altho, in a rapid pronunciation, it approaches to a consonant. [I] It
is however very immaterial, whether we
clafs it with the vowels or confonants;
as all grammarians agree that its found is
that of *oo* fhort. It ought to be named *oo*
or *we*; which would fave children much of
the trouble they now experience, in learning its proper found from that awkward
name *double u*.

The found of *y* in the beginning of
words, is, by fome writers, called a vowel,
but by moft of them a confonant. Lowth
has afferted, that it has every property of a
vowel and not one of a confonant. Sheridan confiders *y* in *youth*, *year*, &c. as the
fhort *ee*. But if thefe writers would attend to the manner in which we pronounce
yes, *ye*; they would acknowlege that *y* has
fome property different from *ee*; for it is
very evident that they are not pronounced
ee-es, *ee-e*. The fact is, that in the American
pronunciation of *y*, the root of the tongue
is preffed againft the upper part of the
mouth, above the palate, more clofely than
it is in pronouncing *ee*, and not fo clofely
as in pronouncing *g* hard. The tranfition
however from *y* to *ee* or to *g*, is extremely
eafy, and hence the miftake that *y* is fhort

ee,

ee, as alſo the convertibility of *y* with *g*. [J]
It appears to me that *y* in the beginning
of words, is more clearly a conſonant than *w*.

In many words, *i* has the power of *y*
conſonant ; particularly after *l* and *n* ; as
filial, union.

The vowels therefore in Engliſh are
all heard in the following words ; late,
half, hall, feet, pool, note, tun, fight, truth.
The five firſt have ſhort ſounds or dupli-
cates; which may be heard in let, hat, hot,
fit, pull ; and the letters *i* and *u* are but
accidentally vowels. The pure primitive
vowels in Engliſh are therefore ſeven.

The dipthongs may be heard in the
following words ; lie or defy, due, voice or
joy, round or now. To theſe we may add
ua in *perſuade* ; and perhaps the combinations of *w* and the vowels, in *well, will,*
&c.

The conſonants in Engliſh are nine-
teen ; but for want of proper characters,
five of them are expreſſed or marked by
double letters. We annex two ſounds to
th ; one to *ſh* ; one to *ng* ; and one to *ſi* or
ſu, as may be heard in the following words;
think,

think, this, shall, bring, confusion or pleasure. These characters should be called, *eth, eſh, eng, ezh*; and *th* should have two names, the aspirate as in *think*, and the vocal as in *this*; the latter found might be diftinguished by a small mark drawn thro *th*. This improvement is so obvious and easy, and would be so convenient for the learners of the language, that I muſt believe it will soon be introduced.

THE consonants may be divided into *mutes* and *semivowels*. When a consonant compreſſes the lips, or the tongue and roof of the mouth, so closely as to check all found, it is called a *perfect mute* : Such are *p*, *k*, and *t*, as may be perceived by pronouncing the syllables, *ep*, *ek*, *et*. When the compreſſion of the organs is more gentle and does not ſtop all found immediately, the letters are called mutes ; ſuch are *b*, *d*, and *g*, as may be perceived by pronouncing the syllables, *eb*, *ed*, *eg*. When a consonant has an imperfect found, or hiſſing, which may be continued, after a contact of the organs, it is denominated a femivowel. Of this kind are ef, el, em, en, er, es, ev, ez, eth,* eth,* efh, ezh, ing. Of theſe, four

are

---

* VOCAL and aſpirate.

are afpirates, ef, es, eth, and efh. The others are vocal, having an imperfect found.

THE whole may be thus arranged.
  Perfect mutes———p, k, t.
  Mutes——————b, d, g.

Semivowels— vocal, } l, m, n, r, v, z, th,
                      } zh, ng,
             afpirate, } f, f, th, fh.

THEY may alfo be claffed according to
the manner in which they are formed by
the organs : Thus, thofe formed
By the lips, are called labials—b, p, f, v.
By the teeth, are called dentals—d, t, th, z, f,
      fh, zh.
By the palate, are called palatine—g, k, l, r.
By the nofe, are called nafal—m, n, ng.

ON the fubject of the alphabet, I have
this remark further ; that for want of a
proper knowlege of the powers of *fh* and
th, fome material errors in printing have
obtained in common practice. *Sh* are u-
fually united in printing, and generally
with propriety, for the combination reprefents a fimple confonant. But in feveral
compound words *f* and *h* have been improperly united, where one is filent or
where each retains its own power, as in
                              dishonor,

dishonor, dishoneſt, dishabille, hogs-head, houſehold, falſehood, and ſome others. The union of *ſh* in theſe words, is embarraſſing, eſpecially to children, who are led to pronounce them *diſh-onor*, *diſh-oneſt*. This error ſtill prevails in printing, except in the laſt mentioned word, which is ſometimes correctly printed, *falſehood*.

*T*ʜ, tho not united in character, have a tendency to produce, in ſome words, a wrong pronunciation. For inſtance, we are very apt to ſay *Wren-tham* inſtead of *Wrent-ham*. *Hotham* is alſo ambiguous; there is nothing in the orthography to direct us, whether to pronounce it *Hot-ham* or *Ho-tham*, altho cuſtom decides in favor of the latter,

Tʜᴇsᴇ remarks ſhow the propriety of attending to our orthography, and of attempting to remove cauſes of error, when it can be done without much trouble or danger of giving offence,

RULES *of* PRONUNCIATION.

HAVING briefly explained the Engliſh alphabet, I proceed to the rules of pronunciation.

Iɴ

In pronunciation, two things demand our notice; the proper founds of the vowels and confonants, and the accent.

In pronouncing both vowels and confonants, the general rule is, *that fimilar combinations of letters fhould be pronounced alike, except when general cuftom has decided otherwife.* Thus if *i* in the words, *bind, find, mind,* has its firft found, it ought to have the fame found in other fimilar combinations, *kind, blind, grind.* This is the rule of *analogy,* the great leading principle that fhould regulate the conftruction of all languages. But as languages are not formed at once by fyftem, and are ever expofed to changes, it muft neceffarily happen that there will be in all languages, fome exceptions from any general rule; fome departures from the principle of uniformity.

The practice of a nation, when univerfal or ancient, has, in moft cafes, the force and authority of law; it implies mutual and general confent, and becomes a rule of propriety. On this ground, fome deviations from the analogy of conftruction and pronunciation muft be admitted in 'all languages. Thus from the analogy already mentioned, *wind* is an exception; for

general

general practice has determined that *i* should, in this word, have its second or short found.*   Whether this deviation was admitted at firft to diftinguifh this word from the verb *to wind*, or whether there were other good reafons which cannot now be explored, or whether it was merely the work of ignorance or accident, it is un-neceffary to enquire ; the common confent of a nation is fufficient to ftamp it with propriety.

ANOTHER rule in Englifh, which admits of no exception, is, when the accent falls on a vowel, it is long, as *o* in ho'-ly ; but when the accent falls on a confonant, the preceding vowel is fhort, as in *flat'-ter*.

IT is alfo a general rule, that when a confonant clofes a fyllable, the preceding vowel is fhort, as in *fan-cy*, *habit* ; altho this rule has its exceptions, as *Cam-bridge*, *dan-ger*, and perhaps *man-ger*.

FROM this rule, the Englifh except alfo *angel*, *ancient*.   In this all the ftandard authors

* ON the ftage, it is fometimes pronounced with *i* long, either for the fake of rhime, or in order to be heard.   Mr. Sheridan marks it both ways ; yet in common difcourfe he pronounces it with *i* fhort, as do the nation in general.

thors agree, except Kenrick and Burn, who mark *a* in *ancient* both long and short. The English pronunciation is followed in the middle and southern states; but the eastern universities have restored these words to the analogy of the language, and give *a* its second sound. It is presumed that no reason can be given for making these words exceptions to the general rule, but practice; and this is far from being universal, there being many of the best speakers in America, who give *a*, in the words mentioned, the same sound as in *anguish*, *annals*, *angelic*, *antiquity*.

THE practice of the eastern universities therefore should be encouraged, rather than discountenanced; as it diminishes the number of anomalies. I shall only remark further, that *a* in these words must formerly have had its third or fourth sound; which is evident from the old orthography; for angel, at least, was spelt like *grant*, *command*, &c. *aungel*, *graunt*, *commaund*. In giving *a* its first sound therefore, the modern English have not only infringed the rule of analogy, but have deviated from former practice.

IN the word *chamber*, *a* has its fourth sound. It is necessary to remark this; as

there

there are many people in America, who give *a* its firſt ſound, which is contrary to analogy and to all the Engliſh authorities.

WITH regard to accent, that particular ſtreſs of voice which ſhould diſtinguiſh ſome ſyllable of a word from others, three things are to be conſidered ; the importance of the ſyllable ; the derivation of the word ; and the terminating ſyllable.

THE importance of a ſyllable is diſcovered by reſolving a word into the parts which compoſe it, or reducing it to its radicals. Thus *ſenſible* is derived from *ſenſus* in Latin or *ſenſe* in Engliſh. The firſt ſyllable therefore is that on which the meaning of the word principally depends ; the others being an acceſſary termination.

THE firſt ſyllable then is the moſt important and requires the accent. For the ſame reaſon, *admire, compare, deſtroy*, &c. have the accent on the ſecond ſyllable in preference to the firſt ; the laſt ſyllables being all derived from verbs, and the firſt being mere particles.*

ANOTHER

* The moſt ſignificant words, and conſequently the moſt important, are nouns and verbs ; then follow adjectives, pronouns, auxiliary verbs and participles.—Particles are the leaſt important,

Another rule for laying the accent of words arifes from derivation. Thus all words that take the terminations *ing*, *ful*, *lefs*, *nefs*, *ed*, *eft*, *ift*, *ly*, retain the accent on the fyllable where it is laid in their primitives; as *proceed*, *proceeding*, *wonder*, *wonderful*, &c.

But the moſt important article to be confidered in the accentuation of words, is the terminating fyllable. From the different terminations of words arife various analogies, the moſt of which are enumerated in the firſt part of my Inſtitute. The principle which has operated to produce thefe analogies, is the eafe of fpeaking or the harmony of enunciation. Confequently this principle muſt take place of all others ; and we find that it frequently interferes with the two foregoing rules, and regulates practice in oppoſition to both.

The general rule, grounded on this principle, is, that words, having the *fame* terminating fyllable, have the accent at the *fame* diſtance from that termination. Thus all words ending in *tion*, *fion*, *cion*, *cial*, *cian*, have the accent on the laſt fyllable but one ;* and this without any regard to

derivation

---

* I consider thefe terminations as fingle fyllables.

derivation or to the number of fyllables in the word.

Thus moſt words in *ty*, if they confiſt of more ſyllables than two, have the accent on the antepenult; as *probity*, *abfurdity*, *probability*. I recollect but two exceptions, viz. *commonalty*, *admiralty*; the accent of which is laid upon the firſt fyllable, as in their primitives.*

But let us obſerve the force of the laſt rule, in oppoſition to the others. *Mortal* has the accent on the firſt fyllable. Here the firſt rule takes place, for the firſt fyllable, having *mors*, death, for its root, is the moſt important. But the derivative, *mortality*, conforms to the analogy of words ending in *ty* and has the accent on the laſt fyllable but two. That the eafe or harmony of pronunciation, is the caufe of this change of accent, will be evident to any perfon who fhall attempt to pronounce words of this claſs, with the accent on any other fyllable than the antepenult.

MOST

* Such is the tendency of people to uniformity, that the *commonally*, for the moſt part, form the word regularly, and pronounce it *commonality*. Analogy requires that both thefe words fhould end in *ity*; but cuſtom has eſtabliſhed them as exceptions.

G

MOST of thefe rules admit a few exceptions, which are to be learnt by practice.
Cuftom has made fome inroads upon the
rules of uniformity, and caprice is ever
bufy in multiplying anomalies. Still, rules
will be of great fervice in afcertaining and
fixing our language ; for tho they may not
root out *old* errors, they may prevent the
introduction of *others*.

BUT befides the principal accent, there
is, in moft polyfyllables, an inferior accent
laid on the third or fourth fyllable from
the principal. Indeed in fome words, the
two accents are fo nearly equal, as to be
fcarcely diftinguifhable.

IT is denied by fome critics that there
are more accents than one, in any word.
But the compofition of words, and the eafe
of fpeaking, both require a plurality of
accent in a very great number of inftances ;
and our ears inform us that fuch a plurality actually exifts in practice. If a man
will affert that in fuch words as *defignation*,
exaltation, there is but one fyllable diftinguifhed from the others by a fuperior ftrefs
of voice, he muft deny the evidence of
fenfe, and would not liften to argument.

I MUST

I MUST however remark that moſt, if not all ſyllables, derived from ſome important word, have ſome degree of accent :* So that in compounds, there are uſually as many accents as radicals. Thus in *ſancti-fy*, which is compoſed of two radicals, *ſanctus* and *fio*, we obſerve two accents ; the ſtrongeſt on the firſt ſyllable. The ſame may be obſerved in *magnanimity*, from *magnus* and *animus* ; in *promogeniture*, &c. except that in theſe the principal accent is on the third ſyllable.

NOTWITHSTANDING it is a general rule, that there are as many accents in a word, as radicals, yet one of them at leaſt is frequently removed from the principal ſyllable, by the analogy of termination, which prevails over all other reaſons. Thus in *mathematics*, the two accents lie on the proper ſyllables ; but in *mathematician*, the laſt accent is removed to a leſs important place. In *imperceptible*, the principal accent,

---

*FROM this remark we muſt except ſome derivatives from the Greek ; as geography, philology, antitheſis, hypotheſis, &c. which have but one accent. Etymology requires theſe words to be accented on the firſt and third ſyllables ; but the genius of the language, or the analogy of termination has prevailed over etymological reaſons. Etymology however reſumes her rights in the derivatives, *geographical*, *philological*, &c. where each radical ſyllable is diſtinguiſhed by an accent,

cent, with propriety, lies on the third fyllable, which being derived from a verb (*ca-
pio*) is the moſt important. The particle
im, being the privative, or that ſyllable
which changes the meaning of the whole
word from affirmative to negative, becomes
important and has ſome degree of accent.
But in the derivative *imperceptibility*, while
the firſt and third ſyllables retain an accent,
the analogy of termination carries the principal accent to the fifth ſyllable, which is
adventitious and leſs important than the
others.*

In many compounds, as, *earth-quake,
rain-bow*, each ſyllable is pronounced with
the ſtreſs that belongs to accented ſyllables;
and there is little or no diſtinction of accent. The reaſon is obvious : There is
no difference in the importance of the ſyllables ; both are equally neceſſary to convey the idea. By giving one ſyllable the
whole

---

* To prove the utility of accent in marking the ſignification of words, it is only neceſſary to advert to the two
words *omiſſion* and *commiſſion*. Theſe words have the accent on the ſecond ſyllable ; but when we uſe them by way
of contraſt, we lay a ſtrong accent on the firſt ſyllable of
each, by which the oppoſition of ſenſe is diſtinguiſhed.
" Sins of o' miſſion and com' miſſion." Thus when we uſe
the word *regain*, we often lay an accent on *re* almoſt equal
to that on *gain* ; becauſe the ſenſe of the word depends
much, or rather wholly, on the particle.

whole accent, such a word lofes its original meaning, or at leaft its force, as may be obferved in the word *huffy*, a corruption of *houfe-wife*; which, from an affectation of a unity of accent, and a hafty pronunciation, has funk into a low word. From the fame ridiculous affectation, *work-houfe* is, by fome people, pronounced *work-us*.

On this head, I fhall only obferve further, that fome words of many fyllables have three accents; of which we have an example in *val'etu'dina'rian*.

It has been already remarked that the compofition of words, and the eafe of fpeaking, require a plurality of accent. The reafon why words of many fyllables have two or three accents, is plain to any man that attempts to pronounce them without an accent.

We cannot pronounce more than two unaccented fyllables with perfect eafe; but four or five can hardly be articulated without an intervening accent. We glide over the unaccented fyllables with fuch rapidity, that we have hardly time to place the organs in a pofition to articulate them. The difficulty is in proportion to the num-

ber :

ber : So that after paffing over two or three, the voice very naturally refts or falls forceably upon a particular fyllable. Hence the words moft difficult to be pronounced, are thofe of four fyllables, accented on the firft ; as *figurative, literature, applicable.* The difficulty is very great, when the middle fyllables abound with confonants, even in triffyllables, as *ag'grandize* ; but is itfelf a fufficient reafon for not accenting the firft fyllable of fuch words as *accepta-ble* and *refractory.* When one of the words which have the accent on the firft, and three fucceeding unaccented fyllables, is followed by two or three particles, the paffage is weak and often occafions hefita-tion in a fpeaker ; as " *applicable to the af-fairs of common life.*"

A REMARKABLE inftance of this, we find in Prieftley's Preface to Letters to a Philofophical Unbeliever ; " Whether of a plea*furcable* or of a painful nature." In this example there are fix weak fyllables following each other without interruption, and fuch paffages are not reduceable to any kind of poetic feet. This affemblage of unimportant fyllables makes a hiatus in language, which fhould, as far as poffible, be avoided by a writer ; for the melody of

profe

profe confifts in a proper mixture of important and unimportant fyllables.*[K]

DIFFERENCES *of* PRONUNCIATION *and* CONTROVERTED POINTS EXAMINED.

HAVING laid down fome general rules refpecting pronunciation, I proceed to examin local differences, and the moft material points of controverfy on this fubject.

IN the eaftern ftates, there is a practice prevailing among the body of the people, of prolonging the found of *i* in the termination *ive*. In fuch words as *motive, relative*, &c. the people, excepting the more polifhed part, give *i* its firft found. This is a local practice, oppofed to the general pronunciation

---

* IN the following paffage, alliteration or the fimilarity of the weak fyllables, has a very bad effect. " We tread, as with*in* an *en*chanted circle, where nothing appears as it truly is."——Blair Serm. 9.

A DIFFICULTY of pronunciation is obvious in the following fentence, " This caution while it *admirably* protects the public liberty, can never bear hard upon individuals." Change the accent from the firft to the fecond fyllable of *admirably*, and the difficulty vanifhes.

" AND yet the labyrinth is more *admirable than the* Pyramids."——Tranf. of Herodotus, Euterpe.

pronunciation of the Englifh on both fides of the atlantic, fometimes to the rules of accent, and always to derivation.   In diffyllables, as *motive*, *active*, the genius of our language requires that the accent fhould be laid on *one* fyllable, and that the other fhould be fhort.*   But by prolonging *i* in the laft, the diftinction of accent is totally deftroyed.

In polyfyllables, which often have two accents, this reafon has lefs force, but the derivation, which is from the French *motif*, *relatif*, always requires that *i* in the termination *ive* fhould have the found of *ee* fhort, as in *live, give*.   This is merely the fhort found of the French *i*, and the confequence of the Englifh accent on the firft fyllable.   Thefe reafons, with the authority of the moft approved practice, fhould operate to difcountenance the fingular drawling pronunciation of the eaftern people.†   The

---

* Except compounds, as *earthquake, bookcafe*.

† The final *e* muft be confidered as the caufe of this vulgar dialect.   It is wifhed that fome bold genius would dare to be right, and fpell this clafs of words without *e*, *motiv*. By reafon of an embarraffing orthography, one half the trouble of learning Englifh, is beftowed in acquiring errors, and correcting them after they are formed into habits.   To prevent the continuance of this erroneous practice, I have, in the firft part of the Inftitute, diftinguifhed the filent *e*, by an Italic character.

THE fame reafons are oppofed to another local practice of a fimilar nature in the middle ftates ; where many people pronounce *practife*, *prejudice*, with *i* long. I know of no authority for this beyond the limits of two or three ftates ; and it is clear that the practice is not warranted by any principle in the language.

ANOTHER very common error, among the yeomanry of America, and particularly in New England, is the pronouncing of *e* before *r*, like *a* ; as *marcy* for mercy. This miftake muft have originated principally in the name of the letter *r*, which, in moft of our fchool books, is called *ar*. This fingle miftake has fpread a falfe pronunciation of feveral hundred words, among millions of people.*

To avoid this difagreeable fingularity fome fine fpeakers have run into another extreme, by pronouncing *e* before *r*, like *u*, *murcy*. This is an error. The true found of the fhort *e*, as in *let*, is the correct and elegant pronunciation of this letter in all words of this clafs.

THERE

---

* To remedy the evil, in fome degree, this letter is named *er*, in the Inftitute. In a few inftances this pronunciation is become general among polite fpeakers, as clerks, fergeant, &c.

THERE is a vulgar fingularity in the pronunciation of the eaftern people, which is very incorrect, and difagreeable to ftrangers; that of prefixing the found of *i* fhort or *e*, before the dipthong *ow*; as *kiow*, *piower* or *peower*. This fault ufually occurs after *p*, *c* hard, or thofe other confonants which are formed near the feat of *ee* in the mouth, or in paffing from which to the fucceeding vowel, the organs naturally take the pofition neceffary to pronounce *ee*. But the moft awkward countryman pronounces *round*, *ground*, &c. with tolerable propriety.

THIS, with fome other peculiarities which prevail among the yeomanry of New England, fprings from caufes that do not exift, in the fame degree, in any other part of America, perhaps not in the world. It may furprize thofe who have not turned their thoughts to this fubject, that I fhould afcribe the manner of fpeaking among a people, to the nature of their government and a diftribution of their property. Yet it is an undoubted fact that the drawling nafal manner of fpeaking in New England arifes almoft folely from thefe caufes.

PEOPLE of large fortunes, who pride themfelves on family diftinctions, poffefs a
certain

certain boldnefs, dignity and independence in their manners, which give a correfpondent air to their mode of fpeaking. Thofe who are accuftomed to command flaves, form a habit of exprefling themfelves with the tone of authority and decifion.

In New England, where there are few flaves and fervants, and lefs family diftinctions than in any other part of America, the people are accuftomed to addrefs each other with that diffidence, or attention to the opinion of others, which marks a ftate of equality. Inftead of commanding, they advife; inftead of faying, with an air of decifion, *you muft*; they afk with an air of doubtfulnefs, *is it not beft?* or give their opinions with an indecifive tone; *you had better, I believe*. Not poffefling that pride and confcioufnefs of fuperiority which attend birth and fortune, their intercourfe with each other is all conducted on the idea of equality, which gives a fingular tone to their language and complexion to their manners.

These remarks do not apply to the commercial towns; for people who are converfant with a variety of company lofe moft of their fingularities, and hence well bred

people

people refemble each other in all countries. But the peculiar traits of national character are found in the internal parts of a country, among that clafs of people who do not travel, nor are tempted by an intercourfe with foreigners, to quit their own habits.*

Such are the caufes of the local peculiarities in pronunciation, which prevail among the country people in New England, and which, to foreigners, are the objects of ridicule. The great error in their manner of fpeaking proceeds immediately from not opening the mouth fufficiently. Hence words are drawled out in a carelefs lazy manner, or the found finds a paffage thro the nofe.

Nothing can be fo difagreeable as that drawling, whining cant that diftinguifhes a certain clafs of people ; and too much pains cannot be taken to reform the practice.

* Hence the furprifing fimilarity between the idioms of the New England people and thofe of Chaucer, Shakefpear, Congreve, &c. who wrote in the true Englifh ftile. It is remarked by a certain author, that the inhabitants of iflands beft preferve their native tongue. New England has been in the fituation of an ifland ; during 160 years, the people except in a few commercial towns, have not been expofed to any of the caufes which effect great changes in language and manners.

tice. Great efforts fhould be made by teachers of fchools, to make their pupils o-pen the teeth, and give a full clear found to every fyllable. The beauty of fpeaking confifts in giving each letter and fyllable its due proportion of found, with a prompt articulation.

THUS in order to pronounce *cow, power,* or *gown* with propriety, the pupil fhould be taught, after placing the organs in the pofition required by the firft confonant, to open his mouth wide; before he begins the found of *ow* : Otherwife in paffing from that pofition to the aperture neceffary to pronounce *ow,* he will inevitably articulate *ee, keow.*

A SIMILAR method is recommended to thofe polite fpeakers who are fo fond of imitating the Englifh ftage pronunciation as to embrace every fingularity, however difagreeable. I refer to the very modern pronunciation of *kind, fky, guide,* &c. in which we hear the fhort *e* before *i, keind,* or *kyind, fkey,* &c. This is the fame barba-rous dialect, as the *keow* and *veow* of the eaftern country people. Yet, ftrange as it may feem, it is the elegant pronunciation of the fafhionable people both in England
and

and America. Even Sheridan, who has laid it down as a rule that *i* is a dipthong, compofed of *aw* and *ee*, has prefixed a *y* fhort to its found in feveral words ; as *kyind, fkyi, gyide*, &c. We may with equal propriety prefix *e* to the dipthong *ow*, or to *o* in *poll*, or to *oo* in *fool*, or to any other vowel. It is prefumed that the bare mention of fuch barbarifms will be fufficient to reftrain their progrefs, both in New England and on the Britifh theater.

Some of the fouthern people, particularly in Virginia, almoft omit the found of *r* as in *ware, there*. In the beft Englifh pronunciation, the found of *r* is much fofter than in fome of the neighboring languages, particularly the Irifh and Spanifh ; and probably much fofter than in the ancient Greek. But there feems to be no good reafon for omitting the found altogether ; nor can the omiffion be defended on the ground, either of good practice or of rules. It feems to be a habit contracted by carelefsnefs.

It is a cuftom very prevalent in the middle ftates, even among fome well bred people, to pronounce *off, foft, drop, crop*, with the found of *a, aff, faft, drap, crap*.
This

This feems to be a foreign and local dialect; and cannot be advocated by any perfon who underftands correct Englifh. [L]

In the middle ftates alfo, many people pronounce a *t* at the end of *once* and *twice*, *oncet* and *twicet*. This grofs impropriety would not be mentioned, but for its prevalence among a clafs of very well educated people; particularly in Philadelphia and Baltimore.

Fotch for *fetch* is very common, in feveral ftates, but not among the better claffes of people. *Cotched* for *caught* is more frequent, and equally barbarous.

Skroud and *fkrouge* for *croud*, are fometimes heard among people that fhould be afhamed of the leaft vulgarifm.

Mought for *might* is heard in moft of the ftates, but not frequently except in a few towns. [M]

Holpe for *help* I have rarely heard except in Virginia. *Tote* is local in Virginia and its neighborhood. In meaning it is nearly equivalent to *carry*. I have taken en great pains to difcover the etymology of the local terms ufed in the feveral ftates; but this word has yet eluded my diligence.*

CHORE, a corruption of *char*, is an Englifh word, ftill ufed in many parts of England, as a *char-man*, a *char-woman*, but in America, it is perhaps confined to New England. It fignifies fmall domeftic jobs of work, and its place cannot be fupplied by any other fingle word in the language.

THESE local words, and others of lefs note, are gradually growing into difufe, and will probably be loft : Except fuch as are neceffary in fome particular occupation.

THE pronunciation of *w* for *v* is a prevailing practice in England and America : It is particularly prevalent in Bofton and Philadelphia.

* I HAVE once met with the word in Chaucer's Plowman's Tale 2014.

" THE other fide ben pore and pale,
And peple yput out of prefe,
And femin caitiffs fore a cale,
And er in one without encreafe ;
Iclepid Lollers and Londlefe ;
Who *toteth* on 'hem thei ben untall ;
They ben arayid all for pece,
But falfhed foule mote it befall."

Philadelphia.* Many people fay *weal, wef-fel*, for *veal, veffel*.

THESE letters are eafily miftaken for each other, and the name of the letter *w* now ufed, is a proof that the letter *v* was formerly called *u* or *oo*. The letter in the Roman language had the found we now give *w* in *will*. *Via* and *vinum*, pronoun-ced *wia, winum*, have fuffered but a fmall change of pronunciation in our *way, wine*. In old Englifh books, down to Shakefpear, *v* was written for the fhort *u*, as *vp, vn-der* ; for *up, under*. On the other hand, *u* was written where we now write *v*, as *uery, euery*, for *very, every*. It feems therefore, that *v* had formerly the found of *w* or *oo* ; and that inftead of corrupting the language, the Cockneys in London, and their imita-tors in America, who fay *weal, wery*, have retained the primitive pronunciation. In confirmation of this opinion, it may be ob-ferved that the Danes, who fpeak a dialect of the Saxon, have no *w* in their language, but where we write *w*, they write *v*, and where

* I AM at a lofs to determine, why this practice fhould prevail in Bofton and not in Connecticut. The firft and principal fettlers in Hartford came from the vicinity of Bofton. Vaft numbers of people in Bofton and the neighborhood ufe *w* for *v*; yet I never once heard this pronunciation in Connecticut.

H

where we write *wh*, they invariably write *hv*; as *vind, wind*; *vej, way*; *vader, wade*; *hvad, what*; *hvide, white*; *hvi, why*. The Germans, whofe language is another branch of the fame ftock, invariably pronounce *w* as we do *v*; *wall, vall*; *wir, vir, we*; *wollen, vollen, will*; and *v* they pronounce as we do *f*; as *vergeſſen, fergeſſen*, which is the fame as the Englifh *forget*.

THE retaining the old found of *v* is a proof of the force of cuftom; but fince the nation in general have annexed to it a precife found, as well as to *w*, every perfon fhould refign his peculiarities for the fake of uniformity.

BUT there are fome points in pronunciation, in which the beft informed people differ, both in opinion and practice.

THE words *ſhall, quality, quantity, qualify, quandary, quadrant*, are differently pronounced by good fpeakers. Some give *a* a broad found, as *ſhol, quolity*; and others, its fecond found, as in *hat*. With refpect to the four firft, almoft all the ftandard writers* agree to pronounce *a* fhort, as in *hat*: And this is

the

* By ftandard writers, I mean, Kenrick, Sheridan, Burn, Perry and Scott.

the ftage pronunciation. . It is correct, for it is more agreeable to the. analogy of the language ; that being the proper found of the Englifh *a* which is heard in *hat* or *bar.* With refpect to the two laft, authors differ; fome give the firft, fome the fecond, and others the fifth found. They all pretend to give us the court pronunciation, and as they differ fo widely, we muft fuppofe that eminent fpeakers differ in practice. In fuch a cafe, we can hardly hefitate a moment to call in analogy to decide the queftion, and give *a* in all thefe words, as alfo in *quafh*, its fecond found.*

THE words *either, neither, deceit, conceit, receipt,* are generally pronounced, by the eaftern people, *ither, nither, defate, confate, refate.* Thefe are errors ; all the ftandard authors agree to give *ei*, in thefe words, the found of *ee.* This is the practice in England, in the middle and fouthern ftates, and, what is higher authority, analogy warrants the practice. Indeed it is very abfurd to pronouce the verb *conceive, conceeve,* and the noun *conceit, confate.* Such

an

* THE diftinction in the pronunciation of *a* in *quality*, when it fignifies the property of fome body, and when it is ufed for high rank, appears to me without foundation in rule or practice.

an inconfiftency will hardly find advocates, except among the prejudiced and uninformed.

IMPORTANCE is, by a few people, pronounced importance; with the firft found of *o*. The reafon alleged is, that it is a derivative of *import*, and *o* fhould preferve the fame found it has in the original. It feems however to be affectation, for the ftandard writers and general practice are oppofed to it. Indeed it may be confidered as a mere imitation of the French pronunciation of the fame word.

DECIS-IVE for *deci-five* is mere affectation.

REESIN for *raifin* is very prevalent in two or three principal towns in America. One of the ftandard authors gives us this pronunciation; and another gives us both *raifin* and *reefin*. But all the others pronounce the word *raifin*, with *a* long; and derivation, analogy and general cuftom, all decide in favor of the practice.

LEISURE is fometimes pronounced *leefure*, and fometimes *lezhure*: The latter is the
moft

moſt general pronunciation in America. It is almoſt ſingular in its ſpelling ; *ſeizure* being the only word in analogy with it ; and this is a derivative from *ſeize*. The true original orthography of *leiſure* was *leaſure* ; this was in analogy with *pleaſure*, *meaſure*, and its ancient pronunciation ſtill remains.

DICTIONARY has been uſually pronounced *dicſonary* ; But its derivation from *diction*, the analogous pronunciation of *tion* in other caſes, and all the ſtandard writers require *dicſhunary*, or *dicſhonary*.

ONE author of eminence pronounces *defile* in three ſyllables, *def-i-le*. In this he is ſingular ; neither general practice, nor rules warrant the pronunciation ; and all the other authorities are againſt him.

WITH reſpect to *oblige*, authorities differ. The ſtandard writers give us both *oblige* and *obleege*, and it is impoſſible to determine on which ſide the weight of authority lies. The direct derivation of the word from the French would incline us to prefer *obleege*, in the analogy of *fatigue, machine, antique, pique, marine, oblique*, which uniformly preſerve the French *i* or Engliſh

lifh *ee*.   Yet Chefterfield called this affectation, and it might be fo in his age ; for
the opinions of men are capricious.   The
Englifh analogy requires *i* long in *oblige* ;
and perhaps this fhould incline all parties
to meet each other on that beft principle.

SOME people very erroneoufly pronouncé
chaife, *fha* in the fingular, and *fhaze* in the
plural.   The fingular number is *fhaze*, and
the plural, *fhazes*.

OUR modern fafhionable fpeakers accent *European* on the laft fyllable but one.
This innovation has happened within a
few years : I fay innovation ; for it is a
violation of an eftablifhed principle of the
language, that words ending in *ean* have
the accent on the laft fyllable but two :
Witnefs *Mediterra′nean*, *Pyré′nean*, *Hercu′-
lean*, *fubterra′nean*.   I do not advert to an
exception,* and why *European* fhould be
made one, it is difficult to determine.   The
reafon given by fome, that *e* in the penul-
tima reprefents the Latin dipthong *æ*, which
was long, is of little weight, oppofed to
the general practice of a nation, and to an

eftablifhed

---

* *HYMENEAN* and *hymeneal* are, by fome writers, accented on the laft fyllable but one ; but erroneoufly.   Other ,
authorities preferve the analogy.

eftablifhed principle. The ftandard authors, in this inftance, as in all others,
where practice is not uniform, very abfurdly give both pronunciations, that we
may take our choice. As this is a very
eafy method of getting over difficulties, ánd
paffing along without giving offence, fo it
is a certain way to perpetuate differences
in opinion and practice, and to prevent the
eftablifhment of any ftandard. Analogy
requires *Euro'pean*, and this is fupported
by as good authorities as the other.

ROME is very frequently pronounced
Room, and that by people of every clafs.
The authors I have confulted give no light
upon this word, except Perry, who directs
to that pronunciation. The practice however, is by no means general in America :
There are many good fpeakers who give *o*
its firft found. It feems very abfurd to
give *o* its firft found in *Romifh*, *Romans*,
and pronounce it *oo* in *Rome*, the radical
word. I know of no language in Europe,
in which *o* has not one uniform found, viz.
the found we give it in *rofe*. It is perhaps
the only vowel, in the found of which all
nations agree. In Englifh it has other
founds ; but the firft is its proper one. A
great proportion of people in America have
reftored

reſtored the analogy of pronunciation in giving *o* its firſt ſound in *Rome* ; and a deſire of uniformity would lead us to extend the practice.*

In the pronunciation of *arch* in many compound words, people are not uniform. The diſputed words are *archangel, archetype, architecture, architrave, archives.* There ſeems to be no ſettled principle of analogy, by which the queſtion can be determined. Etymology would require *ch,* in Greek and Hebrew derivatives, to have uniformly the ſound of *k* ; but before moſt conſonants, ſuch a pronunciation is harſh ; for which reaſon it is generally ſoftened into the Engliſh *ch,* as *archbiſhop.* But before vowels, as in the words juſt enumerated, the beſt practice has decided for the ſound of *k* ; and euphony, as well as derivation, favors the deciſion. [N]

The ſound of *ch* in *chart* is likewiſe diſputed ; and the ſtandard authors are directly oppoſed to each other. There is as good

* This is the ſound which the rhime requires in the following verſes :

" Give eare to me that ten years fought for Rome,
    Yet reapt diſgrace at my returning home."

Rel. An. Poet. p. 204.

good foreign authority on one fide as the other; but in America, *ch* has generally its foft or Englifh found. This muft perhaps be preferred, contrary to etymology; for we uniformly give *ch* that found in *charter*, which is from the fame original; and this alfo diftinguifhes the word from *cart*; a reafon which is not without its weight

THERE are many people who omit the afpirate in moft words which begin with *wh*; as *white*, *whip*, &c. which they pronounce *wite*, *wip*. To fuch it is neceffary only to obferve, that in the pure Englifh pronunciation, both in Great Britain and New England, for it is exactly the fame in both, *h* is not filent in a fingle word beginning with *wh*. In this point our ftandard authors differ; two of them afpirating the whole of thefe words, and three, marking *h* in moft of them as mute. But the omiffion of *h* feems to be a foreign corruption; for in America, it is not known among the unmixed defcendants of the Englifh. Sheridan has here given the true Englifh pronunciation. In this clafs of words, *w* is filent in four only, with their derivatives; viz. *who*, *whole*, *whoop*, *whore*.

ONE

ONE or two authors affect to pronounce *human*, and about twenty other words beginning with *h*, as tho they were spelt *yuman*.* This is a grofs error. The only word that begins with this found, is *humor*, with its derivatives. In the American pronunciation, *h* is filent in the following, *honeft*, *honor*, *hour*, *humor*, *herb*, *heir*, with their derivatives. To thefe the Englifh add *hofpital*, *hoftler*, *humble*; but an imitation of thefe, which fome induftrioufly affect, cannot be recommended, as every omiffion of the afpirate ferves to mutilate and weaken the language.

THE

---

* PARTICULARLY *Perry*. I am furprized that his pronunciation has found fo many advocates in this country, as there is none more erroneous.

I WOULD juft remark here that many writers ufe *an* before *h* afpirate, inftead of *a*; which practice feems not well founded. The rapid found of the article *a* is indiftinct, but opens the mouth to a proper pofition to pronounce *h*; whereas *n* places the end of the tongue under the upper teeth, and the mouth affumes a new pofition, before the afpiration can be formed. *A* hundred, *a* houfe, &c. are therefore much more eafily articulated, than *an* hundred, *an* houfe.

THUS *a* fhould always be ufed before *y* confonant, and confequently before *u* when it has the fame found, as in *union*, *univerfal*, &c. Indeed I cannot account for the ufe of *an* before *y*, on any other principle than this, that the perfons who ufe it do not pronounce *y* at all. If they make *y* the fame as *ee*, it is confiftent to write *an* before it; but this is an error.

THE word *yelk* is fometimes written *yolk* and pronounced *yoke*. But *yelk* is the moft correct orthography, from the Saxon *gealk-we*; and in this country, it is the general pronunciation.

EWE is, by the Englifh, often pronounced *yo*; which is fometimes heard in America. But analogy and the general corresponding practice in this country, with the authority of fome of the moft accurate writers, decide for *yew*.

THE Englifh fpeakers of eminence have fhortened the vowel in the firft fyllable of *tyranny*, *zealous*, *facrifice*, &c. altho in the primitive words, all agree to give the vowel its firft found, This pronunciation has not fpread among the people of this country; but our learned men have adopted it; and it feems in fome degree to be the genius of our language. In *child*, *clean*, *holy*, &c. we uniformly give the firft vowel its long found; but when a fyllable is added, we always fhorten it; *children*, *clenly*, *holyday*.

ON the other hand, many people in America fay *pat-ron*, *mat-ron*; whereas the Englifh fay either *pa-tron* or *pat-ron*, *ma-tron*

tron or *mat-ron* ; but all agree in faying, *pat-ronage*. In *patriot, patriotifm*, the Englifh give *a* its long found ; but a great part of the Americans, its fhort found. In all thefe cafes, where people are not uniform, I fhould prefer the fhort found ; for it appears to me the moft analogous.

WRATH, the Englifh pronounce with the third found of *a* or *aw* ; but the Americans almoft univerfally preferve the analogous found, as in *bath, path*. This is the correct pronunciation ; and why fhould we reject it for *wroth*, which is a corruption ? If the Englifh practice is erroneous, let it remain fo ; we have no concern with it : By adhering to our own practice, we preferve a fuperiority over the Englifh, in thofe inftances, in which ours is guided by rules ; and fo far ought we to be from conforming to their practice, that they ought rather to conform to ours.

IT is difputed whether *g* fhould have its hard or foft found, in *homogeneous* and *heterogeneous* : On this queftion the ftandard authors are not agreed. The hard found, as in *go*, coincides with etymology ; but analogy requires the other, as in *genius*. The fame remarks apply to *g* in *phlogifton*.

IN

IN the middle and southern states, *fierce,
pierce, tierce,* are pronounced *feerce, peerce,
teerce.* To convince the people of the impropriety of this pronunciation, it might
be sufficient to inform them, that it is not
fashionable on the English theater. For
those who want better proofs, before they
relinquish their practice, I would observe,
that these words are derived to us from the
French ; *fierce, tierce,* from *fiers, tiers,* and
pierce from *percer.* In the two former,
the French pronounce both *i* and *e* ; but
it is evident the English originally pronounced *e* only ; for the *i* was omitted in
the spelling of *fierce,* and was not introduced into *pierce* till after Spenser wrote.

> "—WHEN he him knew and had his tale herd,
> As *fers* as a leon pulled out his fwerd."
> Chaucer, Knightes Tale 1600.

> "THE drought of March hath *perced* to the rote."
> Canterbury Tales.

> "FOR they this queen attended ; in whofe fteed,
> Oblivion laid him down on Laura's herfe :
> Hereat the hardeft ftones were feen to bleed,
> And grones of buried ghofts the heavens did perfe."
> Verfes to Edmond Spenfer.

PIERCE is alfo made to rhime with *rehearfe.* Pope makes it rhime with *univerfe.*

" HE, who thro vaft immenfity can pierce,
See worlds on worlds compofe one univerfe."
Effay on Man, 23.

THE rhime in the laft quotation, is not unequivocal proof of the pronunciation in Pope's time ; but the orthography in Chaucer's and Spenfer's writings, are to me fatisfactory evidence that *e* in thefe words was fhort. The ftandard Englifh pronunciation now is *ferce, perce, terce*, and it is univerfal in New England. I have only to add, that the fharp abrupt found of *e* in the two firft words is moft happily adapted to exprefs the ideas.

THE Englifh pronounce *leap, lep* ; and that in the prefent tenfe as well as the paft. Some of our American horfemen have learnt the practice ; but among other people, it is almoft unknown. It is a breach of analogy, at leaft in the prefent tenfe ; the American pronunciation, *leep*, is therefore the moft correct and fhould not be relinquifhed.

IN the fafhionable world, *heard* is pronounced *herd* or *hurd*. This was almoft unknown in America till the commencement of the late war, and how long it has
been

been the practice in England, I cannot determine.   By Chaucer's orthography, one
would imagine that it had been handed
down from remote antiquity ; for he writes
herd, herde, and *herden.**   In reading more
modern poets, I have rarely found any instance of a verse's closing with this word ;
so that it is difficult to say what has been
the general practice among the learned.
But for centuries, the word has been uniformly spelt *heard* ; the verb *hear* is in analogy with *fear, sear,* and yet *e* in the past
time and participle has been omitted, as
heard, not *heared.*   That *herd* was not formerly the pronunciation, is probable from
this circumstance ; the Americans were
strangers to it when they came from England, and the body of the people are so to
this day.†   To most people in this country, the English pronunciation appears like
affectation,

* See Canterbury Tales and Prologue. L. 221, 955,
1599, 15382.

† To prove that the Americans have a corrupt pronunciation, we are often told that our anceftors came from the
western counties of England.   This is but partially true.

The company that purchased New England, was indeed
called the *Plymouth Company,* being composed principally of
persons belonging to the county of Devon.   But many of
the principal settlers in these states came from London and
its vicinity ; some from the middle counties, the ancient
kingdom

affectation, and is adopted only in the capital towns, which are always the moft ready
to diftinguifh themfelves by an implicit
imitation of foreign cuftoms. Analogy
requires that we fhould retain our former
practice; for we may as well change *feared, feared,* into *ferd, ferd,* as to change *beard*
into *herd.*

BEARD is fometimes, but erroneoufly,
pronounced *beerd.* General practice, both
in England and America, requires that *e*
fhould be pronounced as in *were,* and I
know of no rule oppofed to the practice.

DEAF is generally pronounced *deef.* It
is the univerfal practice in the 'eaftern
ftates; and it is general in the middle and
fouthern; tho fome have adopted the Englifh pronunciation, *def.* The latter is evidently a corruption; for the word is in
analogy with *leaf* and *fheaf,* and has been
from time immemorial. So in Sir William
Temple's works, Virg. Ecl.

> ——————————"WE fing not to the deaf,
> An anfwer comes from every trembling leaf."
>
> LEAF

kingdom of Mercia; and a few from the northern counties.
To fhow the falfehood of the charge, with refpect to the
language, it may be afferted with truth, that there is not the
leaft affinity between the language of the New England
people and the fpecimens of the Devonfhire dialect, given
in the Englifh Magazines.

LEAF and *deaf*, with a different orthography, are repeatedly made to rhime in Chaucer's works; as in the Wife of Bath's Prologue, L. 6217,

> "For that I rent out of his book a lefe,
> That of the ftroke mŷn ere wex al *defe*."

So alfo line 6249.

THIS was the orthography of his time, and an almoft conclufive evidence that *deaf* was pronounced *deef*.* This pronunciation is generally retained in America, and analogy requires it.

THIS differtation will be clofed with one obfervation, which the reader may have made upon the foregoing criticifms : That in many inftances the Americans ftill adhere to the analogies of the language, where the Englifh have infringed them. So far therefore as the regularity of conftruction is concerned, we ought to retain our own practice and be our own ftandards. The Englifh practice is an authority; but confidering the force of cuftom and the caprice of fafhion, their practice muft be as liable

to

---

* THE digraph *ea* feems not to have been much ufed in that age; for *fpeak* authors wrote *fpeke*; for *dear*, *dere*; for *leaf*, *lefe*.

I

to changes and to errors, as the practice of a well educated yeomanry, who are governed by habits and not eafily led aftray by novelty. In the inftances where we have adhered to analogy, no confideration can warrant us in refigning our practice to the authority of a foreign court, which, thro mere affectation, may have embraced many obvious errors. In doubtful cafes, to pay a fuitable deference to the opinions of others, is wife and prudent ; but to renounce an obvious principle of propriety becaufe others have renounced it, is to carry our complaifance for the faults of the great, much farther than we can juftify, and in a *nation*, it is an act of fervility that wants a name.

DISSERTATION III.

*Examination of controverted Points, continu-
ed.—Of modern Corruptions in the English
Pronunciation.*

EXAMINATION *of* CONTROVERT-
ED POINTS, *continued.*

N the preceding differtation I have endeavored to fettle a number of controverted points and local differences in pronunciation, on the moft fatisfactory principles hitherto difcovered. I now proceed to fome other differences of confequence to the language, and particularly in America.

GOLD is differently pronounced by good fpeakers, and differently marked by the ftandard writers. Two of them give us

goold

goold, as the ftandard, and three, *gold* or *goold*. But we may find better principles than the opinions or practice of individuals, to direct our judgement in this particular. The word indeed has the pronunciation, *goold*, in fome of the collateral branches of the Teutonic, as in the Danifh, where it is fpelt *guld*. But in the Saxon, it was written *gold*, and has been uniformly written fo in Englifh. Befides, we have good reafon to believe that it was, in early times, pronounced *gold*, with the firft found of *o*, for the poets invariably make it rhime with *old*, *behold*, and other words of fimilar found. Thus in Chaucer :

"With nayles yelwe, and bright as any *gold*,
He hadde a bere's fkin, cole blake for old."
Knight's Tales, L. 2143.

In Pope :

"Now Europe's laurels on their brows behold,
But ftain'd with blood, or ill exchang'd for *gold*."
Effay on Man, Book 4.

The rhime is here a prefumptive proof that the poets pronounced this word with the firft found of *o*, and it is a fubftantial reafon why that pronunciation fhould be preferred. But analogy is a ftill ftronger reafon ; for bold, told, fold, and I prefume
every

every fimilar word in the language, has the firft found of *o*. Thefe are good reafons why *gold* fhould have that found ; reafons which are permanent, and fuperior to any private opinions.

SIMILAR reafons, and equally forceable, are oppofed to the modern pronunciation of *wound*. I fay *modern* ; for in America *woond* is a recent innovation. It was perhaps an ancient dialect ; for the old Saxon and modern Danifh orthography warrant this conjecture.

BUT in Englifh the fpelling has uniformly correfponded with *bound*, *found*, and if we may judge from the rhimes of our poets, the pronunciation has alfo been analogous. Thus in Skelton's Elegy on Henry, Earl of Northumberland, 1489, we have the following lines :

"MOST noble erle ! O foul myfurd* ground
Whereon he gat his finall deadly *wounde*."
Rel. An. Eng. Poet. vol. 1. page 113.

So in a fong which feems to have been written in the reign of Henry VIII.

" WHERE

* MISUSED.

I 3

" WHERE griping grefes the hart would *wounae*
And doleful dumps the mynde oppreffe,
There muficke with her filver found,
With fpeed is wont to fend redreffe."

Ibm. page 165.

SIMILAR rhimes occur in almoft every page of modern poetry.

" WARRIORS fhe fires with animated founds,
Pours balm into the bleeding lover's *wounds*."

Pope.

THE fafhionable pronunciation of *wound* deftroys the rhime and infringes the rule of analogy ; two objections to it which can be removed only by univerfal practice. Does this practice exift ? By no means. One good authority* at leaft, directs to the analogous pronunciation ; and another compiler directs to both—the regular and the fafhionable. But were *woond* the univerfal practice in Great Britain, this fhould not induce us to lay afide our own practice for a foreign one. There is but a fmall part, even of the well bred people in this country, who have yet adopted the Englifh mode ; and the great body of the people uniformly purfue analogy. The

authority

---

* KENRICK, who was not guided folely by the fafhion of the day, but paid fome regard to the regular conftruction of the language.

authority of practice therefore, is, in this country, oppofed to the innovation. Shall we then relinquifh what every man muft acknowlege to be *right*, to embrace the corruptions of a foreign court and ftage? Will not the Atlantic ocean, the total feparation of America from Great Britain, the pride of an independent nation, the rules of the language, the melody of Englifh poetry, reftrain our rage for imitating the errors of foreigners?

BUT it is faid that *wŏond* is fofter than *wound*, and therefore more agreeable. Suppofe the affertion to be true, will it follow that the fofteft pronunciation fhould be preferred?

IT is acknowleged on all hands, that a correfpondence between found and fenfe is a beauty in language, and there are many words in our language, the founds of which were borrowed from the fenfible objects, the ideas of which they are defigned to exprefs. Such are the *dafhing* of waters, the *crackling* of burning faggots, the *hiffing* of ferpents, the *lifping* of infants, and the *ftuttering* of a *ftammerer*. Thefe are confidered as beauties in a language. But there are other words, the founds of which are not

adopted

adopted in imitating audible noifes, which are either foft or harfh, and by the help of affociation are particularly calculated to exprefs ideas, which are either agreeable or difagreeable to the mind. Of this kind are *foft* and *harfh*, *fweet* and *four*, and a multitude of others. On the fuppofition therefore, that *woond* is the fofter pronunciation, this is a good reafon why it fhould *not* be adopted ; for the idea it conveys is extremely difagreeable, and much better reprefented by a harfh word.*

SKEPTIC for *fceptic* is mere pedantry ; a modern change that has no advantage for its object. The Greek derivation will be pleaded as an authority ; but this will not warrant the innovation, without extending

* SHERIDAN has repeated with approbation, a celebrated faying of Dean Swift, who was a ftickler for analogy, in pronouncing *wind* like *mind*, *bind*, with the firft found of *i*. The Dean's argument was, " I have a great mind to find why you pronounce that word *wind*." I would beg leave to afk this gentleman, who directs us to fay *woond*, if any good reafon can be *foond* why he *foonds* that word *woond* ; and whether he expects a rational people, will be *boond* to follow the *roond* of court improprieties ? We acknowlege that *wind* is a deviation from analogy and a corruption ; but who pronounces it otherwife ? Practice was almoft wholly againft Swift, and in America at leaft, it is as generally in favor of the analogy of *wound*. A partial or local practice, may be brought to fupport analogy, but fhould be no authority in deftroying it.

tending it to *scene*, *scepter*, and many others. Will the advocates write and pronounce the latter *skene*, *skepter* ? If not,
they ſhould be ſatisfied with analogy and
former practice. It is remarkable however, that notwithſtanding the authority of
almoſt all the modern dictionaries is in
favor of ſkeptic, no writer of reputation,
whoſe works I have ſeen, has followed the
ſpelling. The old orthography, *ſceptic*,
ſtill maintains its ground.

SAUCE with the fourth ſound of *a* is accounted vulgar ; yet this is the ancient,
the correct, and the moſt general pronunciation. The *aw* of the North Britons is
much affected of late; *ſawce*, *hawnt*, *vawnt*;
yet the true ſound is that of *aunt*, *jaunt*,
and a change can produce no poſſible advantage.

THE words *advertiſement* and *chaſtiſement*
are differently accented by the ſtandard
authors, and by people on both ſides of the
Atlantic. Let us find the analogy. The
original words, *advertiſe* and *chaſtiſe*, are
verbs, accented uniformly on the laſt ſyllable. Let us ſearch thro the language for
verbs of this deſcription, and I preſume we
ſhall not find another inſtance, where, in

nouns

nouns formed from such verbs, by the addition of *ment*, the seat of the accent is changed. We find amusement, refinement, refreshment, reconcilement, and many, perhaps all others, preserve the accent of their primitives ; and in this analogy we find the reason why *chastisement* and *advertisement* should be accented on the last syllable but one. This analogy is a substantial and permanent rule, that will forever be superior to local customs.*

SIMILAR remarks may be made respecting *acceptable, admirable, disputable, comparable*, which our polite speakers accent on the first syllable. The first is indeed accented on the second syllable, by most authors, except Sheridan, who still retains the accent on the first.

IT was an old rule of grammarians, that the genius of our language requires the accent to be carried as far as possible towards the beginning of the word. This is seldom or never true ; on the contrary, the rule is directly opposed to the melody, both of poetry and prose. Under the influence,

---

* *GOVERNMENT, management*, retain also the accent of their primitives ; and the nouns *testament, compliment*, &c. form another analogy.

fluence, however, of this rule, a long catalogue of words loft their true pronunciation, and among the reft, a great number
of adjectives derived from verbs by an addition of the termination *able*. Some of
thefe are reftored to their analogy ; others
retain the accent on the firft fyllable.

NOTWITHSTANDING the authority of
Sheridan, I prefume few people will contend for the privilege of accenting *acceptable* on the firft fyllable.   How the organs
of any man can be brought to articulate
fo many confonants in the weak fyllables,
or how the ear can relifh fuch an unnatu-
ral pronunciation, is almoft inconceiveable.   In fpite of the pedantry of fcholars, the eafe and melody of fpeaking, have
almoft wholly banifhed the abfurd practice, by reftoring the accent to the fecond
fyllable.

BUT with refpect to *admirable*, *comparable* and *difputable*, the authors who are
deemed authorities are divided ; fome are
in favor of the accent on the firft fyllable,
and others adhere to analogy.

SETTING afide cuftom, every reafon for
accenting thefe words on the firft fyllable,
will apply with equal force to *advifeable*,
inclineable,

inclineable, requireable, and a hundred others. They are all formed from verbs accented on the laft fyllable, by annexing the
fame termination to the verb, and they are
all of the *fame* **part** of fpeech. Let us examin them by the rules for accentuation, laid
down in the preceding differtation.

The primitive verbs of this clafs of
words are ufually compounded of a particle and principal part of fpeech ; as *ad-mi-
ro, com-paro, re-quæro*, &c.. The laft fyllable, derived from a verb, is the moft important, and in the primitives, is invariably accented. This is agreeable to the firft
rule. In nine tenths of the derivatives,
the fame fyllable retains the accent ; as,
perceiveable, available, deploreable. In thefe
therefore both rules are obferved. The
third rule, or that which arifes from the
terminating fyllable, is alfo preferved in
moft of this clafs of words. It is therefore much to be regretted, that a falfe rule
fhould have introduced an irregularity into the language, by excepting a few words
from an analogy, which unites in itfelf every principle of propriety.

But the practice, with refpect to the
three words under confideration, is by no
means general. I have taken particular
notice

notice of the pronunciation of people in every part of America, and can teſtify that, in point of numbers, the practice is in favor of analogy. The people at large ſay *admi'reable, diſpu'teable, compa'reable*; and it would be difficult to lead them from this eaſy and natural pronunciation, to embrace that forced one of *ad'mirable*, &c. The people are right, and, in this particular, will ever have it to boaſt of, that among the unlearned is found the purity of Engliſh pronunciation.

Of this claſs of words, there are a few which ſeem to be corrupted in univerſal practice; as *reputable*. The reaſon why the accent in this word is more generally confirmed on the firſt ſyllable, may be this; there is but a ſingle conſonant between the firſt and ſecond ſyllable, and another between the ſecond and third; ſo that the pronunciation of the three weak ſyllables is by no means difficult. This word therefore, in which all authors, and as far as I know, all men, agree to lay the accent on the firſt ſyllable, and the orthography of which renders the pronunciation eaſy, muſt perhaps be admitted as an exception to the general rule.*

ACCESSARY

* It is regretted that the adjectives. *indiſſoluble, irreparable* were derived immediately from the Latin, *indiſſolubilis, irreparabilis,*

Accessary or *accessory*, are differently accented by the best writers and speakers. But the case of speaking requires that they should follow the rule of derivation, and retain the accent of the primitive, *access'ary*.

The fashionable pronunciation of such words as *immediate*, *ministerial*, *commodious*, is liable to particular exceptions. That *i* has a liquid sound, like *y*, in many words in our language, is not disputed ; but the classes of words which will admit this sound, ought to be ascertained.   It appears to me that common practice has determined this point.   If we attend to the pronunciation of the body of people, who are led by their own ease rather than by a nice regard to fashion, we shall find that they

make

reparabilis, and not from the English verbs, *dissolve*, *repair*. Yet *dissolvable*, *indissolvable*, *repairable* and *irrepairable*, are better words than *indissoluble*, *reparable*, *irreparable*.   They not only preserve the analogy, but they are more purely English words ; and I have been witness to a circumstance which alone ought to determine their excellence and give them currency : People of ordinary education have found difficulty in understanding such derivatives as *irreparable*, *indissoluble* ; but the moment the words *irrepairable*, *indissolveable* are pronounced, they are led to the meaning by a previous acquaintance with the words *repair* and *dissolve*. Numberless examples of this will occur to a person of observation, sufficient to make him abhor and reject the pedantry of authors, who have labored to strip their native tongue of its primitive English dress, and load it with fantastic ornaments.

make *i* liquid, or give it the found of *y* confonant, after thofe confonants only, which admit that found without any change of their own powers. Thefe confonants are *l, n, v,* and the double confonant *x* ; as *valiant, companion, behavior, flexion.* Here *y* might be fubftituted for *i,* without any change, or any tendency to a change, of the preceding confonant ; except perhaps the change of *fi* in *flexion* into *fh,* which is a general rule in the language, as it is to change *ti* and *ci* into the fame found.*

But when *i* is preceded by *d,* change it into *y,* and we cannot pronounce it with our ufual rapidity, without blending the two letters into the found of *j,* which is a compound of *dzh* ; at leaft it cannot be effected without a violent exertion of the fpeaker. *Immedyate* is fo difficult, that every perfon who attempts to pronounce it in that manner, will fall into *immejate.* Thus *commodious, comedian, tragedian,* are very politely pronounced *commojus, comejan, trajejan.* Such a pronunciation, changing the true powers of the letters, and introducing a harfh union of confonants,

dzh,

---

* *FLEXION* refolved into its proper letters would be *flekfion,* that is *flekfhun* ; and *fleks-yun* would give the fame found.

i

dxh, in the place of the smooth sound of *dia*, must be considered as a palpable cor‑ruption.

WITH respect to the terminations *ial*, *ian*, &c. after *r*, I must believe it impossi‑ble to blend these letters in one syllable. In the word *ministerial*, for example, I can‑not conceive how *ial* can be pronounced *yal*, without a pause after the syllables, *minister‑*. Sheridan's manner of pronoun‑cing the letters *ryan*, *ryal*, in a syllable, ap‑pears to be a grofs abfurdity: Even allow‑ing *y* to have the sound of *e*, we must of necessity articulate two syllables.

BUT suppofing the modern pronuncia‑tion of *immediate* to be liable to none of these exceptions, there is another objection to it, arifing from the construction of our poetry. To the short syllables of such words as *every*, *glorious*, *different*, *bowery*, *commodious*, *harmonious*, *happier*, *ethereal*, *immediate*, *experience*, our poetry is in a great meafure indebted for the *Dactyl*, the *Amphibrach*, and the *Anapæst*, feet which are neceffary to give variety to verfification, and the laft of which is the moft flowing, melodious and forceable foot in the lan‑guage. By blending the two short sylla‑bles

bles into one, we make the foot an Iambic;
and as our poetry confifts principally of
iambics, we thus reduce our heroic verfe
to a dull uniformity. Take for example
the following line of Pope.

"THAT fees immediate good by prefent fenfe"---

IF we pronounce it thus :

THAT fees|imme|jate good|by pref|ent fenfe ;

the line will be compofed entirely of Iambics. But read it thus :

THAT fees|imme|di-ate good|by pref|ent fenfe ;

and the third foot, becoming an anapæft,
gives variety to the verfe.

IN the following line :

" SOME happier ifland in the watery wafte :"

If we read *happier* and *watry*, as words
of two fyllables, the feet will all be Iambics, except the third, which is a *Pyrrhic.*
But if we read *happier* and *watery,** in three
fyllables, as we ought, we introduce two
anapæfts, and give variety and flowing
melody to the verfe.

THESE

---

* To an ignorance of the laws of verfification, we muft
afcribe the unwarrantable contraction of *watery, wonderous,*
&c. into *watry, wondrous.*

K

THESE remarks will be more fully con-firmed by attending to the laſt verſe of the following diſtich :

> " IN martial pomp he clothes the angelic train,
> While warring myr|iads ſhake|the ethe|rial plain."
> Philoſophic Solitude.

ON Sheridan's principles, and by an eliſ-ion of *e* in *the*, the laſt line is compoſed of pure Iambics ; whereas in fact, the three laſt feet are anapæſts ; and to theſe the verſe is, in ſome meaſure, indebted for its melody and the ſublimity of the deſcrip-tion.

THESE conſiderations are directly oppoſ-ed to the faſhionable pronunciation of *im-mediate*, and that whole analogy of words. In addition to this, I may remark, that it is not the practice of people in general. What-ever may be the charcter and rank of its advocates, in this country they compoſe but a ſmall part, even of the literati.

Of MODERN CORRUPTIONS *in the* ENGLISH PRONUNCIATION.

I PROCEED now to examin a mode of pronouncing certain words, which pre-vails in England and ſome parts of Amer-ica,

ica, and which, as it extends to a vaſt num=
ber of words, and creates a material difference between the orthography and pronunciation, is a matter of ſerious. conſequence.

To attack eſtabliſhed cuſtoms is always
hazardous ; for mankind, even when they
ſee and acknowlege their errors, are ſeldom
obliged to the man who expoſes them.
The danger is encreaſed, when an oppoſition is made to the favorite opinions of the
great ; for men, whoſe rank and abilities
entitle them to particular reſpect, will
ſooner diſmiſs their friends than their prejudices.   Under this conviction, my preſent ſituation is delicate and embarraſſing :
But as ſome ſacrifices muſt often be made
to truth ; and as I am conſcious that a regard to truth only dictates what I write, I
can ſincerely declare, it is my wiſh to
inform the underſtanding of every man,
without wounding the feelings of an individual.

THE practice to which I allude, is that
of pronouncing *d, t,* and *s* preceding *u* ;
which letter, it is ſaid, contains the ſound
of *e* or *y* and *oo* ; and that of courſe *education* muſt be pronounced *edyucation* ; *na-*
K 2

ture,

ture, natyure; and *superior, syuperior*: From
the difficulty of pronouncing which, we
naturally fall into the found of *dzh, tsh,*
and *sh*: Thus education becomes *edzhucation* or *ejucation*; nature becomes *natshure*
or *nachure*; and superior becomes *shupe
rior*.

How long this practice has prevailed in
London, I cannot ascertain. There are a
few words, in which it seems to have been
universal from time immemorial; as, *pleasure*, and the other words of that analogy.
But I find no reason to suppose the practice
of pronouncing *nature, duty, nachure, juty,*
prevailed before the period of Garrick's
reputation on the stage.

On the other hand, the writers on the
language have been silent upon this point,
till within a few years; and Kenrick speaks
of it as a *Metropolitan pronunciation*, sup-
ported by *certain mighty fine speakers,**
which implies that the practice is modern,
and proves it to be local, even in Great
Britain. But the practice has prevailed at
court and on the stage for several years, and
the reputation of a Garrick, a Sheridan
and

* Rhetorical Grammar, prefixed to his Dictionary, page
32. London, 1773.

and a Siddons, has given it a very rapid
and extensive diffusion in the polite world.
As the innovation is great and extends to
a multitude of words, it is neceffary, before
we embrace the practice in its utmoft latitude, to examin into its propriety and confequences.

THE only reafons offered in fupport of
the practice, are, the Englifh or Saxon
found of *u*, which is faid to be *yu* ; and
euphony, or the agreeablenefs of the pronunciation.

BUT permit me to enquire, on what do
the advocates of this practice ground their
affertion, that *u* had in Saxon the found of
eu or *yu* ? Are there any teftimonies to
fupport it, among old writers of authority ? In the courfe of my reading I have
difcovered none, nor have I ever feen one
produced or referred to.

WILL it be faid, that *yu* is the name of
the letter ? But where did this name orig-
inate ? Certainly not in the old Saxon
practice, for the Saxons expreffed this found
by *ew*, or *eo* : And I do not recollect a fingle word of Saxon origin, in which the
warmeft fticklers for the practice, give *u*
K 3   this

this found, even in the prefent age.   Kenrick, who has inveftigated the powers of the Englifh letters with much more accuracy than even Sheridan himfelf, obferves, that we might with equal propriety, name the other vowels in the fame manner, and fay, *ya, ye, yi, yo,* as well as *yu.**

U in *union, ufe,* &c. has the found of *yu* ; but thefe are all of *Latin* origin, and can be no proof that *u* had, in *Saxon,* the found of *ew* or *yu.*

The whole argument is founded on a miftake.   *U* in pure Englifh has not the found of *ew* ; but a found that approaches it ; which is defined with great accuracy by the learned Wallis, who was one of the firft correct writers ·upon Englifh Grammar, and whofe treatife is the foundation of ·Lowth's Introduction and all the beft fubfequent compilations.†

This writer defines the Englifh letter *u* in thefe words, " Hunc fonum Extranei fere affequenter, fi dipthongum *iu* conentur

---

* Rhet. Gram. 33.

† His grammar was written in Latin, in the reign of Charles IId. The work is fo fcarce, that I have never been able to find but a fingle copy. The author was one of the founders of the Royal Society.

nentur pronunciare; nempe *i* exile literæ *u*, vel *w* preponentes; (ut in Hifpanorum *ciudad*, civitas.)   *Non tamen idem eft omnino fonus, quamvis, ad illum proxime, accedat*; eft enim *iu* fonus compofitus, at Anglorum et Gallorum *u* fonus fimplex."*———Gram. Ling. Angl. Sect. 2.

THIS is precifely the idea I have ever had of the Englifh *u*; except that I cannot allow the found to be perfectly fimple.   If we attend to the manner in which we begin the found of *u* in *flute, abjure, truth*, we fhall obferve that the tongue is not preffed to the mouth fo clofely as in pronouncing *e*; the aperture of the organs is not fo fmall; and I prefume that good fpeakers, and am confident that moft people, do not pronounce thefe words *fleute, abjeure, treuth*. Neither do they pronounce them *floote, abjoore, trooth*; but with a found formed by an eafy natural aperture of the mouth, between *iu* and *oo*; which is the true Englifh found. This found, however obfcured by affectation in the metropolis of Great Britain and
the

---

* THIS found of *u*, foreigners will nearly obtain, by attempting to pronounce the dipthong *iu*; that is, the narrow *i* before *u* or *w*; (as in the Spanifh word *ciudad*, a city.) Yet the found (of *u*) is not exactly the fame, altho it approaches very near to it; for the found of *iu* is compound; whereas the *u* of the Englifh and French is a fimple found."

the capital towns in America, is ſtill preſerved by the body of the people in both
countries. There are a million deſcendants of the Saxons in this country who retain the ſound of *u* in all caſes, preciſely
according to Wallis's definition. Aſk any
plain countryman, whoſe pronunciation
has not been expoſed to corruption by
mingling with foreigners, how he pronounces the letters, *t*, *r*, *u*, *th*, and he will
not ſound *u* like *eu*, nor *oo*, but will expreſs
the real primitive Engliſh *u*. Nay, if people wiſh to make an accurate trial, let them
direct any child of ſeven years old, who
has had no previous inſtruction reſpecting
the matter, to pronounce the words *ſuit*,
tumult, *due*, &c. and they will thus aſcertain the true ſound of the letter. Children
pronounce *u* in the moſt natural manner ;
whereas the ſound of *iu* requires a conſiderable effort, and that of *oo*, a forced poſition of the lips. Illiterate perſons therefore pronounce the genuin Engliſh *u*, much
better than thoſe who have attempted to
ſhape their pronunciation according to the
polite modern practice. As ſingular as
this aſſertion may appear, it is literally
true. This circumſtance alone would be
ſufficient to prove that the Saxons never
pronounced *u* like *yu* ; for the body of a
nation,

nation, removed from the reach of conqueft and free from a mixture of foreigners, are the fafeft repofitories of ancient cuftoms and general practice in fpeaking.

But another ftrong argument againft the modern practice is, that the pretended dipthong, *iu* or *yu*, is heard in fcarcely a fingle word of Saxon origin. Almoft all the words in which *d, t* and *f* are converted into other letters, as *education, due, virtue, rapture, fuperior, fupreme*, &c. are derived from the Latin or French ; fo that the practice itfelf is a proof that the principles on which it is built, are falfe. It is pretended that the Englifh or Saxon found of *u* requires the pronunciation, *edzhucation, natfhure*, and yet it is introduced almoft folely into Latin and French words. Such an inconfiftency refutes the reafoning and is a burlefque on its advocates.

This however is but a fmall part of the inconfiftency. In two other particulars the abfurdity is ftill more glaring.

1. The modern refiners of our language diftinguifh two founds of *u* long ; that of *yu* and *oo* ; and ufe both without any regard to Latin or Saxon derivation. The
diftinction

diſtinction they make is founded on a certain principle; and yet I queſtion whether one of a thouſand of them ever attended to it. After moſt of the conſonants, they give *u* the dipthongal ſound of *eu*; as in *blue, cube, due, mute*; but after *r* they almoſt invariably pronounce it *oo*; as *rule, truth, rue, rude, fruit.* Why this diſtinction? If they contend for the Saxon ſound of *u*, why do they not preſerve that ſound in *true, rue, truth*, which are of Saxon original; and uniformly give *u* its Roman ſound, which is acknowleged on all hands to have been *oo*, in all words of Latin original, as *rule, mute, cube?* The fact is, they miſtake the principle on which the diſtinction is made; and which is merely accidental, or ariſes from the eaſe of ſpeaking.

In order to frame many of the conſonants, the organs are placed in ſuch a poſition, that in paſſing from it to the aperture neceſſary to articulate the following vowel or dipthong, we inſenſibly fall into the ſound of *ee.* This in particular is the caſe with thoſe conſonants which are formed near the ſeat of *e*; viz. *k* and *g.* The cloſing of the organs forms theſe mutes; and a very ſmall opening forms the vowel *e.* In paſſing from that cloſe compreſſion occaſioned

by

by *k* and *g*, to the aperture neceſſary to form any vowel, the organs are neceſſarily placed in a ſituation to pronounce *ee*. From this ſingle circumſtance, have originated the moſt barbarous dialects or ſingularities in ſpeaking Engliſh, which offend the ear, either in Great Britain or America.

THIS is the origin of the New England *keow*, *keoward*; and of the Engliſh *keube*, *ackeuſe*, *keind* and *geuide*.

THERE is juſt the ſame propriety in one practice as the other, and both are equally harmonious.

FOR ſimilar reaſons, the labials, *m* and *p*, are followed by *e*: In New England, we hear it in *meow*, *peower*, and in Great Britain, in *meute*, *peure*. With this difference however, that in New England, this pronunciation is generally confined to the more illiterate part of the people, and in Great Britain it prevails among thoſe of the firſt rank. But after *r* we never hear the ſound of *e*: It has been before obſerved, that the moſt awkward countryman in New England pronounces *round*, *ground*, *brown*, as correctly as men of the firſt education; and our faſhionable ſpeakers pronounce *u* after *r* like *oo*. The reaſon

son is the same in both cases : In pronouncing *r* the mouth is necessarily opened (or
rather the glottis) to a position for articulating a broad full sound. So that the vulgar singularities in this respect, and the polite refinements of speaking, both proceed
from the same cause ; both proceed from
an accidental or careless narrow way of
articulating certain combinations of letters;
both are corruptions of pure English ; e-
qually disagreeable and indefensible. Both
may be easily corrected by taking more
pains to open the teeth, and form full bold
sounds.

2. But another inconsistency in the
modern practice, is the introducing an *e**
before the second sound of *u* as in *tun* ; or
rather changing the preceding consonant ;
for in *nature, rapture,* and hundreds of
other words, *t* is changed into *tsh* ; and yet
no person pretends that *u*, in these words,
has a dipthongal sound. On the other
hand, Sheridan and his copier, Scott, have

in

---

*Lowth condemns such a phrase as, " the introducing an
e" and says it should be, " the introducing *of* an *e*." This is
but one instance of a great number, in which he has rejected *good* English. In this situation, *introducing* is a participial noun ; it may take an article before it, like any other
noun, and yet govern an objective, like any transitive verb.
This is the idiom of the language : but in most cases, the
writer may use or omit *of*, at pleasure.

in thefe and fimilar words marked *u* for its
fhort found, which is univerfally acknowleged to be fimple.   I believe no perfon
ever pretended, that this found of *u* contains the found of *e* or *y* ; why then fhould
we be directed to pronounce *nature, nat-
yur* ? Or what is equally abfurd, *natfhur* ?
On what principle is the *t* changed into a
compound confonant ? If there is any thing
in this found of *u* to warrant this change,
does it not extend to all words where this
found occurs ? Why do not our ftandard
writers direct us to fay *tfhun* for *tun*, and
tfhumble for *tumble* ? I can conceive no reafon which will warrant the pronunciation
in one cafe, that will not apply with equal
force in the other.   And I challenge the
advocates of the practice, to produce a
reafon for pronouncing *natfhur, raptfhur,
captfhur*, which will not extend to author-
ize, not only *tfhun, tfhurn*, for *tun, turn*, but
alfo *fatfhal* for *fatal*, and *immortfhal* for *immortal*.*   Nay, the latter pronunciation is
actually heard among fome very refpectable imitators of fafhion ; and is frequent
among

---

* I MUST except that reafon, which is always an invinc-
ible argument with weak people, viz. " It is the practice of
fome great men."   This common argument, which is unan-
fwerable, will alfo prove the propriety of imitating all the
polite and deteftable vices of the great, which are now unknown to the *little vulgar* of this country.

among the illiterate, in thofe ftates where the *tſhu's* are moſt faſhionable. How can it be otherwife ? People are led by imitation ; and when thoſe in high life embrace a fingularity, the multitude, who are unacquainted with its principles or extent, will attempt to imitate the novelty, and probably carry it much farther than was ever intended.

WHEN a man of little education hears a refpectable gentleman change *t* into *tſh* in nature, he will naturally be led to change the ſame letter, not only in that word, but wherever it occurs. This is already done in a multitude of inſtances, and the practice if continued and extended, might eventually change *t*, in all cafes, into *tſh*.

I AM fenfible that fome writers of novels and plays have ridiculed the common pronunciation of *creatur* and *nutur*, by introducing thefe and fimilar words into low characters, fpelling them *creater*, *nater* : And the fupporters of the court pronunciation allege, that in the vulgar practice of fpeaking, the letter *e* is founded and not *u* : So extremely ignorant are they of the nature of founds and the true powers of the Englifh letters. The fact is, we are fo far

from

from pronouncing *e* in the common pronunciation of *natur*, *creatur*, &c. that *e* is
always founded like short *u*, in the unaccented fyllables of *over*, *fober*, *banter*, and
other fimilar words. Nay, moft of the
vowels, in fuch fyllables, found like *i* or *u*
fhort.*   Liar, elder, factor, are pronounced *liur*, *eldur*, *factur*, and this is the true
found of *u* in *creatur*, *nature*, *rapture*, *legiflature*, &c.

I would juft obferve further, that this
pretended dipthong *iu* was formerly expreffed by *ew* and *eu*, or perhaps by *eo*, and
was confidered as different from the found
of *u*.   In modern times, we have, in many
words, blended the found of *u* with that of
ew, or rather ufe them promifcuoufly.   It
is indifferent, as to the pronunciation,
whether we write *fuel* or *fewel*. And yet
in this word, as alfo in *new*, *brew*, &c. we
do not hear the found of *e*, except among
the Virginians, who affect to pronounce
it diftinctly, *ne-ew*, *ne-oo*, *fe-oo*. This affectation is not of modern date, for Wallis

---

* Ash obferves, that " in unaccented, fhort and infignifi-
cant fyllables, the founds of the five vowels are nearly coin-
cident.   It muft be a nice ear that can diftinguifh the difference of found in the concluding fyllable of the following
words, altar, alter, manor, murmur, fatyr."——Gram. Diff,
pref. to Dic. p. 1.

lis mentions it in his time and reprobates it. " Eu, ew, eau, sonanter per *e* clarum et *w* ; ut in *neuter, few, beauty.* Quidem tamen accutius efferunt, acsi scriberentur *niew ter, fiew, bieuty.* At prior pronunciatio rectior est."———Gram. Ling. Ang.

HERE this author allows these combinations to have the sound of *yu* or *iu* ; but disapproves of that refinement which some affect, in giving the *e* or *i* short its distinct sound.

THE true sound of the English *u*, is neither *ew*, with the distinct sounds of *e* and *oo* ; nor is it *oo* ; but it is that sound which every unlettered person utters in pronouncing *solitude, rude, threw,* and which cannot easily be mistaken. So difficult is it to avoid the true sound of *u*, that I have never found a man, even among the ardent admirers of the stage pronunciation, who does not retain the vulgar sound, in more than half the words of this class which he uses. There is such a propensity in men to be regular in the construction and use of language, that they are often obliged, by the customs of the age, to struggle against their inclination, in order to be wrong, and still find it impossible to be uniform in their errors. THE

THE other reafon given to vindicate the polite pronunciation, is *euphony*. But I muft fay with Kenrick,* I cannot difcover the euphony; on the contrary, the pronunciation is to me both difagreeable and difficult. It is certainly more difficult to pronounce two confonants than one. *Ch*, or, which is the fame thing, *tfh*, is a more difficult found than *t*; and *dzh*, or *j*, more difficult than *d*. Any accurate ear may perceive the difference in a fingle word, as in *natur*, *nachur*. But when two or three words meet, in which we have either of thefe compound founds, the difficulty becomes very obvious; as the *nachural feachurs of indiwijuals*. The difficulty is increafed, when two of thefe *churs* and *jurs* occur in the fame word. Who can pronounce

* FOR my part I cannot difcover the euphony; and tho the contrary mode be reprobated, as vulgar, by certain mighty fine fpeakers, I think it more conformable to the general fcheme of Englifh pronunciation: for tho in order to make the word but two fyllables, *ti* and *te* may be required to be converted into *ch*, or the *i* and *e* into *y*, when the preceding fyllable is marked with the accute accent as in *queftion*, *minion*, *courteous*, and the like; there feems to be little reafon, when the grave accent precedes the *t*, as in *nature*, *creature*, for converting the *t* into *ch*; and not much more for joining the *t* to the firft fyllable and introducing the *y* before the fecond, as *nat-yure*. Why the *t* when followed by neither *i* nor *e*, is to take the form of *ch*, I cannot conceive: It is, in my opinion, a fpecies of affectation that fhould be difcountenanced.——Kenrick Rhet. Gram. page 32. Dic.

L

nounce thefe words, " at this *junctfhur* it was *conjectfhured*"—or " the act paffed in a *tfhumultfhuous legiflatfhur*," without a paufe, or an extreme exertion of the lungs ? If this is euphony to an Englifh ear, I know not what founds in language can be difagreeable.   To me it is barbaroufly harfh and unharmonious.

But fuppofing the pronunciation to be relifhed by ears accuftomed to it (for cuftom will familiarize any thing) will the pleafure which individuals experience, balance the ill effects of creating a multitude of irregularities ? Is not the number of anomalies in our language already fufficient, without an arbitrary addition of many hundreds ? Is not the difference between our written and fpoken language already fufficiently wide, without changing the founds of a number of confonants ?

If we attend to the irregularities which have been long eftablifhed in our language, we fhall find moft of them in the Saxon branch.   The Roman tongue was almoft perfectly regular, and perhaps its orthography and pronunciation were perfectly correfpondent.   But it is the peculiar misfortune of the fafhionable practice of pro-

nouncing

nouncing *d*, *t*, and *f*, before *u*, that it deftroys the analogy and regularity of the
Roman branch of our language ; for thofe
confonants are not changed in many words
of Saxon original.   Before this affectation
prevailed, we could boaft of a regular orthography in a large branch of our language ; but now the only clafs of words,
which had preferved a regular conftruction,
are attacked, and the correfpondence between the fpelling and pronunciation, deftroyed, by thofe who ought to have been
the firft to oppofe the innovation.*

SHOULD this practice be extended to all
words, where *d*, *t* and *f* precede *u*, as it
muft before it can be confiftent or defenfible, it would introduce more anomalies
into our tongue, than were before eftablifhed,

* WELL might Mr. Sheridan affert, that " Such indeed is
the ftate of our written language, that the darkeft hiero-
glyphics, or moft difficult cyphers which the art of man has
hitherto invented, were not better calculated to conceal the
fentiments of thofe who ufed them, from all who had not
the key, than the ftate of our fpelling is to conceal the true
pronunciation of our words, from all, except a few well
educated natives." Rhet. Gram. p. 22. Dic.   But if thefe
well educated natives would pronounce words as they
ought, one half the language at leaft would be regular.   The
Latin derivatives are moftly regular to the educated and
uneducated of America ; and it is to be hoped that the modern hieroglyphical obfcurity will forever be confined to a
few well educated natives in Great Britain.

L 2

lished, both in the orthography and con-struction. What a perverted taste, and what a singular ambition must those men possess, who, in the day light of civilization and science, and in the short period of an age, can go farther in demolishing the analogies of an elegant language, than their unlettered ancestors proceeded in centuries, amidst the accidents of a savage life, and the shocks of numerous invasions!

But it will be replied, *Custom is the legislator of language*, and custom authorizes the practice I am reprobating. A man can hardly offer a reason, drawn from the principles of analogy and harmony in a language, but he is instantly silenced with the decisive, *jus et norma loquendi.**

WHAT

---

* "QUEM penes arbitrium est, et jus et norma loquendi." Horace.——"Nothing," says Kenrick, "has contributed more to the adulteration of living languages, than the too extensive acceptation of Horace's rule in favor of custom. Custom is undoubtedly the rule of present practice; but there would be no end in following the variations daily introduced by caprice. Alterations may sometimes be useful—may be necessary; but they should be made in a manner conformable to the genius and construction of the language. Modus est in rebus. Extremes in this, as in all other cases, are hurtful. We ought by no means to shut the door against the improvements of our language: but it were well that some criterion were established to distinguish between improvement and innovation."——Rhet. Gram. page 6, Dict.

WHAT then is cuftom ? Some writer has already anfwered this queftion; "Cuftom is the plague of wife men and the idol of fools." This was probably faid of thofe cuftoms and fafhions which are capricious and varying ; for there are many cuftoms, founded on propriety, which are permanent and conftitute laws.

BUT what kind of cuftom did Horace defign to lay down as the ftandard of fpeaking ? Was it a local cuftom ? Then the *keow* of New England ; the *oncet* and *twicet* of Pennfylvania and Maryland ; and the *keind* and *fkey* of the London theaters, form rules of fpeaking. Is it the practice of a court, or a few eminent fcholars and orators, that he defigned to conftitute a ftandard ? But who fhall determine what body of men forms this uncontrollable legiflature ? Or who fhall reconcile the differences at court ? For thefe eminent orators often difagree. There are numbers of words in which the moft eminent men differ: Can all be right ? Or what, in this cafe, is the *cuftom* which is to be our guide ?

BESIDES thefe difficulties, what right have a few men, however elevated their ftation, to change a national practice ? They may fay, that they confult their own ears, and endeavor to pleafe themfelves. This is their only apology, unlefs they can prove that the changes they make are real improvements. But what improvement is there in changing the founds of three or four letters into others, and thus multiplying anomalies, and encreafing the difficulty of learning a language? Will not the great body of the people claim the privilege of adhering to their ancient ufages, and believing their practice to be the moft correct? They moft undoubtedly will.

If Horace's maxim is ever juft, it is only when cuftom is national; when the practice of a nation is uniform or general. In this cafe it becomes the common law of the land, and no one will difpute its propriety. But has any man a right to deviate from this practice, and attempt to eftablifh a fingular mode of his own? Have two or three eminent ftage players authority to make changes at pleafure, and palm their novelties upon a nation under the idea of *cuftom*? The reader will pardon me for tranfcribing here the opinion of the celebrated Michaelis, one of the moft learned philologers of the prefent century. "It

is

is not," fays he, "for a fcholar to give laws
nor profcribe eftablifhed expreffions : If
he takes fo much on himfelf he is ridiculed,
and defervedly ; it is no more than a juft
mortification to his ambition, and the pen-
alty of his ufurping on the rights of the
people.   Language is a democratical ftate,
where all the learning in the world does
not warrant a citizen to fuperfede a received cuftom, till he has convinced the whole
nation that this cuftom is a miftake. Schol-
ars are not fo infallible that every thing is
to be referred to them.   Were they allowed a decifory power, the errors of language,
I am fure, inftead of diminifhing, would
be continually increafing.   Learned heads
teem with them no lefs than the vulgar ;
and the former are much more imperious,
that we fhould be compelled to defer to
their innovations and implicitly to receive
every falfe opinion of theirs."*

YET this right is often affumed by individuals, who dictate to a nation the rules
of fpeaking, with the fame imperioufnefs
as a tyrant gives laws to his vaffals : And,

ftrange

* SEE a learned " Differtation on the influence of o-
pinions on language and of language on opinions, which
gained the prize of the Pruffian Royal Academy in 1759.
By Mr. Michaelis, court councellor to his Britannic Majefty, and director of the Royal Society of Gottingen."

ſtrange as it may appear, even well bred people and ſcholars, often ſurrender their right of private judgement to theſe literary governors. The *ipſe dixit* of a Johnſon, a Garrick, or a Sheridan, has the force of law ; and to contradict it, is rebellion. Aſk the moſt of our learned men, how they would pronounce a word or compoſe a ſentence, and they will immediately appeal to ſome favorite author whoſe deciſion is final. Thus diſtinguiſhed eminence in a writer often becomes a paſſport for innumerable errors.

THE whole evil originates in a fallacy. It is often ſuppoſed that certain great men are infallible, or that their practice conſtitutes cuſtom and the rule of propriety. But on the contrary, any man, however learned, is liable to miſtake ; the moſt learned, as Michaelis obſerves, often teem with errors, and not unfrequently become attached to particular ſyſtems, and imperious in forcing them upon the world.* It is not the particular whim of ſuch men, that conſtitutes *cuſtom* ; but the common practice

* THE vulgar thus by imitation err,
As oft the learn'd by being ſingular.
So much they ſcorn the croud, that if the throng,
By chance go right, they purpoſely go wrong."
POPE.

practice of a nation, which is conformed to their *general* ideas of propriety. The pronunciation of *keow*, *keind*, *drap*, *juty*, *natſhur*, &c. are neither right nor wrong, becauſe they are approved or cenſured by particular men ; nor becauſe one is local in New England, another in the middle ſtates, and the others are ſupported by the court and ſtage in London. They are wrong, becauſe they are oppoſed to national practice ; they are wrong, becauſe they are arbitrary or careleſs changes of the true ſounds of our letters ; they are wrong, becauſe they break in upon the regular conſtruction of the language ; they are wrong, becauſe they render the pronunciation difficult both for natives and foreigners ; they are wrong, becauſe they make an invidious diſtinction between the polite and common pronunciation, or elſe oblige a *nation* to change their general cuſtoms, without preſenting to their view one *national* advantage. Theſe are important, they are permanent conſiderations ; they are ſuperior to the caprices of courts and theaters ; they are reaſons that are interwoven in the very ſtructure of the language, or founded on the common law of the nation ; and they are a living ſatire upon the licentiouſneſs of modern

ſpeakers,

fpeakers, who dare to flight their authority.

But let us examin whether the practice
I am cenfuring is general or not ; for if
not, it cannot come within Horace's rule. ·
If we may believe well informed gentlemen, it is not general even in Great Britain.   I have been perfonally informed, and
by gentlemen of education and abilities,
one of whom was particular in his obfervation, that it is not general, even among
the moft eminent literary characters in
London.   It is lefs frequent in the interi-
or counties, where the inhabitants ftill
fpeak as the common people do in this
country.   And Kenrick fpeaks of it as an
affectation in the metropolis which ought
to be difcountenanced,

But whatever may be the practice in
England or Ireland, there are few in America who have embraced it, as it is explained
in Sheridan's Dictionary.   In the middle
and fouthern ftates, there are a few, and
thofe well bred people, who have gone far
in attempting to imitate the fafhion of the
day.*   Yet the body of the people, even

in

* There are many people, and perhaps the moft of them
in the capital towns, that have learnt a few common place
words,

in thefe ftates, remain as unfafhionable as ever ; and the eaftern ftates generally adhere to their ancient cuftom of fpeaking, however vulgar it may be thought by their neighbors.* Suppofe cuftom therefore to be the *jus et norma*, the rule of correct fpeaking, and in this country, it is directly oppofed to the plan now under confideration.

As a nation, we have a very great intereft in oppofing the introduction of any plan of uniformity with the Britifh language, even were the plan propofed perfectly unexceptionable. This point will be afterwards difcuffed more particularly ; but I would obferve here, that the author who has the moft admirers and imitators in this country, has been cenfured in London, where his character is highly efteemed, and that too by men who are confeffedly partial to his general plan. In the critical review of Sheridan's Dictionary, 1781,

words, fuch as *forchin, nachur, virchue* and half a dozen others, which they repeat on all occafions ; but being ignorant of the extent of the practice, they are, in pronouncing moft words, as vulgar as ever.

*It fhould be remarked that the late Prefident of Pennfylvania, the Governor of New Jerfey, and the Prefident of New York college, who are diftinguifhed for erudition and accuracy, have not adopted the Englifh pronunciation,

1781, there are the following exceptions to his ſtandard.

" Nevertheless our author muſt not be ſurprized if, in a matter, in its nature ſo delicate and difficult, as that concerning which he treats, a doubt ſhould here and there ariſe, in the minds of the moſt candid critics, with regard to the propriety of his determinations. For inſtance, we would wiſh him to reconſider, whether, in the words which begin with *ſuper*, ſuch as *ſuperſtition*, *ſuperſede*, he is right in directing them to be pronounced *ſhooper*. Whatever might be the caſe in Queen Ann's time, it doth not occur to us, that any one at preſent, above the lower ranks, ſpeaks theſe words with the ſound of *ſh* ; or that a good reaſon can be given, for their being thus ſounded. Nay their being thus ſpoken is contrary to Mr. Sheridan's own rule; for he ſays that the letter *ſ* always preſerves its own proper ſound at the beginning of words."

Here we are informed by this gentleman's admirers, that, in ſome inſtances, he has impoſed upon the world, as the ſtandard of purity, a pronunciation which is not heard, except among the *lower ranks of people,*

ple, and directly oppofed to his own rule. The reviewers might have extended their remarks to many other inftances, in which he has deviated from general practice and from every rule of the language. Yet at the voice of this gentleman, many of the Americans are quitting their former practice, and running into errors with an eagernefs bordering on infatuation.

CUSTOMS of the court and ftage, it is confeffed, rule without refiftance in monarchies. But what have we to do with the cuftoms of a foreign nation? Detached as we are from all the world, is it not poffible to circumfcribe the power of *cuftom*, and lay it, in fome degree, under the influence of propriety? We are fenfible that in foreign courts, a man's reputation may depend on a genteel bow, and his fortune may be loft by wearing an unfafhionable coat. But have we advanced to that ftage of corruption, that our higheft ambition is to be as particular in fafhions as other nations? In matters merely indifferent, like modes of drefs, fome degree of conformity to local cuftom is neceffary ;* but

when

* NOT between different nations, but in the fame nation. The manners and fafhions of each nation fhould arife out of their circumftances, their age, their improvements in commerce and agriculture.

when this conformity requires a facrifice of any principle of propriety or moral rectitude, fingularity becomes an honorable teftimony of an independent mind. A man of a great foul would fooner imitate the virtues of a cottage, than the vices of a court ; and would deem it more honorable to gain one ufeful idea from the humble laborer, than to copy the vicious pronunciation of a fplendid court, or become an adept in the licentious principles of a Rochefter and a Littleton.

It will not be difputed that Sheridan and Scott have very faithfully publifhed the prefent pronunciation of the Englifh court and theater. But if we may confult the rules of our language and confider them as of any authority ; if we may rely on the opinions of Kenrick and the reviewers ; if we may credit the beft informed people who have travelled in Great Britain, this practice is modern and local, and confidered, by the judicious and impartial, even of the Englifh nation, as a grofs corruption of the pure pronunciation.

Such errors and innovations fhould not be imitated, becaufe they are found in authors of reputation. The works of fuch
authors

authors fhould rather be confidered as lights to prevent our falling upon the rocks of error.   There is no more propriety in our imitating the practice of the Englifh theater, becaufe it is defcribed by the celebrated Sheridan, than there is in introducing the manners of Rochefter or the principles of Bolingbroke, becaufe thefe were eminent characters ; or than there is in copying the vices of a Shylock, a Lovelace, or a Richard III. becaufe they are well defcribed by the mafterly pens of Shakefpear and Richardfon.   So far as the correctnefs and propriety of fpeech are confidered as important, it is of as much confequence to oppofe the introduction of that practice in this country, as it is to refift the corruption of morals, which ever attends the wealthy and luxurious ftage of national refinements.

HAD Sheridan adhered to his own rules and to the principle of analogy ; had he given the world a confiftent fcheme of pronunciation, which would not have had, for its unftable bafis, the fickle practice of a changeable court, he would have done infinite fervice to the language : Men of fcience, who wifh to preferve the regular conftruction of the language, would have rejoiced

rejoiced to find such a respectable authority on the side of propriety ; and the illiterate copiers of fashion must have rejected
faults in speaking, which they could not
defend.*

THE corruption however has taken such
deep root in England, that there is little
probability it will ever be eradicated. The
practice must there prevail, and gradually
change the whole structure of the Latin
derivatives. Such is the force of custom,
in a nation where all fashionable people
are drawn to a point, that the current of
opinion is irresistible ; individuals must
fall into the stream and be borne away by
its violence ; except perhaps a few philofophers, whose fortitude may enable them to
hold their station, and whose sense of propriety may remain, when their power of
oppofition has ceafed.

BUT

* SHERIDAN, as an improver of the language, ftands a-
mong the firft writers of the Britifh nation, and defervedly. His Lectures on Elocution and on Reading, his Treatifes on Education, and for the moft part his Rhetorical
Grammar, are excellent and almoft unexceptionable per-
formances. In thefe, he encountered practice and prejudices, when they were found repugnant to obvious rules of
propriety. But in his Dictionary he feems to have left
his only defenfible ground, *propriety*, in purfuit of that
phantom, *fashion*. He deferted his own principles, as the
Reviewers obferve : and where he has done this, every
rational man fhould defert his *ftandard*.

BuT our detached fituation, local and political, gives us the *power*, while pride, policy, and a regard for propriety and uniformity among ourfelves, fhould infpire us with a *difpofition*, to oppofe innovations, which have not utility for their object.

WE fhall find it difficult to convince Englifhmen that a corrupt tafte prevails in the Britifh nation. Foreigners view the Americans with a degree of contempt; they laugh at our manners, pity our ignorance, and as far as example and derifion can go, obtrude upon us the cuftoms of their native countries. But in borrowing from other nations, we fhould be exceedingly cautious to feparate their virtues from their vices; their ufeful improvements from their falfe refinements. Stile and tafte, in all nations, undergo the fame revolutions, the fame progrefs from purity to corruption, as manners and government; and in England the pronunciation of the language has fhared the fame fate. The Auguftan era is paft, and whether the nation perceive and acknowlege the truth or not, the world, as impartial fpectators, obferve and lament the declenfion of tafte and fcience.

M   THE

THE nation can do little more than read the works and admire the beauties of the original authors, who have adorned the preceding ages. A few, ambitious of fame, or driven by neceffity, croud their names into the catalogue of writers, by imitating fome celebrated model, or by compiling from the productions of genius. Nothing marks more ftrongly the declenfion of genius in England, than the multitude of plays, farces, novels and other catchpenny pieces, which fwell the lift of modern publications ; and that hoft of compilers, who, in the rage for felecting beauties and abridging the labor of reading, disfigure the works of the pureft writers in the nation. Cicero did not wafte his talents in barely reading and felecting the beauties of Demofthenes ; and in the days of Addifon, the beauties of Milton, Locke and Shakefpear were to be found only in *their works*. But tafte is corrupted by luxury ; utility is forgotten in pleafure ; genius is buried in diffipation, or proftituted to exalt and to damn contending factions, and to amufe the idle debauchees that furround a licentious ftage.*

THESE

---

* FROM this defcription muft be excepted fome arts which have for their object, the pleafures of fenfe and imagination;

THESE are the reasons why we should
not adopt promiscuously their taste, their
opinions, their manners. Customs, habits,
and *language*, as well as government should
be national.   America should have her
own distinct from all the world.   Such is
the policy of other nations, and such must
be *our* policy, before the states can be either independent or respectable.   To copy
foreign manners implicitly, is to reverse
the order of things, and begin our political existence with the corruptions and vices
which have marked the declining glories
of other republics.

agination ; as music and painting ; and sciences which depend
on fixed principles, and not on opinion, as mathematics
and philosophy.   The former flourish in the last stages of
national refinement, and the latter are always proceeding
towards perfection, by discoveries and experiment.   Criticism also flourishes in Great Britain : Men read and judge
accurately, when original writers cease to adorn the sciences.   Correct writers precede just criticism.

DISSERTATION

DISSERTATION IV.

Of the Formation of Language. Horne Tooke's Theory of the Particles. Examination of particular Phrases.

FORMATION of LANGUAGE.

HAVING difcuffed the fubject of pronunciation very largely in the two preceding Differtations, I fhall now examin the *ufe of words in the conftruction of* fentences.

SEVERAL writers of eminence have attempted to explain the origin, progrefs and ftructure of languages, and have handled the fubject with great ingenuity and profound learning ; as Harris, Smith, Beatie, Blair, Condillac, and others. But the

M 3

discovery

difcovery of the true theory of the conftruction of language, feems to have been
referved for Mr. Horne Tooke, author of
the " Diverfions of Purley." In this treatife, however exceptionable may be particular inftances of the writer's fpirit and
manner, the principles on which the formation of languages depends, are unfolded
and demonftrated by an etymological analyfis of the Saxon or Gothic origin of
the Englifh particles. From the proofs
which this writer produces, and from various other circumftances, it appears probable, that the *noun* or fubftantive is the
principal part of fpeech, and from which
moft words are originally derived.

THE invention and progrefs of articulate
founds muft have been extremely flow.
Rude favages have originally no method of
conveying ideas, but by looks, figns, and
thofe inarticulate founds, called by grammarians, *Interjections*. Thefe are probably the firft beginnings of language. They
are produced by the paffions, and are perhaps very little fuperior, in point of articulation or fignificancy, to the founds which
exprefs the wants of the brutes.*

BUT

* IT is a difpute among grammarians, whether the in-
terjection is a part of fpeech ; and the queftion, like many
others

But the firſt ſounds, which, by being often repeated, would become articulate, would be thoſe which ſavages uſe to convey their ideas of certain viſible objeƈts, which firſt employ their attention. Theſe ſounds, by conſtant application to the ſame things, would gradually become the *names* of thoſe objeƈts, and thus acquire a permanent ſignification. In this manner, rivers, mountains, trees, and ſuch animals as afford food for ſavages, would firſt acquire names ; and next to them, ſuch other objeƈts as can be noticed or perceived by the ſenſes. Thoſe names which are given to ideas called *abſtraƈt* and *complex*, or, to ſpeak more correƈtly, thoſe names which expreſs a combination of ideas, are invented much later in the progreſs of language. Such are the words, faith, hope, virtue, genius, &c.

It

others upon ſimilar ſubjeƈts, has employed more learning than common ſenſe. The ſimple truth is this ; the involuntary ſounds produced by a ſudden paſſion, are the language of nature which is ſubjeƈt only to nature's rules. They are, in ſome degree, ſimilar among all nations. They do not belong to a grammatical treatiſe, any more than the looks of fear, ſurpriſe or any other paſſion. The words, ah me! oh me! are mere exclamations, as are bleſs me! my gracious! and numberleſs other ſounds, which are uttered without any preciſe meaning, and are not reduceable to any rules.

IT is unneceſſary, and perhaps impoſſible, to deſcribe the whole procefs of the
formation of languages ; but we may reaſon from the nature of things that the *neceſſary* parts of ſpeech would be the firſt
formed ; and it is very evident from etymology that all the others are derived from
theſe, either by abbreviation or combination. The neceſſary parts of ſpeech are
the *noun* and *verb* ; and perhaps we may
add the *article*. Pronouns are not necef-
ſary, but from their utility, muſt be a very
early invention.

THAT the noun and verb are the only
parts of ſpeech, abſolutely neceſſary for a
communication of ideas among rude nations, will be obvious to any perſon who
conſiders their manner of life, and the
ſmall number of their neceſſary ideas.
Their employments are war and hunting;
and indeed ſome tribes are ſo ſituated as to
have no occupation but that of procuring
ſubſiſtence. How few muſt be the ideas
of a people, whoſe ſole employment is to
catch fiſh, and take wild beaſts for food!
Such nations, and even ſome much farther advanced towards civilization, uſe few
or no prepoſitions, adverbs and conjunctions, in their intercourſe with each other,

and

and very few adjectives. Some tribes of savages in America use no adjectives at all ; but express qualities by a particular form of the verb ; or rather blend the affirmation and quality into one word.* They have, it is said, some connecting words in their own languages, some of which have advanced towards copiousness and variety. But when they attempt to speak English, they use nouns and verbs long before they obtain any knowlege of the particles. They speak in this manner, go, way———sun, shine———tree, fall———give, Uncas, rum ; with great deliberation and a short pause between the words. They omit the connectives and the abbreviations, which may be called the " wings of Mercury." Thus it is evident, that, among such nations, a few nouns and verbs will answer the purposes of language.

Many of this kind of expressions remain in the English language to this day. *Go away* is the savage phrase with the article *a*, derived perhaps from *one*, or what is more probable, added merely to express the found, made in the transition from one word to the other ; for if we attend to the

manner

* See Dr. Edwards on the Mohegan tongue. New Haven. 1788.

manner in which we pronounce thefe or two fimilar words, we fhall obferve that we involuntarily form the found expreffed by *a* or *aw*. In fome fuch manner are formed *aftray, awhile, adown, aground, a-fhore, above, abaft, among,* and many others. They are ufually called adverbs and prepofitions; but they are neither more nor lefs than nouns or verbs, with the prefix *a*.* That all the words called adverbs and prepofitions, are derived in like manner, from the principal parts of language, the noun and verb, is not demonftrable; but that *moft* of them are fo derived, etymology clearly proves.

HORNE TOOKE's THEORY *of the* PARTICLES.

THIS theory derives great ftrength from analizing the words called *conjunctions.* It will perhaps furprize thofe who have not attended to this fubject, to hear it afferted, that the little conjunction *if,* is a *verb* in

the

---

* *WHILE* is an old Saxon noun, fignifying *time*; and it is ftill ufed in the fame fenfe, *one while, all this while. Adown* is of uncertain origin. The Saxon *aduna* cannot eafily be explained. *Above* is from an old word, fignifying *head. Among* is from the Saxon *gemengan* to mix. The etymology of the others is obvious.

the Imperative Mode. That this is the fact
can no more be controverted than any
point of hiftory, or any truth that our
fenfes prefent to the mind. *If* is radically
the fame word as *give*; it was in the Saxon Infinitive, *gifan*, and in the Imperative,
like other Saxon verbs, loft the *an*; being
written *gif*. This is the word in its purity; but in different dialects of the fame
radical tongue, we find it written *gife*, *giff*,
gi, *yf*, *yef*, and *yeve*. Chaucer ufed *y* inftead of *g*.*

> " UNTO the devil rough and blake of hewe
> *Yeve* I thy body and my panne alfo."
> Freres Tale, 7204.

BUT the true Imperative is *gif*, as in the
Sad Shepherd. Act 2. Sc. 2.

> —————————" MY largeffe
> Hath lotted her to be your brother's miftrefs
> *Gif* fhe can be reclaimed; *gif* not, his prey."

THIS is the origin of the conjunction *if*;
and it anfwers, in fenfe and derivation to
the Latin *fi*, which is but a contraction of
fit. Thus what we denominate the Subjunctive

---

* IT has been remarked that *y* and *g* are gutturals which
bear nearly the fame affinity to each other as *b* and *p*.
Thus it happens that we find in old writings a *y* in many
words where *g* is now ufed; as *ayen*, *ayenft*, for again, againft.
Thus *bayonet* is pronounced *bagonet*.

junctive mode is refolvable into the Indicative. "*If* ye love me, ye will keep my commandments," is refolvable in this manner ; " Give, (give the following fact, or fuppofe it) ye love me, ye will keep my commandments." Or thus, "Ye love me, give that, ye will keep my commandments." But on this I fhall be more particular when I come to fpeak of errors in the ufe of verbs.

An is ftill vulgarly ufed in the fenfe of *if*. "*An* pleafe your honor," is the ufual addrefs of fervants to their mafters in England ; tho it is loft in New England. But a word derived from the fame root, is ftill retained ; viz. the Saxon *anan*, to give ; which is fometimes pronounced *nan*, and fometimes *anan*. It is ufed for *what*, or *what do you fay* ; as when a perfon fpeaks to another, the fecond perfon not hearing diftinctly, replies, *nan*, or *anan* ; that is, *give* or *repeat* what you faid. This is ridiculed as a grofs vulgarifm ; and it is indeed obfolete except among common people ; but is ftrictly correct, and if perfons deride the ufe of the word, it proves at leaft that they do not underftand its meaning.

Unless,

Unless, *left* and *else*, are all derivatives of the old Saxon verb *lefan*, *to difmifs*, which we preferve in the word *leafe*, and its compounds. So far are thefe words from being conjunctions, that they are, in fact, verbs in the Imperative mode; and this explanation ferves further to lay open the curious ftructure of our language. For example :

" Unless ye believe ye fhall not underftand," may be thus refolved; " Ye believe ; *difmifs* (that fact) ye fhall not underftand." Or thus, " *Difmifs* ye believe, (that circumftance being away) ye fhall not underftand." Thus by analizing the fentence we find no Subjunctive mode ; but merely the Indicative and Imperative.

" Kiss the Son, left he be angry," is refolvable in the fame manner· " Kifs the Son, *difmifs* (that) he will be angry." *Elfe* is ufed nearly in the fame fenfe, as in Chaucer, Freres Tale, 7240 :

" Axe him thyfelf, if thou not troweft me,
Or *elles* ftint a while and thou fhalt fee."

That is, " If thou doft not believe me, afk him thyfelf, or *difmiffing* (omitting that) wait and thou fhalt be convinced.

Though,

THOUGH, or *tho*, commonly called a conjunction, is also a verb in the Imperative Mode. It is from the verb *thafian* or *thafigan*, which, in the Saxon, signified to grant or *allow*. The word in its purity is *thaf* or *thof*; and so it is pronounced by many of the common people in England, and by some in America.

" *THO* he slay me, yet will I trust in him," may be thus explained; " *Allow* (suppose) he should slay me, yet will I trust in him." That this is the true sense of *tho*, is evident from another fact. The old writers used *algife* for *although*; and its meaning must be nearly the same.

"————————WHOSE pere is hard to find,
" *Algife* England and France were thorow faught."
Rel. An. Poet. 115.

SINCE is merely a participle of the old verb *seon*, to see. In ancient authors we find it variously written; as *sith*, *sithence*, *sin*, *sithen*, &c. and the common people in New England still pronounce it *sin*, *sen* or *sence*. Of all these, *sin* or *sen*, which is so much ridiculed as vulgar, comes nearest to the original *seen*.* This explanation
of

---

* FOUR hundred years ago, the purest author wrote *sen* or *sin* which is now deemed vulgar:
" SIN

of *fince* unfolds the true theory of languages, and proves that all words are originally derived from thofe which are firft ufed to exprefs ideas of fenfible objects. Mankind, inftead of that abftract fenfe which we annex to *fince*, if we have any idea at all when we ufe it, originally faid, *feen the fun rofe, it has become warm* ; that is, after the fun rofe, or that circumftance being *feen* or *paft*. We ufe the fame word now, with a little variation ; but the etymology is loft to moft people, who ftill employ the word for a precife purpofe, intelligible to their hearers.

But has two diftinct meanings, and two different roots. This is evident to any perfon who attends to the manner of ufing the word. We fay, " *But to proceed* ;" that is, *more* or *further*. We fay alfo, " All left the room, *but* one ;" that is, except one. Thefe two fignifications, which are conftantly and infenfibly annexed to the word, will perhaps explain all its ufes ; but cannot be well accounted for, without fuppofing it to have two etymologies. Happily the early writers furnifh us with the

means

" Sin thou art rightful juge, how may it be,
That thou wolt fuffren innocence to fpill,
And wicked folk to regne in profperitee ?"
Chaucer, Cant. Tales. 5504.

means of folving the difficulty. Gawen Douglafs the poet, was cotemporary with Chaucer, or lived near his time, was Bifhop of Dunkeld in Scotland, and probably wrote the language in the purity of his age and country. As the Scots in the Low Lands, are defcendants of the Saxons, in common with the Englifh, and from their local fituation, have been lefs expofed to revolutions, they have preferved more of the Saxon idiom and orthography than their fouthern brethren. In Douglafs we find two different words to exprefs the two different meanings, which we now annex to one ; viz. *bot* and *but*. The firft is ufed in the fenfe of *more, further* or *addition* ; and the laft in the fenfe of *except* or *take away*.

> " *BOT* thy work fhall endure in laude and gloric,
> *But* fpot or falt condigne eterne memorie."

The firft Mr. Horne derives from *botan, to boot, to give more* ; from which our Eng-lifh word *boot*, which is now for the moft part confined to jockies, is alfo derived ; and the other from *be utan,** to be out* or *away*. That thefe etymologies are juft

is

---

* *CUT* was originally a verb. So in the firft line of the celebrated Chevy Chace.

" THE

is probable, both from old writings and from the prefent diftinct ufes of the word *but*. This word therefore is the blending or corruption of *bot* and *beut*, the Imperatives of two Saxon verbs, *botan* and *beutan*.*

AND

> " The Perfé *owt* of Northombarlande,
> And a vow to God made he," &c.

I HAVE, in one or two inftances, obferved the ufe of it ftill among the lower claffes of people, in this country ; and I find *outed* in fome good writers, as late as Charles I.

* MR. Horne remarks that the French word *mais* was formerly ufed in the fenfe of *more*, or *bot*. The Englifh word *more* was formerly often fpelt *mo*.

> " TELLE me anon withouten wordes *mo*."
> Chaucer, Prol. to Cant. Tales, 810.

Is it not poffible that *mo* or *more* and the French *mais* may be radically the fame word ?

THE following paffage will confirm the foregoing explanation of *beutan*. It is taken from the Saxon verfion of the Gofpels.——Luke, chap. 1. v. 74. of the original.

> " HÆT we *butan* ege of ure feonda handa alyfede, him theowrian."

THIS verfion of the Gofpels was doubtlefs as early as the tenth or eleventh century. In Wickliffs verfion, made about three centuries later, the paffage ftands thus : " That we *without* drede, delyvered fro the hand of oure enemyes, ferve to him." Where we find *butan* and *without* are fynonimous.

THE word *bot* or *bote* is ftill retained in the law language, as *fire-bote*, *houfe-bote* ; where it is equivalent to *enough* or *fufficiency*.

And is probably a contraction of *anan*, to give, the verb before mentioned; and *ad*, the root of the verb *add*, and signifying *series* or *remainder*. *An ad, give the remainder.*

THE word *with*, commonly called a prepofition, is likewife a verb. It is from the Saxon *withan*, to join; or more probably from *wyrth*, to be, or the German *werden*, devenir, to be. The reafon for this latter conjecture, is that we have preferved the Imperative of *wyrth* or *werden*, in this ancient phrafe, " woe *worth* the day;" that is, woe be to the day. The German verb, in its inflections, makes *wirft* and *wurde*; and is undoubtedly from the fame root as the Danifh *værer*, to be. But whether *with* has its origin in *withan*, to join, or in *werden*, to be, its fenfe will be nearly the fame; it will ftill convey the idea of connection. This will plainly appear to any perfon who confiders, that *by* is merely a corruption of *be*, from the old verb *beon*; and that this word is ftill ufed to exprefs connection or nearnefs; " He lives *by* me;" " He went *by* me;" that is, he lives *be* me.

THIS verb *be* was formerly ufed in this phrafe; *be my faith, be my troth*; that is,

by

by my faith, as in Chevy Chace.* We ftill find the fame verb in a multitude of compounds, *be-come*, *be-yond*, *be-tween*, *be-fide*, *be-fore*. Thus we fee what are called *prepofitions*, are mere combinations or corruptions of verbs; they are not a primitive part of language, and if we refolve this phrafe, *he went beyond me*, we fhall find it compofed of thefe words, *he went*, *be*, *gone*, *me*; *yond* being nothing but the participle of *go*.

WILL my grammatical readers believe me, when I affert that the affirmation *yea*, or *yes*, is a verb? That it is fo, is undeniable. The Englifh *yea*, *yes*, and the German *ja*, pronounced *yaw*, are derived from a verb in the Imperative Mode; or rather, they are but corruptions of *aye*, the Imperative of the French *avoir*, to have. The pure word *aye*, is ftill ufed in Englifh. The affirmation *yea* or *yes*, is *have*, an expreffion of affent, *have what you fay*.†

THAT

---

* So in Mandeville's works. " And right as the fchip men taken here avys here, and govern hem *be* the lode fterre, right fo don fchip men bezonde the parties, *be* the fterre of the Southe, the which apperethe not to us."

† The French *oui* is faid to be a derivative or participle of the verb *ouir* to hear. The mode of affent therefore is by the word *heard*; as what you fay is *heard*; a mode equally expreffive with the Englifh.

THAT all the words, called *adverbs*, are abbreviations or combinations of nouns, verbs and adjectives, cannot perhaps be proved ; for it is extremely difficult to trace the little words, *when, then, there, here,* &c. to their true origin.* But excepting a few, the whole clafs of words, denominated *adverbs,* can be refolved into other parts of fpeech. The termination *ly,* which forms a large proportion of thefe words, is derived from the Saxon *liche, like.*

"AND as an angel heaven*lich* fhe fung."
Chaucer, Cant. Tales, 1057.

WE have in a few words retained the original pronunciation, as *Godlike* ; but in ftrictnefs of fpeech, there is no difference between *Godlike* and *Godly.*†

NOTWITHSTANDING

---

* IT is moft probable that many of the Englifh words beginning with *wh* are from the fame original as the Latin qui, quæ, quod ; and both coeval with the Greek. Qui and who ; quod and what ; are from the fame root, and a blending of the Greek και ο and και οτι. This fuppofition is ftrongly fupported by the ancient Scotch orthography of *what, where,* &c. which was *quhat, quhar.*

† THE termination *ly,* from *liche,* added to *adjectives,* forms the part of fpeech called *adverbs* ; as *great, greatly ; gracious, gracioufly.* But when this termination is added to a noun, it forms an adjective, as God, *Godly ;* heaven, *heavenly ;* and thefe words are alfo ufed adverbially ; for they will not admit the addition of another *ly. Godlily,*
which

NOTWITHSTANDING· it is evident that conjunctions, prepofitions, and adverbs are not original and neceffary parts of fpeech, yet as fpecies of abbreviations, or compound terms to exprefs affemblages of ideas, they may be confidered as very ufeful, and as great improvements in language. Every perfon, even without the leaft knowlege of etymology, acquires a habit of annexing a certain idea, or certain number of ideas to *unlefs*, *left*, *yes*, *between*, and the other particles ; he ufes them with precifion, and makes himfelf underftood by his hearers or readers. Thefe words enable him to communicate his ideas with greater facility and expedition, than he could by mere names and affirmations.ʹ They have loft the diftinguifhing characteriftics of verbs, perfon, time, and inflection. It is therefore convenient for grammatical purpofes, to affign them diftinct places and give them names, according to their particular ufes. Such of thefe old verbs as exhibit fome connection between the members of a difcourfe, may be properly denominated *conjunctions*. Others, that are ufed to fhow certain relations
between

which has been fometimes ufed, that is, *Godlikelike*, and other fimilar words, are not admiffible, on any principle whatever.

between words and are generally prefixed to them, may be well called *prepofitions*. A third fpecies, which are employed to qualify the fenfe of other words, may, from their pofition and ufes in a difcourfe, be denominated *adverbs*. But the foregoing inveftigation is neceffary to unfold the true principles on which language is conftructed, and the philofophical enquirer is referred for a more general view of the fubject, to Mr. Horne Tooke's *Diverfions of Purley.*

THE *verb* or *word* is fo called by way of eminence ; the ancient grammarians having confidered it as the principal part of fpeech. The *noun* is however entitled to the precedence ; it is of equal importance in language, and undoubtedly claims priority of origin. Philofophy might teach us that the *names* of a few vifible objects would be firft formed by barbarous men, and afterwards the words which exprefs the moft common actions. But with refpect to names of abftract ideas, as they are ufually called, they not only precede the formation of the verbs which reprefent the action, but it often happens that the fame word is ufed, with a prefix to denote the action of the object to which the name is
given.

given.   For example, *love* and *fear* are the names of certain paffions or affections of the mind.   To exprefs the action or exertion of thefe affections, we have not invented diftinct terms ; but cuftom has for this purpofe prefixed the word *do* or *to*, which, in its primitive fenfe, is *to act, move, or make.** Thus I *do love*, or *do fear*, are merely, I *act, love*, or *act, fear* ; and *to love* and *to fear* in the Infinitive, are *act, love*, and *act, fear*.

To confirm thefe remarks, let it be confidered that formerly *do* and *did* were almoft invariably ufed with the verb ; as *I do fear, he did love* ; and the omiffion of thefe words in affirmative declarations is of a modern date.   They are ftill preferved in particular modes of expreffion ; as in the negative and interrogative forms, and in emphatical affertions.

THE prefent hypothefis will derive additional ftrength from another circumftance.   Grammarians allege that the termination of the regular preterit tenfe, *ed*, is a corruption of *did*.   If fo, it feems to have been originally optional, either to

place

---

* *DO* and *to* are undoubtedly from the fame root ; *d* and *t* being convertible letters.

place the word *did*, which expreſſed the *action* of the objeƈt, before or after the *name*. Thus, *he feared,* is reſolvable into *he fear did*, and muſt be a blending of the words in a haſty pronunciation.   But it was alſo a praƈtice to ſay *he did fear*, which arrangement is not yet loſt nor obſcured ; but in no caſe are both theſe forms uſed, *he did feared* ; a preſumptive evidence of the truth of the opinion, that *ed* is a contraƈtion of *did*. Indeed I ſee no objeƈtion to the opinion but this, that it is not eaſy on this ſuppoſition, to account for the formation of *did* from *do*.   If *did* is itſelf a contraƈtion of *doed*, the regular preterit, which is probable, whence comes *ed* in this word ? To derive *ed* in other words from *did* is eaſy and natural ; but this leaves us ſhort of the primary cauſe or principle, and conſequently in ſuſpenſe, as to the truth of the opinion. Yet whatever may be the true derivation of the regular ending of the paſt time and perfeƈt participle of Engliſh verbs, the uſe of *do*, *did* and *to* before the verb, is a ſtrong evidence, that at leaſt one claſs of affirmations are formed by the help of *names*, with a prefix to denote the aƈtion of the objeƈts expreſſed by the names.   *I fear*, therefore, is a phraſe, compoſed of the pronoun *I*, and the noun *fear* ; and the affirmation,

contained

contained in the phrafe, is derived from the fingle circumftance of the pofition of the name after *I*. *I fear* is a modern fubftitute for *I do fear*; that is, *I act, fear*; all originally and ftrictly *nouns*. But by a habit of uniting the perfonal name *I* with the name of the paffion *fear*, we inftantly recognize an affirmation that the paffion is exerted; and *do*, the primitive name of *act*, has become fuperfluous.

EXAMINATION *of* PARTICULAR PHRASES.

HAVING made thefe few remarks on the formation of our language, I fhall proceed to examin the criticifms of grammarians on certain phrafes, and endeavor to fettle fome points of controverfy with refpect to the ufe of words; and alfo to detect fome inaccuracies which prevail in practice.

N O U N S.

WRITERS upon the fubject of propriety in our language, have objected to the ufe of *means*, with the article *a* and the definitive pronouns fingular, *this* and *that*.

The

The objection made is, that as this word
ends in *s*, it muft be plural, and cannot be
joined in conftruction with words in the
fingular.   This objection fuppofes that all
nouns ending with *s* are plural ; but this
would perhaps prove too much, and make
it neceffary to confider all nouns, *not* ending in *s*, as fingular, which cannot be true,
even on the principles of thofe who bring
the objection.   The fuppofition in both
cafes would be equally well founded.

It appears to me however, that the fenfe
of the word, and particularly the univerfal
practice of the Englifh nation, ought to
have induced the critical grammarian, who
wifhed to reduce the language to fome certainty, to fupprefs the objection.   The
word *means*, applied to a fingle inftrument
of action, or caufe, conveys a *fingle* idea ;
and I prefume, was generally ufed for this
purpofe, till Bifhop Lowth queftioned the
propriety of the practice ; at leaft *mean* is
fcarcely ufed as a noun, in any author
from Chaucer to Lowth.   On the contrary, the beft writers have ufed *means* either
in the fingular or plural number, according as they had occafion to exprefs by it
an idea of one caufe or more.

"By

" By *this means*, it became every man's intereft, as well as his duty to prevent all crimes."———Temple, Works, vol. 3. p. 133.

" And by *this means* I fhould not doubt," &c.———Wilkins Real Character, book 1.

" And finding themfelves by *this means* to be fafe."———Sidney on Gov. chap. 3. fect. 36.

" For he hopeth by *this means* to acquit himfelf."———Rawley's Sylva Sylvarum.

" And by *that means* they loft their bar-rier."———Moyle on the Lacedem. Gov.

" Clodius was now quæftor and by *that means* a fenator."———Middleton L. of Cic. vol. 1. p. 261.

" By *this means* however, there was nothing left to the Parliament of Ireland."——— Blackftone's Com. vol. 1. p. 102.

In this manner was the word ufed by the elegant writers in Queen Anne's reign.

But we have not only the authority of almoft every good writer in the language, for this ufe of *means* in the fingular as well as plural number, but we have the
authority

authority of almoſt unanimous national practice in ſpeaking. It is rare to hear *mean* uſed as a noun, and by thoſe only who are fettered by the arbitrary rules of grammarians. I queſtion whether the word, in the ſingular form, has obtained ſuch an eſtabliſhment, as to be entitled to a place among the Engliſh nouns. The uſe of it appears like pedantry. No man, whatever may be his rank and abilities, has a right to rejеɛt a mode of ſpeech, eſtabliſhed by immemorial uſage and univerſal conſent. Grammars ſhould be formed on *praɛtice* ; for praɛtice determines what a language is. I do not mean a *local* praɛtice, for this would ſubjeɛt us to perpetual variety and inſtability ; but *national* or *general* praɛtice. The latter, it has been remarked, is the ſtandard of propriety, to which all local idioms and private opinions ſhould be ſacrificed. The buſineſs of a grammarian is not to examin whether or not national praɛtice is founded on philoſophical principles ; but to *aſcertain* the national praɛtice, that the learner may be able to weed from his own any local peculiarities or falſe idioms.

 If *this means* and *a means* are now, and have immemorially been, uſed by good au-

thors

thors and the nation in general, neither Johnson, Lowth, nor any other person, however learned, has a right to say that the phrases are not *good English*. That this is the fact, every person may satisfy himself, by consulting the good authors and observing the universal practice in discourse.

BESIDES, the general practice of a nation is not easily changed, and the only effect that an attempt to reform it can produce, is, to make *many* people doubtful, cautious, and consequently uneasy ; to render a *few* ridiculous and pedantic by following nice criticisms in the face of customary propriety ; and to introduce a distinction between the learned and unlearned, which serves only to create difficulties for both.

DR. Priestley is the only writer upon this subject who seems to have been guided by just principles. He observes, with great propriety, that " Grammarians have leaned too much to the analogies of the Latin language, contrary to our mode of speaking and to the analogies of other languages, more like our own. It must be allowed, that the custom of speaking, is the original

al and only juft ftandard of any language."
Pref. to Gram. page 9. His criticifms are
exceedingly judicious, and are entitled to
the confideration of the ftudent, in preference to thofe of Lowth, or any other Englifh author. He confiders *means* as belonging " to that clafs of words which do not
change their termination on account of
number." It is ufed in both numbers, *a
means*, or *thefe means*, with equal propriety.

To the fame clafs of words belong *pains,
news*, and perhaps fome others. Every
perfon who has read good Englifh authors,
or lived where the language is fpoken in
purity, muft have obferved that the word
pains is ufually preceded by *much*, and followed by a verb in the fingular number ;
much pains was taken. If the word is a
plural noun, it fhould neither be followed
by a fingular verb, nor preceded by *much* ;
for we never prefix *much* to plurals. The
moft untutored ear would be offended at
much papers, much labors. But do we not
always fay *much pains ?* Do we ever fay
many pains were taken ? I confefs I never
yet heard or faw the expreffion. Yet
Lowth contends that *pains* is plural. This
criticifm upon the word is an authority in

vindication

vindication of an erroneous practice of using it with a plural verb, even when it is preceded by *much*. So in Sheridan's Art of Reading, we obferve thefe words; "If fo *much pains were* thought neceflary among them," &c. Temple indulges the fame miftake; "I know how *much pains have been* taken to deduce the words *Baro* and *feudum* from the Latin and Greek, and even from the Hebrew and Egyptian tongue." Works, vol. 3. p. 365.

MIGHT not thefe writers have ufed, *much fheep were killed*, with the fame propriety?

THE fenfe of the word *pains* does not require that we fhould confider it as a plural; for it fignifies *labor* or *fatigue*, in contradiftinction to thofe uneafy fenfations, each of which fingly is called a *pain*, and to exprefs a number of which *pains* is ufed as a plural. On the other hand we have the authority of general practice for uniting with it *much*, which can in no cafe be ufed with a plural, and alfo a verb in the fingular number.

—"AND taken *much pains* fo to proportion the powers of the feveral magiftrates."——Sidney on Gov. fect. 1.

"I FOUND

"I FOUND *much art* and *pains* employed."——Middleton.

"HE will affemble materials with *much
pains*."——Bolling. on Hift. letter 4.

"As to our own language, feveral perfons have taken *much pains* about the orthography of it."——Wilkins Real Char.
book 1. chap. 5.

THERE are a few inftances in which
good authors have confidered *news* as a
plural ; as

"FROM all regions where the beft *news
are* made."——B. Johnfon, Staple of News.

"AND feal the news and iffue *them*."——
The fame.

BUT can an Englifh ear relifh this affected correctnefs ? Hear the language of
Cowley and Shakefpear, who wrote as the
nation fpoke :

"A GENERAL joy at *this glad newes* appear'd."
Cowley's Davideis, book 1.

"Now by St. Paul *this news is* bad indeed !"
The fame.

"No news fo bad abroad as *this* at home."
Rich. III. fcene 1.
SUCH

Such is the language at this day, and a man would expofe himfelf to ridicule, who fhould fay, *thefe news are good.*

Late writers feem to confider *riches* as plural; but erroneoufly. It is merely a contraction of *richeffe,* the French fingular, which was probably introduced into England under the Norman kings. Chaucer ufes *richeffe* as the fingular:

> " But for ye fpeken of fwiche gentilleffe,
> As is defcended out of old *richeffe.*"
> > Cant. Tales, 6691.

> —" And he that ones to love doeth his homage
> Full oftentymes dere bought *is the richeffe.*"
> > La Belle Dame fans mercy, 323.

The word *richeffe* here is no more plural than *gentilneffe, diftreffe, doubleneffe,* which the author ufes in the fame poem; and *riches* now, in ftrictnefs of fpeech, is no more plural than *gentlenefs, diftrefs,* or any other word of fimilar ending. When Chaucer had occafion for a plural, he wrote the word *richeffes;* as in the Tale of Me-libeus: " Thou haft dronke fo muche hony of fwete temporal *richeffes* and delices and honors of this world," &c.——Works, vol. 4. p. 170. Bell's edit.

THE

The word *riches* therefore is in the singular number and merely an abbreviation of *richeſſe* ; as *diſtreſs* is of *diſtreſſe* ; *weakneſs*, of *weakneſſe*, &c. and the reaſon why the plural *richeſſes* has been neglected, may be, that the idea it conveys does not admit of number any more than that of *wealth*, which is alſo deſtitute of a plural form.

" Was ever *riches* gotten by your golden mediocrities ?"——Cowley on Cromwell's Gov.

"When love has taken all thou haſt away,
His ſtrength by too *much riches* will decay."
. Cowley.

" The envy and jealouſy which great *riches* is always attended with."——Moyle's Eſſay on Lacedem. Gov. 48.

" In one hour *is* ſo great *riches* come to nought."——Bible.

Here *riches* is conſidered in its true light. Notwithſtanding this, the termination of the word has led late writers into the opinion, that it is plural ; ſo that we generally ſee it followed by a plural verb : Should this become the unanimous opinion and a general correſpondent practice enſue, *riches* will be eſtabliſhed as a

plural,

plural, contrary to etymology and ancient ufage.

Alms is alfo in the fingular number ; being a contraction of the old Norman French, *almeffe*, the plural of which was *almeffes*.   So in Chaucer :

> "Ye knowen wel that I am poure and olde,
> Kithe (fhow) your *almeffe* upon me poure wretche."
>   Freres Tale, 7190.

"*This almeffe* fhouldeft thou do of thy propre thinges," &c.——Vol. 5. p. 217. Bell.

"These ben generally the *almeffes* and werkes of charitie of hem that have temporel richeffes."——The fame.

Alms is ufed as a noun fingular in the Bible ; "To afk *an alms*."   "He gave *much alms*;" that is, *almeffe*, or charity. The plural of this word is not ufed.

Largess is a word of this clafs.   It is from the old French *largeffe* ; but the idea admits of number, and accordingly we find the plural, *largeffes*, ftill in ufe.

Laches, from the French *lacheffe*, is ftill retained in the law ftile ; but cuftom has

                      abbreviated

abbreviated the word into *lache*, a single syllable.

AMENDS may properly be considered as in the singular number, and so it is used by one of our best writers. " They must needs think that this honor to him, when dead, was but *a* necessary *amends* for the injury which they had done him, when living." ———Middleton's L. of Cic. vol. 3. p. 131.

THE idea here conveyed by *amends* is as single as that expressed by *compensation*. The word has no change of termination, and may be considered as singular or plural, at the choice of the writer.

WAGES is a word of the same kind.

VICTUALS is derived from the old French *vitaille*,* and was formerly used in the singular form, *victual*. But the latter is now wholly disused, and *victuals* generally used with a singular verb and pronoun. So Swift uses the word. " We had such very fine *victuals* that I could not eat *it*."† The editor

* THIS word is not used in modern French ; but *its* derivatives, *avitailler*, *avitaillment*, &c. are still retained.

† CORRESPONDENCE, letter 53.

editor of his works remarks, *that here is false concord*; but I believe Swift has followed the general practice of the English. The word seems to have lost the plurality of ideas, annexed to many different articles included in the term, and to have assumed the general meaning of the word *food*, which does not admit of the plural.

THE word *odds* seems to be of the same kind. We sometimes find a plural verb united to it, as in Pope's translation of Homer :

"On valor's side the *odds* of combat *lie*,
The brave live glorious, or lamented die."
Iliad, b. 15. l. 670.

BUT in common practice *odds* is considered as in the singular number. We always say, "What *is* the *odds* ;" and I should rank this among the words, which, altho they have the termination of regular plurals, more properly belong to the singular number.

THE word *gallows* is evidently of this class. "Let *a gallows* be made," say the translators of the Bible, with perfect propriety. Indeed I cannot conceive how any man who has read English authors, can consider this word as in the plural.

O 3   *BELLOWS*

BELLOWS, tongs, sheers, scissors, snuffers, pincers, have no change of termination, and it is the practice to prefix to them the word *pair*. Yet notwithstanding these articles are composed of two principal parts, both are necessary to form a single indivisible instrument, and the names might have been considered as nouns in the singular.* *Pair* is more properly applied to two separate articles of the same kind, and used together ; a *pair of shoes*, or *gloves*. Custom, however, has sanctioned the use of it before the words just enumerated, and therefore a pair of tongs, &c. must be admitted as good English.†

THERE are many other words in our language which have the plural termination ; as *billiards, ethics, metaphysics, mathematics, measles, hysterics,* and many others;
which

* SOME of these articles, in other languages, have names in the singular number, as in Latin, *forceps,* pincers ; *forfex,* sheers or scissors ; *follis,* bellows. In French, *soufflet* is singular, and *pincettes,* plural. *A bellows* is sometimes heard in English, and is perfectly correct.

† WILL the same authority justify our farmers in prefixing *pair* to a sett of *bars,* and other people, in prefixing it to *stairs,* when there are five or six of the former, and perhaps twenty of the latter? A *pair of bars,* a *pair of stairs,* in strictness of speech, are very absurd phrases : but perhaps it is better to admit such anomalies, than attempt to change universal and immemorial practice.

which properly belong to the fingular number. *Ethics is a fcience*, is better Englifh than *ethics are*.

ON the other hand, there are many words, which, without ever taking the plural termination, often belong to the plural. *Sheep, deer* and *hofe*, are often mentioned as belonging to this defcription. To thefe we may add many names of fifh ; as *trout, falmon, carp, tench* and others, which are in fact names of fpecies ; but which apply equally to the individuals of the fpecies. We fay *a trout*, or *five trout* ; but never *five trouts*.

POSSESSIVE CASE.

IN many inftances we find two or three words ufed to defcribe or defignate a particular perfon or thing ; in which cafe they are to be confidered as a fingle noun or name, and the fign of the poffeffive annexed to the laft ; as, " the *King of France's* army."

"*FLETCHER of Salton's plan* of a militia differs little from that of Harrington."*——— Home, Sketch 9.   ARTICLE

*" THE *King of England's court*, toto nempe illi aggregato, The *King of England*, tamquam uni fubftantivo potponitur litera formativa *s*."——— Wallis.

ARTICLE.

MOST grammarians have given the article the firft rank among the parts of fpeech. To me this arrangement appears very incorrect; for the article is a mere appendage of the noun, and without it cannot even be defined. The *noun* is the primary and principal part of fpeech, of which the *article*, *pronoun* and *adjective* are mere adjuncts, attendants, or fubftitutes, and the latter therefore fhould follow the former in grammatical order and definition.

UNDER this head I will introduce a few obfervations on the ufe of *a*. Grammarians have fuppofed that *a*, in the phrafes *a going*, *a hunting*, is a corruption of the prepofition *on* ; a fuppofition, which, if we attend to the fenfe of the phrafes, appears highly abfurd, but which etymology, in a great meafure, overthrows.

IN the firft place, the prepofition is not among the original parts of language ; its ufe, and confequently its formation, are not neceffary among rude nations ; it is a part of fpeech of a late date in the progrefs of language, and is itfelf a derivative from

other

other words.   I have, in another place,*
given some reasons to prove *on* to be an
abbreviation of the numeral *one*, or *top one*.
It is very evident that *on* is a contraction
of *upon*, which was formerly written *uppone* ; and there are good reasons for believing the latter to be derived from *top one*.
In addition to the authorities quoted in
the Institute, an example or two from
Chaucer will almost place the question beyond a doubt.

"THERE lith on—up myn hed."
Cant. Tales, 4288.

That is, there lieth one upon my head ;
where *up* is used for *upon*, as it is in other
places.

"No more, *up paine* of lesing of your hed."
Ibm. 1709.

That is, *upon pain of losing your head.*

THE word *up* is undoubtedly but a corruption of *top*, or a noun derived from the
same root, and this hypothesis is support-
ed by the true theory of language ; which
is, that rude nations converse mostly by
names. *Up myn hed*, is *top mine head.* An
improvement of this phrase would be the
use

*SECOND part of the Grammatical Institute. Tit. Notes.

ufe of *one*, *ane* or *an*, to afcertain particular things ; *uppone*, *upon*. In the progrefs of language, thefe words would be contracted into *on*, which we denominate a prepofition.

I am very fenfible that Chaucer ufed *on* in the manner mentioned by Lowth ; *on live* for *alive* ; *on hunting* ; *on hawking* ; which would feem to warrant the fuppofition of that writer, that *a* is a contraction of *on*, confidering *on* originally as a prepofition. But it is contrary to all juft ideas of language to allow fuch a primitive part of fpeech. On the other hand, Chaucer ufes *on* for other purpofes, which cannot be explained on Lowth's hypothefis.

> "His brede, his ale, was alway *after on*."
> Cant. Tales, 343.

So alfo in line 1783. In this example *on* is allowed on all hands to be a contraction of *one* ; *after one* (way, manner) that is, *alike*, or in the fame manner.

" They were *at on* ;" line 4195. They were *at one* ; that is, together or agreed.

" Ever *in on* ;" line 1773, and 3878 ; ever *in one* (way, courfe, &c.) that is, *continually*.

If

IF therefore we suppose *on* to be merely a corruption of *one*, we can easily explain all its uses. *On hunting*, or contractedly, *a hunting*, is *one hunting*. *On live, on life*, or *alive*, is merely *one life*. This form of expression is very natural, however childish or improper it may appear to us. It seems very obvious to resolve *ashore, abed*, into *on shore, on bed*; but even Lowth himself would be puzzled to make us believe that *adry, athirst*, came from *on dry, on thirst*; and Wallis would find equal difficulty to convince us that they came from *at dry, at thirst*. If we suppose *a* to be a contraction of *one*, or the Saxon *ane* or *an*, the solution of all these phrases is perfectly easy, and corresponds with Horne's theory of the particles. For if rude nations converse without particles, they must say *go shore*, or *go one shore*; *he is bed*, or *he is one bed*; *he is dry*, or *one dry*; *I am thirst*, or *I am one thirst*. Indeed every person who will attend to the manner of speaking among the American savages, must believe this explanation of the phrases to be probably just.

THAT *on* was formerly used both as a preposition and an adjective, is acknowleged by the Editor of the British Poets;* but

---

✝ CHAUCER's Works, Glossary, p. 151.

but its ufes in all cafes may be eafily explained on the fingle principle before mentioned.

This hypothefis however will be con-
firmed by the fact, that the Englifh article
a, "is nothing more than a corruption of
the Saxon adjective, *ane* or *an* (one) before
a fubftantive beginning with a confonant."
Editor of Chaucer's works, Gloff. p. 23.
And the article *a* and the numeral *one* have
ftill the fame fignification. That *ane* or
an, and *one* are originally the fame, is a
point not to be controverted. We have
therefore the ftrongeft reafon to believe that
a in the phrafes *a going, a hunting, a fifhing*
is derived from *one*. *On*, as a contraction
of *upon*, has, in modern language, a different fenfe, and cannot be well fubftituted
for *a*; for *on going, on fifhing*, have an awkward appearance and will not obtain in
the language, to the exclufion of *a going,
a fifhing*. The vulgar practice is more
correct than Lowth's correction, and ought
by no means to be rejected.

"O let my life, if thou fo many deaths *a coming* find,
With thine old year its voyage take."——
Cowley's Ode to the New Year.

" But thefe fantaftic errors of our dream,
Lead us to folid wrong ;
We pray God, our friend's torments to prolong,
And

And wifh uncharitably for them,
To be as long *a dying* as Methufalem."
Cowley.

IF the foregoing opinion of the origin of *a* in fuch phrafes, fhould not be deemed fatisfactory, we may perhaps afcribe its origin to a mere cuftom of forming expletive founds in the tranfition from one word to another.*

THE following phrafes, *three fhillings a piece*, *a day*, *a head*, *a bufhel*, it is faid are elliptical forms of fpeech ; fome prepofition being implied, as, *for* or *by*. This affertion can proceed only from an imperfect view of the fubject. Unlefs grammarians can prove that fome prepofition was formerly ufed, which is now omitted, they cannot prove that any is implied, nor fhould they have recourfe to implication to find a rule to parfe the phrafes. The truth is, no fuch prepofition can be found, nor is their need of any. *A,* in this form of
fpeech,

---

* THE Editor of Chaucer's Works before mentioned, remarks, " that *a*, in compofition with words of Saxon original, is an abbreviation of *af* or *of*, *at*, *on* or *in* ; and often a corruption of the prepofitive particle *ge* or *y*." According to this writer, *a* is any thing and every thing ; it has fo many derivations and ufes, that it has no certain derivation or meaning at all. In the phrafe *a coming*, *a* feems now to be a mere expletive ; but otherwife *a*, *one*, and *an* have the fame meaning in all cafes,

fpeech, carries the full meaning of the Latin *per*, and the fubftitution of the latter, for want, as it is faid, of an Englifh word, in the phrafes, *per day*, *per head*, *per pound*, is a burlefque upon the Englifh to this day. We fee continually a wretched jargon of Latin and Englifh in every merchant's book, even to the exclufion of a pure Englifh phrafe, more concife, more correct, and more elegant. It is to be wifhed that *a* might be reftored to its true dignity, as it is ufed by fome of the pureft Englifh writers.

" HE had read almoft conftantly, twelve or fourteen hours *a day*;" that is, *one day*. ——Bollingbroke on Hiftory, letter 4.

" To the fixteen fcholars twenty pounds *a piece*."——Cowley.

THIS is pure elegant Englifh, and the common people have the honor of preferving it, unadulterated by foreign words.

VERB.

THE moft difficult branch of this fubject is the verb. Next to the noun, this is the moft important part of fpeech, and as it includes all the terms by which we exprefs

exprefs action and exiftence, in their numberlefs varieties, it muft, in all languages,
be very comprehenfive.

THE Englifh verb fuffers very few inflections or changes of termination, to exprefs the different circumftances of perfon,
number, time and mode. Its inflections
are confined to the three perfons of the
fingular number, in the prefent tenfe, indicative mode, and the firft and fecond perfons of the paft tenfe ; unlefs we confider
the irregular participles as a fpecies of inflection belonging to the verb. All the
other varieties of perfon, number, time and
mode, are expreffed by prefixing other
words, by various combinations of words,
or by a particular manner of utterance.

THIS fimplicity, as it is erroneoufly called, is faid to render our language eafy of
acquifition. The reverfe however of this
is true ; for the ufe of auxiliaries or combinations of words, conftitutes the moft
perplexing branch of grammar ; it being
much eafier to learn to change the termination of the verb, than to combine
two, three or four words for the fame
purpofe.

GRAMMARIANS

Grammarians have ufually divided the English verbs into *active*, *paffive* and *neuter*. "*Active* verbs," fay they,* " exprefs action, and neceffarily imply an agent and an object acted upon." But is not a man *paffive* in *hearing*? Yet *hear* is called an *active* verb.

" A verb *neuter* expreffes being, or a ftate or condition of being ; when the agent and object coincide, and the event is properly neither action nor paffion, but rather fomething between both." But is there neither *action* nor *paffion* in *walking*, *running*, *exifting*? One would think that *running* at leaft might be called *action*.

The common definitions, copied, in fome meafure, from the Latin Grammars, are very inaccurate. The moft correct and general divifion of Englifh verbs, is, into *tranfitive* and *intranfitive* ; the former term comprehending all verbs that may be followed by any object receiving the action, or of which any thing is affirmed ; the latter, all thofe verbs, the affirmation in which is limited to the agent. Thus *hear* is a *tranfitive* verb, for it affirms fomething of an object ; *I hear the bell* :

Run

---

* Lowth's Introduction. Tit. verb.

Run is an *intranfitive* verb, for the action mentioned is confined to the agent ; *he runs.* Yet the laft is an *active* verb, and the firft, ftrictly fpeaking, is not ;* fo that there is a diftinction to be made between a verb *active* and *tranfitive.*

In ftrict propriety, we have in Englifh no paffive verb ; that is, we have no fingle word which conveys the idea of paffion or fuffering, in the manner of the Greek or Latin paffive verb. It may be ufeful, in teaching Englifh to youth or foreigners, to exhibit a fpecimen of the combinations of the verb *be,* with the participles of other verbs in all their varieties ; but each word fhould be parfed as a diftinct part of fpeech ; altho two or more may be neceffary to convey an idea which is expreffed by a fingle word in another language.

T I M E.

TIME is naturally divided into *paft, prefent* and *future.* The Englifh verb has but two variations of ending to exprefs time ; the prefent, as *love, write* ; and the
paft,

---

* *RUN*, like many other verbs, may be ufed either tranfi-tively or intranfitively. Simply *to run,* is intranfitive ; *to run a horfe,* tranfitive.

P

paſt, as *loved, wrote.* The uſual diviſion of tenſes, or combinations of words corresponding to the Latin tenſes, is not wholly accurate. The definition of the ſecond tenſe, in the ordinary arrangement of them in Latin grammars, may be correct, as it relates to the Roman tongue; but does not apply to the Engliſh tenſe, which is commonly called by the ſame name, the *Imperfect.* The Latin words *movebam, legebam,* are tranſlated *I moved, I read.* Now the Engliſh words expreſs actions *perfectly paſt,* and therefore the time or tenſe cannot be juſtly denominated *imperfect.* If the Latin words expreſſed, in the Roman tongue, actions *imperfectly paſt,* they ſhould be rendered by us, *I was moving, was reading,* which convey ideas of actions, as taking place at ſome preceding period, but not then paſt. In this ſenſe, the name of the tenſe might have been uſed with propriety. But the Engliſh form of expreſſion, *he moved,* conveys the idea of an action completely paſt, and does not fall within the definition of the Latin *Imperfect.*

It is ſurprizing that the great Lowth ſhould rank this form of the verb, *they moved,* under the head of *indefinite* or *undetermined* time; and yet place. this form,

have

have moved, or what is called the perfect tenfe, under the head of *definite* or *determined* time. The truth is, the firft is the moft *definite*. *I have loved*, or *moved*, exprefses an action performed and completed, generally within a period of time not far diftant; but leaves the particular *point* of time wholly *indefinite* or *undetermined*. On the other hand, *I loved* is necefsarily employed, when a particular *period* or *point* of time is fpecified. Thus it is correct to fay, *I read a book yefterday, laft week, ten years ago*, &c. but it is not grammatical to fay, *I have read a book yefterday, laft week*, &c. fo that, directly contrary to Lowth's rule, *I moved*, is the *definite*, and *I have moved*, the *indefinite* time.

GREAT inaccuracy is likewife indulged in the ufual defcription of the Englifh future tenfe. There is no variation of the verb to exprefs a future action; to remedy this defect, the Englifh ufe *fhall* and *will*, before the verb in its radical form. But thefe words are both in the prefent time; being merely the Teutonic verbs *follen* and *wollen*, which formerly had, and in the German ftill have, moft of the inflections of regular verbs. Thus:

Ind.

Ind. Pref. *Ich foll*, I ought or fhould. *Ich will*, I will.

Imp. *Ich follt*, I ought or fhould. *Ich wollt*, I would.

Preter. *Ich habe gefollt*, I ought or fhould have. *Ich habe gewollt*, I would or would have, &c. &c.*

I will go is really nothing more than a *prefent* promife of a *future* action. I *fhall go* is a *prefent* prediction of a *future* action. In the fecond and third perfons, *will* expreffes the prediction ; and as one cannot promife for a fecond or third perfon, *fhall*, in thefe perfons, implies a promife of the firft perfon, that he will *command* or *oblige* the fecond or third perfon to do an action in fome future time. The whole may be thus explained :

I will go,

Is my own *prefent* promife to do a future action.

Thou

* LOWTH obferves a diftinction between the verb *to will*, and the auxiliary, *will*; the firft being regularly inflected, *I will, thou willeft, he wills*, and the latter, *I will, thou wilt, he will*. But altho this diftinction actually exifts in modern practice, yet the words are, in both cafes, the fame—derived from the fame root, and ftill retaining nearly the fame meaning.

Thou wilt go—He will go,

Are my (the speaker's) *present* predictions that the persons mentioned will do a future action ; or perhaps more properly, a declaration of their inclination or intention.

I shall go,

Is my *present* prediction of a future action.

Thou shalt go—He shall go,

Are my (the speaker's) *present* promise that the second and third persons will do a future action.   But as a man cannot compel a superior, he can promise only for himself or inferiors ; therefore these last expressions imply a promise in the speaker, and a right to command the second and third persons to do the thing promised ; for which reason they are used only in addressing or speaking of, inferiors or subjects. The same remarks apply to the three persons in the plural number.

HENCE we observe the inaccuracy of translating the future tense of the Greeks, Romans, and French, by *shall* or *will* indifferently.   It is probable that the future tense in those languages, and perhaps in others, where the tense is formed by inflections, was employed merely to *foretell.*

If

If fo, *fhall* only fhould be ufed in the firft perfon of the Englifh tranflation, and *will*, in the fecond and third.   Thus:

Latin,	*French,*	*Englifh,*
Habebo,	J'aurai,	I fhall have.
Habebimus,	nous aurons,	we fhall have.
Habebis,	tu auras,	thou wilt have.
Habebit,	il aura,	he will have.
Habebitis,	vous aurez,	you will have.
Habebunt,	ils auront,	they will have.

On the other hand, a promife in the firft perfon expreffed in Englifh by *will*, and a promife or command in the fecond and third, expreffed by *fhall*, feem, in thefe languages, to be communicated by other words or a circumlocution.

In ftrictnefs of fpeech therefore, we have no future tenfe of the verb in Englifh; but we ufe auxiliaries, which, in the prefent tenfe, exprefs a prediction of an action, or a difpofition of mind to produce an action.   Thefe auxiliaries, united with the verb or affirmation, anfwer the purpofes of the future tenfes of verbs in other languages; and no inconvenience can arife from calling fuch a combination a *tenfe*.

MODE

M O D E.

MOST languages are fo conftructed, that the verbs change their terminations for the purpofe of expreffing the *manner* of being or action. In this particular, the Englifh is fingular ; there being but one inflection of a fingle verb, which can be faid to be peculiar to the conditional or fubjunctive mode.* In all other refpects, the verbs in the declaratory and conditional modes are the fame ; and the condition is known only by fome other word prefixed to the verb.

IT is aftonifhing to fee how long and how ftupidly Englifh grammarians have followed the Latin grammars in their divifions of time and mode ; but in particular the latter. By this means, we often find *may, can, fhould* and *muft* in a conditional mode, when they are pofitive declarations and belong to the indicative. All unconditional declarations, whether of an action, or of a *right, power* or *neceffity* of doing an action, belong to the *indicative* ; and the diftinction between the *indicative* and *potential* is totally ufelefs. *Should* is commonly

monly

---

* *IF I were, thou wert, he were,* in the prefent hypothetical tenfe of the fubjunctive mode, are not ufed in the indicative.

monly placed in the imperfect time of the
subjunctive ; yet is frequently used to express an unconditional obligation, as *he
should go* ; and belongs to the present time
of the indicative, as much as *he ought*, or
the French *il faut* or *il doit*.

WOULD is sometimes employed in a declaratory sense to express a present volition,
and then belongs to the indicative.   In the
past time, *should, would, might, could*, often
express unconditional ideas, and belong to
the indicative.   In short, the usual arrangement of the English verbs and auxiliaries in our grammars is calculated to perplex and mislead a learner ; and I have
never found a foreigner who could use
them with tolerable propriety.

NUMBER *and* PERSON.

UNDER this head, I shall remark on a
single article only, the use of *you* in the
singular number, with a plural verb.   The
use of the plural *nos* and *vos*, for *ego* and *tu*
in Latin ; of *nous* and *vous* for *je* and *tu* in
French ; seems to have been very ancient,
and to have been originally intended to
soften the harshness of egotism, or to make
a respectful distinction in favor of great
personages,

perfonages.   But the practice became gen-eral in the French nation, was introduced by them into England, and gradually imi-tated by the Englifh in their own tongue. *You*, in familiar difcourfe, is applied to an individual, except by a fingle fect of chrift-ians ; the practice is general and of long ftanding ; it has become correct Englifh, and ought to be confidered, in grammar, as a pronoun in the fingular number.   It may be objected, that we unite with it a verb in the plural number, *you are, you have*; this is true, but the verb, in thefe in-ftances, becomes fingular ; and both the pronoun and verb fhould be placed in the fingular number.

In the union of *you* with a plural verb in the prefent time, we are all unanimous; but in the paft time, there is a difference between books and common practice in a fingle inftance.   In books, *you* is common-ly ufed with the plural of the verb *be*, *you were* ; in converfation, it is generally fol-lowed by the fingular, *you was*.   Notwith-ftanding the criticifms of grammarians, the antiquity and univerfality of this prac-tice muft give it the fanction of propriety ; for what but practice forms a language ? This practice is not merely vulgar ; it is

general

general among men of erudition who, do not affect to be fettered by the rules of grammarians, and some late writers have indulged it in their publications. I should therefore inflect the verb *be* in the past time after this manner; *I was, thou waſt*, or *you was, he was*, &c. Whatever objections may be raiſed to this inflection, *it is the language of the Engliſh*, and rules can hardly change a general practice of ſpeaking; nor would there be any advantage in the change, if it could be effected.

AUXILIARIES.

THERE are ſeveral verbs in Engliſh, which, from the neceſſity of their union with other verbs, have obtained the name of *auxiliaries*. Originally they were principal verbs, with regular Saxon infinitives, and the uſual inflections; as may be obſerved by any perſon, who has the ſmalleſt acquaintance with the modern German, which retains more of the ancient ſtructure, than any other branch of the primitive language.

The verbs, called *auxiliaries* or *helpers*, are *do, be, have, ſhall, will, may, can, muſt*. The three firſt are often employed alone, and are therefore acknowleged to be ſometimes principal verbs. That the others

were

were fo, will be made obvious by a fpecimen from the German, with the corref-
ponding Englifh.

	German,	*Englifh,*
Inf.	*Wollen,*	to will.
Ind.Pref.	Ich will,	I will.
	Wir wollen,*	we will.
Imper.	Ich wolte,	I would.
Preterit.	Ich habe gewolt,	I have would,or willed.
Plup.	Ich hatte gewolt,	I had would.
Fut.	Ich werde wollen,	I fhall will.
Imp.	Wolle du,	will thou.
Subj.	*Ich wolle,*	(if) I would,&c.
Inf.	Wollen,	to will.
	Gewolte haben,	to have would, or willed.
Part.	Wollend,	willing.
	Gewollte,	having would, or willed.

Sollen, to fhall, is inflected in the fame
manner. *Koennen*, to can, or be able, is
inflected much in the fame manner. *Ich
kann*, I can, &c. Imperfect, *Ich konnte*, I
could. Preterit, *Ich habe gehonnt*, I have
could (or been able.) Participle, *Kœn-
nend, canning*, being able. Thus *mœgen*, to
may,

-may, makes, in the paſt tenſes, *Ich mochte,* I might or mought, as the vulgar ſome-times pronounce it ; *Ich habe gemocht, I have might.* *Muſt* alſo, which in Engliſh has loſt all inflection, is varied in the German ; *muſſen,* to muſt, or be obliged ; Imperfect, *Ich muſte,* I muſt, or was obliged.

But whatever theſe verbs may have once been, yet from their loſs of ſeveral inflections and the participles, with their ſingular uſe in combination with other verbs, they may very well be denominated *auxiliary verbs.* Their true force in Engliſh ſhould be aſcertained and explained in grammars for the benefit of learners, and particularly for the aſſiſtance of foreign-ers ;* yet in reſolving ſentences, each ſhould be conſidered as a verb or diſtinct part of ſpeech.

For want of a clear and accurate knowl-ege of the Engliſh auxiliaries, foreigners are apt to fall into material errors in con-ſtructing ſentences. The moſt numerous errors appear in the uſe of *will* and *ſhall,* and their inflections. The Scots and I-riſh, even of the firſt rank, generally uſe

will

---

* See the ſecond part of the Grammatical Inſtitute. Appendix.

will for *shall* in the first person ; by which means, they substitute a *promise* for an intended *prediction*.   Several errors of this kind have escaped the notice of the most celebrated writers.

" WITHOUT having attended to this, we *will* be at a loss in understanding several passages in the classics, which relate to the public speaking, and the theatrical entertainments of the ancients."——Blair's Lectures, p. 48. Philad. edit.

" IN the Latin language, there are no two words, we *would* more readily take to be synonimous, than *amare* and *diligere*."——The same, p. 83.

IN these and several other instances which occur in Blair's writings, the words *will* and *would* are used very improperly, for *shall* and *should*.   The author means only to *foretell* certain events, and has employed words which carry, to an English ear, the full force of a *promise*.

ENGLISH writers have rarely fallen into this error ; yet a few instances may be found in authors of reputation.

" IF I draw a catgut or any other cord to a great length between my fingers, I
will

will make it fmaller than it was before,"
&c.——Goldfmith's Survey of Experi-
mental Philofophy, book 2. chap. 2.

In the middle and fouthern ftates of A-
merica, this error is frequent, both in writing and converfation.

" Let us fuppofe the charter repealed
and the bank annihilated ; *will* we be better fituated ?"——Argument againft re-
pealing the charter of the Bank of North
America.

This is very incorrect ; there is hardly
a poffible cafe, in which *will* can be properly employed to afk a queftion in the firft
perfon.

" As foon as the diploma is made out, I
will have the honor to tranfmit it to you."
——Letter to Count Rochambeau.

Is not this *promifing* to have the honor of
a communication, an engagement which
delicacy forbids ? It is impoffible for a foreigner to have a juft idea of the abfurdity
of ufing *will* in this manner ; but a correct
Englifh ear revolts at the practice.

Dr. Prieftley obferves very juftly, that
the form of the auxiliaries, *fhall, will,*

which

which is generally conditional, viz. *should* and *would*, is elegantly used to express a slight assertion, with modest diffidence.

"THE royal power, *it should seem*, might be intrusted in their hands."——Hume's History, vol. 3. p. 383.

WE say also, "I *would* not choose any." In these cases, the verbs are not conditional; they modestly declare a fact, and therefore properly belong to the indicative mode. But in the following passage, *should* is improperly employed :

"IN judging only from the nature of things, and without the surer aid of divine revelation, one *should* be apt to embrace the opinion of Diodorus Siculus," &c.——Warburton's Divine Legation, vol. 2. p. 81.

SHOULD, in the second and third persons, expresses *duty*, and the idea of the author was, to express an event, under a condition, or a modest declaration ; he *should* have used *would*.

"THERE is not a girl in town, but let her have her will in going to a mask, and she *shall* dress as a shepherdess.—"Spect. No. 9.

SHALL,

Shall, in this example, expresses *command*, an idea very different from the author's meaning.

" Think what reflection *shall* most probably arise."———Blair, Serm. 9.

" A person, highly entertained at a play, *shall* remember perfectly the impression made on him by a very moving scene."———Nugent's Tranf. of Condillac, p. 1. f. 1.

I would just remark here, that the errors in the use of the auxiliary verbs before mentioned, are not English ; that they are little known among the inhabitants of South Britain, and still less among their descendants in New England. This is a new proof of the force of national customs. I do not remember to have heard once in the course of my life, an improper use of the verbs *will* and *shall*, among the unmixed English descendants in the eastern states.

But of all the errors or inaccuracies in speaking or writing the English language, the most numerous clafs appear in the improper use of verbs in the subjunctive mode. Not only illiterate men, but authors of the first rank, often use the prefent

ent tenfe for the future, the future for the prefent, and the paft for both.

"If any member *abfents* himfelf, he fhall forfeit a penny for the ufe of the club, unlefs in cafe of ficknefs and imprifonment."——Rules of the Two Penny Club, Spect. No. 9.

"If thou *neglectefl* or *dofl* unwillingly what I command, I'll rack thee with old cramps."——Temp. act 1. f. 4.

In both thefe examples, the events mentioned in the verbs are *future*; " if any member *fhall* abfent himfelf;" " if thou *fhalt* neglect;" therefore the auxiliary verb *fhall* fhould have been employed, or the fentences fhould have been elliptical, " if any member *abfent* himfelf;" " if thou *neglect*;" where *fhall* is underftood and eafily fupplied by the reader.

Numberless examples of the fame kind of inaccuracy may be found in good authors. Thus in Haley's Happy Prefcription, act 2.

"And if my fcheme *profpers*, with joy I'll confefs,
What a whimfical trifle produced our fuccefs."

The idea is, " if my fcheme *fhall* profper;" and this is obvious by the fubfequent

Q

part

part of the fentence, where the future is employed, " with joy *I'll* confefs."

" IF Punch *grows* extravagant, I fhall reprimand him very freely; if the ftage *becomes* a nurfery of folly and impertinence, I fhall not be afraid to animadvert upon it."——Spect. No. 35.

THESE fhould have been *grow* or *fhould grow*; *become* or *fhould become*.

" IF any thing *offers* (fhall offer) from Dublin, that may ferve either to fatisfy or divert you, I will not fail," &c.—— Swift's Correfp. letter 2.

IN the following paffage, the fame writer is much more correct.

" IF any one matter in it *prove* (that is, *fhall prove*) falfe, what do you think will become of the paper ?"——Letter 8.

BUT the ufe of the future for the prefent is much more frequent.

" IF reverence, gratitude, obedience and confidence *be* our duty."——Prieftley, let. 7 to a Phil. Unbeliever.

" IF he *have* any knowlege of actual exiftence, he muft be fatisfied."——Same, letter 8.

THE

THE author doubtlefs intended thefe fentences to be ftrictly grammatical, by placing the verbs in the prefent tenfe of the
fubjunctive. But in the firft example, *be* is
wrong even on Lowth's principles. The rule
of the Bifhop, with refpect to the ufe of the
indicative and fubjunctive modes, is this :
That when fomething conditional, hypothetical, or doubtful, is expreffed, the verb
fhould be in the fubjunctive mode ; but
when the fact is certain, or taken for granted, the verb fhould be in the indicative.
He gives for examples of the former, feveral
paffages from fcripture : " If thou *be* the
fon of God." Matth. iv. 3.   " Tho he *flay*
me, yet will I truft in him." Job xiii. 15.
" Unlefs he *wafh* his flefh." Lev. xxii. 6.
" No power except it *were* given from a-
bove." John xix. 11.   " Whether it *were*
I or they, fo we preach." 1 Cor. xv. 11.
" The fubjunctive in thefe inftances," fays
the Bifhop, " implies fomething contingent
or doubtful ; the indicative would exprefs
a more abfolute and determinate fenfe."
To illuftrate the latter part of his rule,
he quotes a paffage from Atterbury's Sermons.   " Tho he *were* divinely infpired,
and fpake therefore as the oracles of God,
with fupreme authority ; .tho he *were*
endued with fupernatural powers," &c.

Q 2

That

That our Savior was divinely infpired, and endued with fupernatural powers, are pofitions that are here taken for granted, as admitting not of the leaft doubt; they would therefore have been better exprefled in the indicative mode; "tho he *was* divinely infpired," &c. Even on thefe principles, the verb in the firft example from Prieftley, juft quoted, fhould have been in the indicative; for there is no doubt that reverence, gratitude, &c. *are* our duty to the Supreme Being.

But I apprehend, that however juft Lowth's diftinction between the modes, may have formerly been, it is not warranted by the prefent idiom of the language. Indeed I cannot think the rule juft. In the *firft*, *fourth* and *fifth* examples quoted by the Bifhop, the indicative might be fubftituted for the fubjunctive, and the paffages rendered more correct, according to the prefent practice of fpeaking and writing. "If thou *art* the fon of God." "No power except it *was* given from above." "Whether it *was* I, or they, fo we preach." Every Englifh ear muft acknowlege that thefe expreffions are more agreeable to our prefent practice, than thofe employed by

the

the tranflators of the Bible, and they convey an idea of condition or doubt, as fully
as the other form.   But why did the tranflators deviate from the original ? In the
Greek, the verbs, in the two firft examples,
are in the indicative mode ; and in the laft,
the verb is not expreffed.   Ει υιος ει του Θεου,
literally, If thou *art* the fon of God.   Ουκ
εχεις εξουσιαν ουδεμιαν κατ' εμου, ει μη ην σοι δεδομενον
ανωθεν ; literally, Thou haft no power (or
authority) againft me, except it *was* given
thee from above.   In the laft inftance the
verb is omitted ; Ειτε δε εγω, ειτε εκεινοι ; Whether I or they.   In thefe inftances therefore the
tranflators of the Bible, and Bifhop Lowth
have evidently miftaken the true ftructure
of the Englifh verbs.   The tranflators
deviated from the original Greek, in
changing the modes ; and the Bifhop has
taken their error, as the foundation of a
diftinction which does not exift in the language.   The indicative mode is employed
to exprefs conditional ideas, more frequently
than the fubjunctive, even by the beft Englifh writers.   Take the following examples.

   " And if the fame accident *is* able to reftore them to us."——Bollingbroke, Re-
flec. on Exile.

" If

Q 3

"IF this being, the immediate maker of the univerſe, *has* not exiſted from all eternity, he muſt have derived his being and power from one who has."——Prieſtley, let. 4 to Phil. Unb.

"IF there *is* one, I ſhall make two in the company."——Merry Wives of Windſor, act 3. ſc. 11.

"IF thou *loveſt* me then
Steal forth thy father's houſe tomorrow night."
Midſum. Night's Dream, act 1. ſ. 2.

"IF thou *beeſt** Stephano, touch me and ſpeak to me;
If thou *beeſt* Trinculo, come forth."
Tempeſt, act 2. ſ. 3.

"IF thou *art* any thing beſides a name."
Cowley's Requeſt.

"FOR if he *lives* that hath you doen deſpight."
Spenſer's Fairy Queen, book 2. chap. 1.

"IF any one *imagines*."——Moyle.

"WHY did Caligula wiſh that the people had but one neck, that he might ſtrike it off at a blow, if their welfare *was* thus reciprocal."——Sidney on Gov. ſect. 5.

"IF

* It muſt be remembered that *be* is the old original ſubſtantive verb, and belongs to the indicative. *Am* and *art* are of later introduction into Engliſh.

" I_F Governments *are* conftituted."———
Sidney.

" W_ELL, keep your own heart, if filence *is* beft,
Tho a woman, for once, I'll in ignorance reft."
Haley's Happy Prefcription.

" I_F fhe *has* ftolen the color of her rib-
bons from another."———Spect. No. 4.

" I_F we *are* rightly informed."———Same,
No. 8.

" I_F fhe *is* tall enough, fhe is wife e-
nough."———No. 66.

" I_F you *are* in fuch hafte, how came you
to forget the mifcellanies ?"———Swift's
Letter to Mr. Tooke.

" I_F men's higheft affurances *are* to be
believed."———Same.

S_HALL we fay that the ufe of the indicative after *if* in the foregoing examples is improper or ungrammatical? By
no means. Yet the verbs exprefs fomething conditional or doubtful ; and therefore Lowth's rule cannot be well founded.

L_ET the foregoing paffages be contraft-
ed with the following.

" B_UT

" But if he *say* true, there is but one government in the world that can have any thing of juſtice in it."———Sidney, ſeɛt. 1.

" If he *have* any knowlege of aɛtual exiſtence, he muſt be ſatisfied."———Prieſtley, let. 8.

" But tho criticiſm *be* thus his only declared aim, he will not diſown," &c.——— Introd. to Elements of Criticiſm.

" But if a lively piɛture, even of a ſingle emotion, *require* an effort of genius, how much greater the effort to compoſe a paſſionate dialogue, with as many different tones of paſſion as there are ſpeakers?"——— Elements of Criticiſm, vol. 1. chap. 16.

" Here we muſt alſo obſerve, that tho THOU *be* long in the firſt part of the verſe, it becomes ſhort when repeated in the ſecond."———Sheridan's Art of Reading.

The Scotch writers, who learn the Engliſh language grammatically, are the moſt particular in the uſe of this ſubjunɛtive form of the verb ; in conſequence of which their ſtile generally appears ſtiff and fettered. In all the foregoing examples, and in every inſtance where the affirmation reſpeɛts preſent time, the indicative form is the

moſt

moſt correct, and the only form that cor-
reſponds with the actual preſent ſtate of
the language. *If he ſays, if he has, if he
requires*, are the true expreſſions univerſally uſed in ſpeaking; and grammars ſhould
exhibit and enforce this practice, rather
than amend it.

THERE are few or no Engliſh writers,
who ſeem to have adhered uniformly to
any rule in the uſe of the verbs after the
conjunctions. In conſequence, either of
ignorance or inattention, the moſt correct
writers have fallen into inconſiſtencies, e-
ven in the ſame ſentence. This will appear by the following examples.

"IF life and health enough *fall* to my
ſhare, and I *am* able to finiſh what I med-
itate."——Bolingbroke, let. 4, on Hiſtory.

THE author intended the verbs, *fall* and
am, to be in the preſent time; but this
would make him write nonſenſe; for the
events were future at the time of writing.
The firſt part of the ſentence, to make
ſenſe, muſt be conſidered as elliptical, " if
life and health enough *ſhall* or *ſhould fall*
to my ſhare;" in the laſt part therefore *be*
ſhould be ſubſtituted for *am*, if *I ſhall be
able :*

able : This would make the whole fentence correct and confiftent.

" WHETHER our conduct *be* infpected, and we *are* under a righteous government, or under no government at all."——Prieft-ley's Pref. to Let. to a Phil. Unb.

WHAT a confufion of modes ! or rather of tenfes !

" THO THOU *be* long, in the firft part of the verfe," fays Sheridan, in the paffage juft quoted; yet foon after ufes the indicative in a phrafe precifely fimilar ; " And tho it *is* impoffible to prolong the found of this word."   Can this great critic give a reafon for this change of modes ? Such examples ferve to fhow at leaft the neceffity of ftudying our language with more attention, than even many eminent fcholars are willing to beftow.

IT has been remarked by Lowth, and many other writers on this fubject, that "the verb itfelf in the prefent, and the auxiliary both of the prefent and paft imperfect times, often carry with them fome-what of a future fenfe."*   Thus, *if he*
come

* Lowth's Introduction, p. 39. Note.

come tomorrow, if he should or would come to-morrow, carry *somewhat of a future sense.* The writer should have gone farther, and said that these expressions are in future time ; for they form the English future, and belong to no other tense.   This would have been the truth, and have prevented the numberless errors which have proceeded from his arranging them in the present tense of the subjunctive.   Let us attend to the following passages,

" THIS can never happen till patriotism *flourish* more in Britain."—Home's Sketches, book 2. f. 9.

" PRAY heaven, he *prove* so, when you come to him."——Two Gent. of Verona, act 2. f. 10.

" BUT if thou *linger* in my territories." ——Same, act 3. f. 2.

" LEST, growing ruinous, the building *fall.*"——Same, act 5. f. 6.

" IF the second *be* pronounced thus, the verse will be degraded into hobbling prose." ——Sheridan's Art of Reading.

IT is needless to multiply similar passages ; the same use of the verb, without
the

the perfonal termination, occurs in almoft every page of our beft writings, and it is perfectly correct.

But will any perfon contend that the verbs in thefe paffages are in the prefent tenfe? The fenfe is entirely future, and could not be tranflated into Latin or French, without employing the future tenfe. The expreffions are elliptical, and cannot be clearly underftood, without inferting *fhall* or *fhould* before the verbs. This pretended prefent tenfe of the fubjunctive is therefore the real future of the indicative. To confirm this remark, let us attend to fome other paffages.

"Tho he *flay* me, yet will I truft in him."

"Unlefs he *wafh* his flefh, he fhall not eat of the holy thing."

In the original Hebrew thefe verbs are in the future tenfe; and fo are moft fimilar expreffions.*

MATTH.

* "The prefent tenfe in Englifh hath often the *fenfe of the future*; as *when do you go out of town?* I go tomorrow: that is, when will you, fhall you go? I fhall go. *If you do well*, that is, fhall do well, you will be rewarded: *As foon as*, or *when you come there*; that is, fhall come, turn on your right hand: With thefe forms of fpeaking, the verb is always

placed

MATTH. vii. 10.—Or if he *ask* a fish, will he give him a serpent ? Και εαν ιχθυν αιτησῃ μη οφιν επιδωσει αυτῳ;

ROM. xiv. 15.—But if thy brother *be* grieved with thy meat. Ει γαρ δια βρωμα ὁ αδελφος σου λυπειται.

LUKE xvii. 3.—If thy brother *trespass* against thee. Εαν αμαρτησῃ ὁ αδελφος σου. 4. And seven times in a day *turn* again to thee. Και επτακις της ημηρας επιστρεψῃ.

LUKE xvi. 28.—Lest they also *come* into this place of torment. Μη και αυτοι ελθωσιν εις τουτον τον τοπον της βασανου.*

Is

placed in the future in Latin, Greek and Hebrew."——— Bayley's Intro. to Lan. Lit. and Phil. 99.

THIS critical writer has explained this mode of speaking with accuracy ; but it would be more correct to call this form of the verb, an *elliptical future*, than to say, *the present tense has the sense of the future.*

* So in the law stile. " If a man *die* intestate ;" " if a man *die* seised of an estate in fee ;" " if Titius *enfeoff* Gaius," &c. are future ; and in most such phrases used in translations from the Latin and French, the verbs in the original are future. But in law the same form is used in the present very frequently, agreeable to the ancient practice. The reason may be, the convenience and necessity of copying words and phrases with great exactness. But Blackstone, the most accurate and elegant law writer, uses the other form, " if a man *has* heirs ;" " if a good or valuable consideration *appears* ;" and too often, when the sense requires the future. He generally gives *be* its subjunctive form, as it is called, and most other verbs the indicative.

Is not the fenfe of the foregoing verbs *future* ? Are not the verbs in the original, either in the future tenfe, or in the indefinite tenfes, which, in the fubjunctive mode, *ufually* have the fenfe of the future, and perhaps *never* the fenfe of the prefent ? Why then fhould we confider the Englifh verbs as in the prefent time ? Either the tranflators made a miftake, and placed the verbs in a wrong tenfe ; or Lowth and his followers have miftaken the tenfe, and called that prefent which is really future.

THAT the fault is, in fome meafure, to be afcribed to the tranflators, is evident from their ufing the fame form of the verb, after a conjunction, when the original Greek is in the prefent of the indicative.

1 COR. xvi. 22.—If any man *love* not the Lord Jefus Chrift, let him be, &c. Ει τις ου φιλει τον Κυριον Ιησουν Χριϛον, ητω, &c.

1 COR. xiv. 37.—If any man think himfelf a prophet. Ει δε τις δοκει προφηϙης ειναι. 38.—If any man *be* ignorant, let him be ignorant ftill. Ει δς.τις αϛνοει, αϛνοειϙω.

IN thefe inftances, the verbs exprefs conditional facts in the prefent time. In the original they are in the indicative prefent ;

and

and on what authority did the tranflators introduce a different mode in Englifh ? Can they be juftified by the idioms of the language at the time when they lived ? Was the fubjunctive always ufed after a conjunction ? By no means : Their own tranflation of other paffages proves the contrary.

1 Cor. xv. 13.—And if their *is* no refurrection of the dead. Ει δε αναϲαϲις νεκρων ουκ εϲιν.

Here is the prefent tenfe of the indicative ufed, where the fact mentioned is fuppofed, by the argument, to be at leaft doubtful.   In other places the prefent time of the fame mode is ufed, where the future would have been more accurate.

Prov. ii. 3, 4.—" Yea if thou *crieft* after knowlege, and *lifteft* up thy voice for understanding ; if thou *feekeft* for her as for hid treafures, then fhalt thou underftand," &c.

What conclufion fhall we draw from this ftate of facts ? This at leaft may be faid with fafety, either that the Englifh modes and tenfes have not been afcertained and underftood, or that the beft of our writers have been extremely negligent.

After

AFTER an attentive and accurate examination of this subject, I believe I may venture to assert, that nine times out of ten, when the pretended subjunctive form of the verb is used after a conjunction, either in the vulgar translation of the Bible, or in our best profane authors, the sense is actually future, and to render the sentences complete, it would be necessary to insert *shall* or *should*.* This will be more obvious by attending to the Latin translation of the New Testament, where the future is almost always employed to express the Greek future and aorifts. *Igitur si munus tuum attuleris ad altare*—If thou *bring* thy gift to the altar ; *et illic memineris*—and there *rememberest* ; (what confusion of modes.) If his son *ask* bread—*Si filius ejus* petierit *panem.* And if the house *be* worthy—*Et si quidem* fuerit *domus digna* ; and so throughout the whole New Teftament.

WILL any person pretend to say that the verbs *bring*, *ask* and *be*, in the foregoing passages, are present time ; or that *rememberest* is not bad English ? The elliptical future, *If thou be, if he ask*, &c. is correct English, but should by no means be confounded

---

* In some inftances, the time is present, and the ellipfis may be supplied by *may* or fame other auxiliary.

founded with the prefent tenfe, which, in Englifh, has but one form.

I do not deny that good authors have ufed this form, after conjunctions, in the prefent time ; but I deny that the genius of the language requires it, that it is agreeable to the ancient or modern elegant languages, and that it has been or is now the general practice.

With refpect to the ancient practice, examples fufficient have been already produced, to fhow that authors have confidered the prefent of the indicative, after conjunctions, denoting uncertainty or doubt, as at leaft correct ; and the prefent practice in fpeaking is wholly on this fide of the argument.

With refpect to the Roman and Greek languages, I believe examples enough may be brought to prove, that the fubjunctive mode after the conditional conjunctions or adverbs, was not generally ufed, except when the idea was fuch as we fhould exprefs by *may, might, fhould, let,* or fome other auxiliary before the verb. "Quid eft autem, quod deos *veneremur* propter admirationem ejus naturæ, in qua egregium ni-

R.   hil

hil videmus ?" " Ut, quos ratio non pof-
fet, eos ad officium religio *duceret*."—Cicero, De nat Deorum, l. 1. 42. To render
veneremur and *duceret* into Englifh, *fhould*
may be prefixed to *adore*, and *might* to
lead.

At any rate, the conditional conjunctions do not all, nor generally require the
fubjunctive mode : " Quæ, *fi* mundus *eft*
Deus, quoniam mundi partes funt, Dei
membra parim ardentia, partim refrigera-
ta dicenda funt."—Ibm. l. 1. 10. " *Si* Di
poffunt effe fine fenfu," &c. The indicative
after this conjunction occurs frequently in
the beft Roman authors.

In Greek the cafe is nearly the fame.
Several inftances of the indicative after the
conditional conjunction ει (if) have already
been quoted from fcripture ; and fimilar
inftances without number may be produced from profane writers.

" Ει ουν ουτως εχει, εφη, ω Κῦρε, τι αν αλλο τις κρειτ]ον
ευροι, ἢ πεμπειν εις Περσας, και αμα μεν διδασκειν αυτους
οτι ει τι πεισονται Μηδοι, εις Περσας το δεινον ηξει, αμα
δε αιτειν πλειον σρατευμα ;"———Xenoph. de Cyri.
Inft. l. 2. p. 80. Lond. Ed.

Here the verb εχει is in the prefent tenfe
of the indicative, after a conjunction denoting

noting condition or doubt ; " if the affair *is* fo—if fuch *is* the true ftate of affairs, Cyrus, what better method *can be taken* (ευροι) than to fend to the Perfians, and inform them that *if* any accident *happen* to the Medes (fo we fhould render πεισονlαι, which is in the future) calamity will fall upon the Perfians alfo, and let us afk for a greater force."

In French, the conditional conjunctions do not require the fubjunctive mode. " Si ma prédiction *eft* fauffe, vous ferez libre de nous immoler dans trois jours."—Telemaque, liv. 1. " S'il *eft* vrai que vous aimiez la juftice."—Liv. 4. If my prediction *is* falfe—if it *is* true—are correct modes of fpeaking in French. No argument therefore in favor of the ufe of the Englifh fubjunctive, can be drawn from the analogy of other languages.

But this fubjunctive form is not agreeable to the ftructure of the language. It has been demonftrated that our conjunctions are moftly old Saxon verbs in the imperative mode. Let us refolve fome fentences where the fubjunctive form is ufed ; for example, the paffages before quoted.

" If he *have* any knowlege of actual exiftence, he muft be fatisfied."———Prieftley's
Letters.

Resolved—" He have any knowlege of
actual exiftence, (if) give that, he muft be
fatisfied."   Is this Englifh ?

" If thou be the fon of God, command
that thefe ftones be made bread."——
Matth. iv .3.

Resolved—" Thou be the fon God,
give that, command," &c.

" Tho he flay me, yet will I truft in
him."

Resolved—" He flay me, grant it, yet
will I truft in him."

This is the literal conftruction of thofe
fentences ; the two firft are prefent time,
the laft, which is future, is merely elliptical.

If therefore, *I be, he have*, are good Englifh in the prefent tenfe of the indicative,
the foregoing are correct expreffions ; if
not, they are incorrect ; for every fuch conditional fentence is refolvable into two or
more declaratory phrafes. Let us fubftitute the Latin derivative, which precifely
anfwers

anſwers to *if*, viz. *ſuppoſe* ; thus, in place of "if thou be the ſon of God," write, "*ſuppoſe* thou be the ſon of God," does not every ear acknowlege the impropriety ? The only difference between the two expreſſions is this ; *if* is a *Saxon* verb in the imperative mode, and *ſuppoſe*, a *Latin* one in the ſame mode.

WITH reſpect to *be*, it may be ſaid very juſtly, that it was anciently uſed after the conjunctions in almoſt all caſes. But it muſt be obſerved alſo, it was uſed *without* the conjunctions. *Be*, from the Saxon *be-on*, is the true radical verb, ſtill preſerved in the German, *Ich bin*, I be, *du biſt*, thou beeſt, in the indicative. The old Engliſh writers employed *be* in the ſame mode and tenſe.

" O, THERE *be* players that I have ſeen play."———Shakeſp. Hamlet to the Players.

" THEY that *be* drunken, are drunken in the night."———1 Theſſ. v. 7.

" As we *be* ſlanderouſly reported."——— Rom. iii. 8.

THE common people in New England ſtill employ *be* in the preſent tenſe of the indicative,

dicative,

dicative, except in the third perſon. They almoſt univerſally ſay, *I be, we be, you be,* and *they be.* While *be* remained the proper ſubſtantive verb in the indicative, it was very correctly employed after the conjunctions, *If he be, tho he be,* but when *am, are, art* and *is* were ſubſtituted in the indicative, they ſhould likewiſe have been employed in the ſubjunctive ; for the latter is reſolvable into the former.

FROM the facts produced, and the remarks made, we may draw the following concluſions ; that the diſtinction made by grammarians between the preſent tenſe of the indicative and ſubjunctive mode in Engliſh, is not well founded ; that it is not warranted by the conſtruction of the language, nor by the analogy of other languages ; that the expreſſions commonly ſuppoſed to be in the preſent tenſe of the ſubjunctive, are moſtly in fact an elliptical form of the future in the indicative, and that the preſent tranſlation of the Bible cannot be vindicated on any other ſuppoſition ; that the preſent practice, both in ſpeaking and writing, is generally in favor of the indicative after the conjunctions ; and conſequently, that the arrangement of the verbs by Lowth and his followers, is

calculated

calculated to lead both foreigners and natives into error.

I HAVE been more particular upon this article, becaufe the Scotch writers, many of whom ftand among the firft authors of the Britifh nation, follow the ufual grammatical divifion of verbs, and thus write a ftile not conformed to the prefent practice of fpeaking.

IN the ufe of what is called the *imperfect* tenfe, after the conjunctions, there is fomething peculiar, which has not yet been fufficiently explained. On examination it will probably be found that cuftom has eftablifhed one fingular diftinction in the fenfe of verbs in different tenfes, a knowlege of which is neceffary to enable us to fpeak and write with precifion. This diftinction will readily be underftood by a few examples.

A SERVANT calls on me for a book, which his mafter would borrow. If I am uncertain whether I have that book or not, I reply in this manner ; " If the book *is* in my library, or if I *have* the book, your mafter fhall be welcome to the ufe of it."

BUT

But if I am certain I do not possess the book, the reply is different ; " I have not the book you mention ; if I *had*, it should be at your master's service."

Both these forms of speaking are correct ; but the question is, what is the difference ? It cannot be in *time* ; for both refer to the same. The ideas both respect present time ; " If I *have* it *now*, it *shall* be at your master's service"—" If I *had* it *now*, it *should* be." The distinction in the meaning is universally understood, and is simply this ; the first expresses *uncertainty* ; the last implies *certainty*, but in a peculiar manner ; for an affirmative sentence implies a positive negation ; and a negative sentence implies a positive affirmation. Thus, *if I had the book*, implies a positive denial of having it ; *if I had not the book*, implies that I have it : And both speak of possessing or not possessing it at this *present* time.

The same distinction runs thro all the verbs in the language. A man, shut up in an interior apartment, would say to his friend, " *if it rains* you cannot go home." This would denote the speaker's uncertainty. But on coming to the door and ascertaining the fact, he would say, " *if it rain-*
ed,

ed, you fhould not go ;" or, " *if it did not rain,* you might go."   Can thefe verbs be in *paft* time ? By no means ; *if it did not rain now, you could go,* is prefent, for the prefent exiftence of the fact prevents the man from going.

THESE forms of fpeech are eftablifhed by unanimous confent in practice.

" IT remaineth that they who have wives, be as tho they *had* none, and they that weep, as tho they *wept* not ; and they that rejoice, as tho they *rejoiced* not ; and they that buy, as tho they *poffeffed* not."——1 Cor. vii. 29, 30.*

" NAY, and the villains march wide betwixt the legs, as if they *had* gyves on."——1 Henry IV.

" WE have not thefe antiquities ; and if *we had* them, they would add to our uncertainty.——Bolingbroke on Hift. let. 3.

" WHEREAS, *had* I (if I had) ftill the fame woods to range in, which I once *had,*

when

* IN the original, the participle of the prefent time is employed : ἱνα και εχονίες γυναικας, ὡς μη εχονίες ; and fo in the other inftances.   The Greek is correct ; " thofe *having* wives as *not having* them."   The tranflation is agreeable enough to the Englifh idiom ; but the verbs reprefent the prefent time.

when I was a fox hunter, I fhould not re-fign my manhood for a maintenance."——
Spect. No. 14.

" I confefs I have not great tafte for po-etry ; but if *I had*, I am apt to believe I fhould read none but Mr. Pope's."*——
Shenftone on Men and Manners.

WHATEVER thefe verbs may be in de-claratory phrafes, yet after the conditional conjunctions *if* and *tho*, they often exprefs prefent ideas, as in the foregoing examples. In fuch cafes, this form of the verb may be denominated the *hypothetical* prefent tenfe. This would diftinguifh it from the fame form, when it expreffes uncertainty in the paft time ; for this circumftance muft not be paffed without notice. Thus,
" If

---

* A SIMILAR ufe of the verb occurs after *wifh ;* " *I wifh I had* my eftate *now* in poffeffion ;" this would be expreffed in Latin. *Utinam me habere,* ufing the prefent of the infin-itive, or *Utinam ut haberem ;* but this Imperfect tenfe of the Subjuctive, both in Latin and French, is ufed to convey the fame ideas as Englifh verbs after if; *if I had, fi haberem, fi j'aurois,* and whatever may be the name annexed to this form of the verb, it cannot, in the foregoing fenfe, have any reference to paft time.

THE common phrafes, *I had rather, he had better,* are faid to be a corruption of *I would rather, he would better,* rapidly pronounced, *I'd rather.* I am not fatisfied that this is a juft account of their origin ; *would* will not fupply the place of *had* in all cafes. At any rate, the phrafes have become good Englifh.

" If he *had* letters by the laft mail," denotes the fpeaker's uncertainty as to a paft
fact or event.   But, " if *he had* a book, he
would lend it," denotes a prefent certainty
that he has it not.   The times referred to
are wholly diftinct.

As the practice of all writers and good
fpeakers, and even of the vulgar, is nearly
uniform in the diftinction here mentioned,
it is needlefs to produce more examples for
illuftration.   One verb however deferves a
feparate confideration ; which is *be*.   In
the ufe of this verb in the hypothetical
fenfe, there is a difference between good
authors and common parlance ; the firft
write *were*, but moft people in converfation fay, *was*.   Thus,

" EVERY rich man has ufually fome fly
way of jefting, which would make no great
figure, *were* he not rich."——Spect. No. 2.

" HE will often argue, that if this part
of our trade *were* well cultivated, we fhould
gain from one nation," &c.——Same.

" *WERE* I (if I were) a father, I fhould
take a particular care to preferve my children from thefe little horrors of imagination."——Same, No. 12.

" NOR

"Nor think, tho men *were* none,
That heaven would want fpectators, God want praife."
Milton, P. L.

"What then he *was*, oh, *were* your Neftor now."
Pope, Iliad, b. 7. 189.

"Yes, if the nature of a clock *were* to fpeak, not ftrike."——Ben Johnfon.

"Where the poor knave erroneoufly believes,
If he *were* rich, he would build churches, or
Do fuch mad things."————Same.

Were, in thefe examples, is the fame hypothetical prefent tenfe juft defcribed, having not the leaft reference to the paft.* But in converfation, we generally hear *was*; " if I *was* in his place ;" " if he *was* here *now*," &c. and I obferve that modern writers are copying the general practice.

" If I *was* not afraid of being thought to refine too much."—Boling. Refl. on Exile.
Both

* The following tranflation of a paffage in Cicero is directly in point. " Vivo tamen in ea ambitione et labore tanquam id, quod non poftulo, *expectem*."——Cicero ad Quintum. 2. 15.

" I live ftill in fuch a courfe of ambition and fatigue, as if *I were expecting* what I do not really defire."——Middleton, Life of Cicero, vol. 2. p. 97.

Here *tanquam expectem* are rendered very juftly, " as if I *were* expecting ;" *now*, in prefent time, agreeable to the original. The words carry a negative : *if I were expecting*, implying, that *I do not expect*.

Both thefe forms have fuch authorities to fupport them, that neither can be confidered as wholly incorrect; they are both Englifh. But cuftom will eventually eftablifh the latter, *was*, as the hypothetical form of the fubftantive verb. It is now almoft univerfally ufed, except in books; and the tide of general practice is irrefiftible.

The following examples will illuftrate what has been advanced.

Prefent time.   Affirmative.

If he *has* or *is*—denotes uncertainty. If he *had* or *were* or *was*—denote certainty that he has not, or is not.

Negative.

If he *has* not or *is* not—uncertainty. If he *had* not, *were* not or *was* not—certainty that he has or is.

Paft time.   Affirm.

If he *had* or *was* yefterday—uncertainty. If he had have,* or had been yefterday—certainty that he had not, or was not.

Negative.

---

* This tenfe is not admitted to be good Englifh; yet is often ufed in fpeaking; the *have* being contracted or corrupted into *a*, *had a written, if he had a received.*

Negative.

If he *had* or *was* not—uncertainty. If he had not have, or had not been—certainty that he had or was.*

I CANNOT clofe my remarks on the tenfes of the Englifh verb, without noticing a common error, which muft have fprung from inattention, and is perhaps too general now to admit of correction. It is the ufe of the paft tenfe after another verb or *that*, when the fenfe requires a change of tenfes. Thus,

" SUPPOSE I were to fay, that to every art there *was* a fyftem of fuch various and well approved principles."——Harris.

THE firft part of the fentence is hypothetical, *fuppofe I were to fay*; but the laft becomes declaratory under the fuppofition, and therefore the form of the verb fhould be changed to the prefent, indicative, *that to every art there* is *a fyftem*: For it muft be remarked that when the Englifh fpeak of general exiftence, they ufe the prefent time;

* WE have derived our fubftantive verb from two radical verbs; *beon*, whence come the Englifh *be*, and the German *bift*; and *weorthan*, to be or *become*, fieri; from which probably the Danes have their *varer*, and the Englifh their *were*.

time ; as, truth *is* great above all things ; the fcriptures *are* a rule of faith ; the heavens *difplay* the glory of the Lord. The paft or the future, in fuch cafes, would be highly improper. Hence the abfurdity of the paffage juft quoted ; the fuppofition is that every art *has* (generally—at all times) a fyftem of principles.

" If the taxes laid by government *were* the only ones we *had* to pay."

THE author's meaning is, "the only taxes we have to pay ;" and he was probably led into the miftake by not underftanding the preceding hypothetical verb, *were*, which actually fpeaks of the prefent time conditionally.

THE error will be more ftriking in the following paffages.

" If an atheift would well confider the arguments in this book, he would confefs there *was* a God."

THERE *was* a God ! And why not confefs that there *is* a God ? The writer did not confider that the firft part of the fentence is *conditional*, and that the laft ought to be *declaratory* of a fact always exifting.

" Two

" Two young men have made a difcovery that there *was* a God."——Swift's Arg. againft Abolifhing Chriftianity.

A curious difcovery indeed ! Were the Dean ftill alive, he might find there *is* a great inaccuracy in that paffage of his works.

"Yet were we to ufe the fame word, where the figure *was* manifeft, we fhould ufe the prepofition *from*."——Prieftley, Gram. p. 158.

Here is the fame error, and the author may live to correct it.

But of all this clafs of miftakes, the following is the moft palpable.

" I am determined to live, as if there *was* a *future* life."——Hammon, quoted by Price and Prieftley.

Hammon is an atheift, and it would require the fame abilities to reconcile the two words *was future*, as to reconcile his principles with the common fenfe of mankind.*

THE

---

* The great fource of thefe errors is this : Grammarians have confidered *that* as a conjunction, and fuppofed that
" conjunctions

.THE following paſſage, from *Gregory's Comparative View of the State and Faculties of Man*, is remarkable for this error.

"MEN have been taught that they *did* (do) God acceptable ſervice, by abſtracting themſelves from all the duties they *owed* (owe) to ſociety; and by inflicting on themſelves the ſevereſt tortures which nature can ſupport. They have been taught that it *was* (is) their duty," &c.

"AND yet one would think that this *was* the principal uſe of the ſtudy of hiſtory." ——Bolingbroke on Hiſt. letter 3.

A SIMILAR fault occurs in one of Mrs. Thale's letters to Dr. Johnſon, Aug. 9, 1775.
"——YET

"conjunctions couple like caſes and modes;" a Latin rule that does not always hold in Engliſh. But Mr. Horne Tooke has clearly proved the word *that* to be always a relative pronoun: It always relates to a word or ſentence; and the reaſon why grammarians have called it a conjunction, may be this; they could not find any word to govern it as a relative, and therefore did not know what to do with it. But it is in fact a relative word, thus, "two men have made a diſcovery;" this is one aſſertion. What diſcovery? "*that* or *this* is the diſcovery;" the word *that* carrying the force of a complete affirmation; "there *was* a God." Here we ſee the abſurdity of Swift's declaration and the common notions of a ſubjunctive mode. There is no ſubjunctive; in ſtrictneſs of ſpeech, all ſentences are reſolvable into diſtinct declaratory phraſes. "There *is* a God;" "two young men have diſcovered *that*;" ſo the ſentence ſhould be written to ſhow the true conſtruction.

S

"—Yet I have always found the best supplement for talk *was* writing."

So in Blackstone's Commentaries, book 1. chap. 7.

" It was observed in a former chapter, that one of the principal bulwarks of civil liberty, or, in other words, of the British constitution, *was* the limitation of the king's prerogative."

The observation had been made in time past, but respecting a fact that exists *now*, and at all times while the British constitution exists. The sentence therefore should run thus ; " it *was* observed that one principal bulwark of civil liberty, *is* the limitation of the king's prerogative."

No fault is more common ; we every day hear such expressions as these ; " If I thought it *was* so ;" " suppose I should say she *was* handsome ;" " I did not think it *was* so late," &c. *Was*, in the first and last examples, should be the infinitive, *to be* ; and in the second, the present time, *is*. Had proper attention been paid to our language, so many palpable mistakes would not have crept into practice, and into the

most

moſt correct and elegant writings.   Dr. Reid is perhaps the only writer who has generally avoided this error.

The Greek and Roman writers were not guilty of ſuch miſtakes.   Either the varieties of inflection in their languages, or ſuperior care in the writers, made them attentive to the nice diſtinctions of time. In the following paſſage, the tranſlators of the Bible, by adhering cloſely to the original, have avoided the common error before mentioned.

"I *knew* thee that thou art an hard man."—Matth. xxv. 24.   "Εγνων ὁτι σκληρος ει ανθρωπος ;" literally, *having known* that thou *art* an hard man.   So alſo ver. 26, " Thou wicked and ſlothful ſervant, thou *kneweſt* that I *reap*, where I ſowed not ;" " ηδεις ὁτι θεριζω."   Had theſe paſſages been tranſlated into the careleſs ſtile of modern converſation, and even of many excellent writings, they would have ſtood thus—"I knew thee that thou *waſt* an hard man"—" thou kneweſt that I *reaped* where I ſow not." But the general character and conduct of the perſon mentioned in this parable, are ſuppoſed to exiſt at all times while he is living ; and this general nature of the fact
S 2

requires

requires the verb to be in the prefent time. To confirm this remark let the fentences be inverted ; " thou art an hard man, I knew thee to be fuch, or I knew it." " I reap where I fowed not, thou kneweft that." This is an indubitable evidence of the accuracy of the tranflation.*

AN

* A passage in Dr. Middleton's Life of Cicero, is remarkably accurate ; " The celebrated orator, L. Caffius, died of the fame difeafe (the pleurify,) which might probably be then, as I *was* told in Rome it *is now*, the peculiar diftemper of the place." *Was* refers to time completely *paft ;* but *is* declares a fact that exifts generally, at all times ; the verb is therefore in the prefent tenfe, or as Harris terms it,† the *aorift of the prefent.* So alfo in Dr. Reid's Effays, vol. 1. p. 18. " Thofe philofophers *held*, that there *are* three firft principles of all things ;" which is correct Englifh. " Ariftotle *thought* every object of human underftanding *enters* at firft by the fenfes."—Page 110. The following paffage is equally correct. " There *is* a courage depending on nerves and blood, which *was* improved to the higheft pitch among the Greeks."——Gillies, Hift. of Greece, vol. 1. p. 248. This courage is derived from the conftitution of the human body ; it exifts therefore at *all times ;* and had our author faid, " there *was* a courage depending on nerves and blood, which the Greeks *improved* to the higheft pitch," the fenfe would have been left imperfect. Here then we fee the indefinite ufe of this form of the prefent tenfe ; for were the verb *is*, in the foregoing example, limited to time *now prefent*, it would make the author write nonfenfe ; it being abfurd to fay, " the Greeks 2000 years ago *improved* a courage which exifts only *at the prefent time.*" So that verbs, in the *prefent* tenfe, exprefs facts that have an uninterrupted exiftence in *paft, prefent,* and *future* time.

† HERMES, page 123.

An inverfion of the order of the fentence in the paffages firft quoted, will fhow the common error in a moft ftriking light.

" There *was* a God, two young men have made that difcovery." " Men *did* God acceptable fervice, by abftracting themfelves, &c. they have been taught this ; it *was* their duty, they have been taught this." " The taxes we *had* to pay to government, if thefe were the only ones." This will not make fenfe to a man who *has* taxes *ftill* to pay ; the writer's *had to pay* will not difcharge the public debt. But it is unneceffary to multiply examples and arguments; the reader muft be already convinced that thefe errors exift, and that I ought not to have been the firft to notice them.

Sometimes this hypothetical tenfe is ufed with an infinitive for the future. In the following paffage it feems to be correct.

" I wish I *were* to go to the Elyfian fields, when I die, and then I fhould not care if I *were* to leave the world tomorrow."——Pope.

But the following are hardly vindicable.

" Suppose they *marched* up to our mines with a numerous army, how could they

fubfift

ſubſiſt for want of proviſion."——Moyle, Diſſ. on the Rev. of Athens,

" If they foraged in ſmall parties."—— Same.

The ſenſe is future, and therefore *ſhould march*, *ſhould forage*, would have been more correct.

" I should not act the part of an impartial ſpectator, if I *dedicated* the following papers to one who is not of the moſt conſummate and acknowleged merit."—— Spect. Dedic.

If I ſhould dedicate, would have been more accurate.

A similar fault occurs in the following paſſage.

" If nature *thunder'd* in his opening ears,
And *ſtunn'd* him with the muſic of the ſpheres."
                              Pope, Eſſay on Man.

If nature *ſhould thunder* and *ſtun* him, is the meaning.

There is another article that deſerves to be mentioned ; which is, the uſe of a verb after *as* or *than*, apparently without a nominative.

" This

"THIS unlimited power is what the beft legiflators of all ages have endeavored to depofit in fuch hands, as *would preferve* the people from rapine."——Swift, vol. 2. Contefts, &c.

"*WOULD preferve*" feems to have no nominative, for *hands* cannot be inferted without changing the form of the fentence; *in thofe hands which would preferve.*

"A HYPOCRITE hath fo many things to attend to, *as make* his life a very perplexed and intricate thing."——Tillotfon.

THIS mode of expreffion is however well eftablifhed and occafions no obfcurity. The truth is, *as* is an article or relative e-quivalent to *that* or *which* ; and the criti-cifms of Lowth on the conjunctions, where he condemns the ufe of *as* and *fo* in a num-ber of inftances, prove that he knew noth-ing about the true meaning of thefe words. See Diverfions of Purley, page 283.

ANOTHER form of expreffion, peculiar to our language, is the *participial noun*, a word derived from a verb, and having the properties, both of a verb and a noun ; as, "I heard of *his acquiring* a large eftate." *Acquiring* here expreffes the *act done*, the acquifition ;

acquisition; yet governs the following objective case, *estate*. When a noun precedes the participle, it takes the sign of the possessive, " I heard of a *man's acquiring* an estate." This is the genuin English idiom; and yet modern writers very improperly omit the sign of the possessive, as, I heard of a *man acquiring* an estate. This omission often changes the sense of the phrase or leaves it ambiguous.

The omission of the sign of the possessive in the following example is a very great fault.

" Of a general or public act, the courts of law are bound to take notice judicially and *ex officio*, without the *statute being* particularly pleaded."———Blackstone Comment. vol. 1. p. 86.

The preposition *without* here governs the phrase following, which might otherwise be properly arranged thus, without *the particular pleading of the statute*, or without *pleading the statute particularly*. But as the sentence stands, there is nothing to show the true construction, or how the sentence may be resolved : *Being* and *pleaded* both stand as participles ; whereas the

construction

conftruction requires that they fhould be confidered as ftanding for a noun ; for *without* does not govern *ftatute* ; *without the ftatute*, is not the meaning of the writer. But it governs *pleading*, or refers immediately to that idea or union of ideas, exprefled by *being particularly pleaded*. As thefe laft words reprefent a noun, which is immediately governed by the prepofition, *without*, the word *ftatute* fhould have the fign of the poffeffive, as much as any word in the genitive cafe, *without the ftatute's being particularly pleaded* ; that is, without the particular pleading *of the ftatute* by the parties ; for in order to make grammar or fenfe, *ftatute* muft be in the poffeffive.

To confirm thefe remarks, I would juft add, that when we fubftitute a pronoun in fuch cafes, we always ufe the poffeffive cafe. Suppofe the word *ftatute* had been previoufly ufed, in the fentence ; the writer then would have ufed the pronoun in the clofe of the fentence, thus ; " without *its* being particularly pleaded ;" and I prefume that no perfon will contend for the propriety of, " without *it* being pleaded."

So we fhould fay, " a judge will not proceed to try a criminal, without *his* being

ing prefent." But would it be correct to fay, without *him* being prefent ? This mode of fpeaking will not, I am confident, be advocated : But unlefs I am miftaken, this laft expreffion ftands on a footing with the example cited, *without the ftatute being pleaded.* Numberlefs fimilar examples occur in thofe modern writers who aim at refinement of language. " If we can admit the doctrine of the *ftomach having* a general confent with the whole fyftem."—" On account of the *fyftem being* too highly toned," &c. It is ftrange the writers of fuch language do not fee that there are in fact two poffeffives in fuch phrafes—" on account *of* the too high toning *of* the fyftem," and that both fhould be expreffed; thus, " on account *of* the *fyftem's* being too high toned."

IT may be queftioned whether the verb *need* may not with propriety be ufed in the third perfon fingular of the indicative, prefent, without the ufual termination of that perfon. Practice will at leaft warrant it.

" BUT tho the principle is to be applauded, the error cannot, and, in this enlightened age, happily *need* not be defended."——Erfkine, Orat. Temp. vol. I. p. 95.

" Now

" Now a perſon *need* but enter into him-
ſelf and reflect on the operations of his
own mind."——Nugent's Burlamaqui, 1. 9.

" HENCE it was adjudged, that the *uſe*
need not always be executed the inſtant the
conveyance is made."——Blackſtone, Com.
b. 2. chap. 20.

NUMBERLESS authorities of this kind
may be produced ; but we may ſpare the
trouble, and only advert to the conſtant
practice of ſpeakers of every claſs ; " he
need not ;" " it need not."   Indeed, *he needs
not*, altho grammatically correct, is ſo of-
fenſive to moſt ears, that we have little
reaſon to expect people will be perſuaded
to uſe it.

THE ſame may be ſaid of *dare* ; " he dare
not."

I AM miſtaken, Lowth reprobates as bad
Engliſh ; aſſerting that the phraſe is equivalent to *I am miſunderſtood.*   In this criticiſm the Biſhop *is miſtaken* moſt groſsly.
Whether the phraſe is a corruption of *am
miſtaking* or not, is wholly immaterial ; in
the ſenſe the Engliſh have uſed it from
time immemorial and univerſally, *miſtaken*

is

is a mere adjective, fignifying that one is in an error ; and this fenfe the Bifhop fhould have explained, and not rejected the phrafe.

PARTICLES.

THE fame author difapproves of *to* after *averfe* ; another example of his hafty decifion.   The practice of good writers and fpeakers is almoft wholly in favor of *to*, and this is good authority ; the propriety of the Englifh particles depending almoft folely on their ufe, without any reference to Latin rules.   *Averfe* is an adjective, defcribing a certain ftate or quality of the mind, without regard to motion, and therefore *averfe from* is as improper as *contrary from, oppofed from*, or *reluctant from*. Indeed in the original fenfe of *from*, explained by Mr. Horne Tooke, as denoting *beginning*, *averfe from* appears to be nonfenfe.

THE following phrafes are faid to be faulty ; *previous to, antecedent to*, with others of a fimilar nature.   The criticifm on thefe expreffions muft have been made on a very fuperficial view of the fubject.   In this fentence, "previous to the eftablifhment

ment of the new government, the refolutions of Congrefs could not be enforced by
legal compulfory penalties ;" *previous* refers to the word *time* or fomething equivalent implied, *at the time previous*, or *during
the time or period, previous* to the eftablifhment of the new government.   This is the
ftrict grammatical refolution of the phrafe;
and the ufual correction, *previoufly*, is
glaringly abfurd; *during the time previoufly
to the eftablifhment*; into fuch wild errors
are men led by a flight view of things, or
by applying the principles of one language
to the conftruction of another.*

"*AGREEABLE to his promife*, he fent me
the papers ;" here *agreeable* is correct; for
it refers to the fact done ; he fent me the
papers, which fending was agreeable to his
promife.   In fuch cafes, practice has often
a better foundation than the criticifms
which are defigned to change it.

ACCORDING is ufually numbered among
the prepofitions ; but moft abfurdly ; it is
always

---

* *PREVIOUS* may be vindicated on another principle;
viz. by confidering it as qualifying the whole fubfequent
member of the fentence.   " The refolutions of Congrefs
could not be enforced by legal penalties ; this *fact* was *previous* to the eftablifhment," &c.   But the other is the real
conftruction.

always a participle, and has always a reference to fome noun or member of a fentence. "*According to his promife*, he called on me laft evening." Here *according* refers to the whole fubfequent member of the fentence ; "he called on me laft evening, which (the whole of which facts) was *according* to his promife." No perfon pretends that "*accordingly* to his promife" is good Englifh ; yet the phrafe is not more incorrect than "*agreeably* to his promife,". or "*previoufly* to this event," which the modern critics and refiners of our language have recommended.

"*Who* do you fpeak *to* ?" "*Who* did he marry ?" are challenged as bad Englifh ; but *whom* do you fpeak *to* ? was never ufed in fpeaking, as I can find, and if fo, is hardly Englifh at all. There is no doubt, in my mind, that the Englifh *who* and the Latin *qui*, are the fame word with mere variations of dialect. *Who*, in the Gothic or Teutonic, has always anfwered to the Latin nominative, *qui* ; the dative *cui*, which was pronounced like *qui* ; and the ablative *quo* ; in the fame manner as *whofe* has anfwered to *cujus*, in all genders ; *whom* to *quem*, *quam*, and *what* to *quod*. So that *who* did he fpeak *to* ? *Who* did you go *with* ?

were

were probably as good Englifh, in ancient times, as *cui dixit ? Cum quo ivifti ?* in Latin.   Nay, it is more than probable that *who* was once wholly ufed in afking queftions, even in the objective cafe ; *who* did he marry ? until fome Latin ftudent began to fufpect it bad Englifh, becaufe not agreeable to the Latin rules.   At any rate, *whom* do you fpeak *to* ? is a corruption, and all the grammars that can be formed will not extend the ufe of the phrafe beyond the walls of a college.

THE foregoing criticifms will perhaps illuftrate and confirm an affertion of Mr. Horne Tooke, that " Lowth has rejected much *good* Englifh."   I fhould go farther and affert that he has criticized away more phrafes of *good* Englifh, than he has corrected of *bad*.   He has not only miftaken the true conftruction of many phrafes, but he has rejected others that have been ufed generally by the Englifh nation from the earlieft times, and by arbitrary rules, fubftituted phrafes that have been rarely, or never ufed at all.   To detect fuch errors, and reftrain the influence of fuch refpectable names, in corrupting the true idiom of our tongue, I conceive to be the duty of every friend to American literature.

ON

On examining the language, and comparing the practice of speaking among the yeomanry of this country, with the stile of Shakespear and Addison, I am constrained to declare that the people of America, in particular the English descendants, speak the most *pure English* now known in the world. There is hardly a foreign idiom in their language; by which I mean, a *phrase* that has not been used by the best English writers from the time of Chaucer. They retain a few obsolete *words*, which have been dropt by writers, probably from mere affectation, as those which are substituted are neither more melodious nor expressive. In many instances they retain correct phrases, instead of which the pretended refiners of the language have introduced those which are highly improper and absurd.

Let Englishmen take notice that when I speak of the American yeomanry, the latter are not to be compared to the illiterate peasantry of their own country. The yeomanry of this country consist of substantial independent freeholders, masters of their own persons and lords of their own soil. These men have considerable education. They not only learn to read, write

and

and keep accounts; but a vaſt proportion of them read newſpapers every week, and beſides the Bible, which is found in all families, they read the beſt Engliſh ſermons and treatiſes upon religion, ethics, geography and hiſtory; ſuch as the works of Watts, Addiſon, Atterbury, Salmon, &c. In the eaſtern ſtates, there are public ſchools ſufficient to inſtruct every man's children, and moſt of the children are actually benefited by theſe inſtitutions. The people of diſtant counties in England can hardly underſtand one another, ſo various are their dialects; but in the extent of twelve hundred miles in America, there are very few, I queſtion whether a hundred words, except ſuch as are uſed in employments wholly local, which are not univerſally intelligible.

BUT unleſs the rage for imitating foreign changes can be reſtrained, this agreeble and advantageous uniformity will be gradually deſtroyed. The ſtandard writers abroad give us local practice, the momentary whims of the great, or their own arbitrary rules to direct our pronunciation; and we, the apes of faſhion, ſubmit to imitate any thing we hear and ſee. Sheridan has introduced or given ſanction

T

to

to more arbitrary and corrupt changes of pronunciation, within a few years, than had before taken place in a century ; and in Perry's Dictionary, not to mention the errors in what he moſt arrogantly calls his "*Only ſure Guide* to the Engliſh Tongue," there are whole pages in which there are ſcarcely two or three words marked for a juſt pronunciation. There is no Dictionary yet publiſhed in Great Britain, in which ſo many of the analogies of the language and the juſt rules of pronunciation are preſerved, as in the common practice of the well informed Americans, who have never conſulted any foreign ſtandard: Nor is there any grammatical treatiſe, except Dr. Prieſtley's, which has explained the real idioms of the language, as they are found in Addiſon's works, and which remain to this day in the American practice of ſpeaking.

THE reſult of the whole is, that we ſhould adhere to our own practice and general cuſtoms, unleſs it can be made very obvious that ſuch practice is wrong, and that a change will produce ſome conſiderable advantage.

DISSERTATION

DISSERTATION V.

*Of the Construction of English Verse.—Pauses.
—Expression.—Of reading Verse.*

Of the CONSTRUCTION *of* ENGLISH VERSE.

S poetry has ever been numbered among the *fine arts*, and has employed the pens of the firſt geniuſes in all nations, an inveſtigation of the ſubjeĉt muſt be gratifying to readers of taſte. And it muſt be the more agreeable, as it has been much neglecĉted, and the nature and conſtrucĉtion of Engliſh verſe have frequently been miſunderſtood.

Moſt proſodians who have treated particularly of this ſubjecĉt, have been guilty of a fundamental error, in conſidering the

 movement

movement of Englifh verfe as depending on long and fhort fyllables, formed by long and fhort vowels. This hypothefis has led them into capital miftakes. The truth is, many of thofe fyllables which are confidered as *long* in verfe, are formed by the fhorteft vowels in the language; as *ftrength, health, grand.* The doctrine, that long vowels are requifite to form long fyllables in poetry, is at length exploded, and the principles which regulate the movement of our verfe, are explained; viz. *accent* and *emphafis.* Every emphatical word, and every accented fyllable, will form what is called in verfe, a long fyllable. The unaccented fyllables, and unemphatical monofyllabic words, are confidered as fhort fyllables.

But there are two kinds of emphafis; a natural emphafis, which arifes from the importance of the idea conveyed by a word; and an accidental emphafis, which arifes from the importance of a word in a particular fituation.

The firft or natural emphafis belongs to all nouns, verbs, participles and adjectives, and requires no elevation of voice; as,

"Not *half* fo *fwift* the *trembling doves* can *fly.*"
                                             The

THE laft or accidental emphafis is laid on a word when it has fome particular meaning, and when the force of a fentence depends on it; this therefore requires an elevation of voice; as,

"PERDITION catch my foul—but I *do* love thee."

So far the profody of the Englifh language feems to be fettled; but the rules laid down for the conftruction of verfe, feem to have been imperfect and difputed.

WRITERS have generally fuppofed that our heroic verfe confifts of five feet, all pure Iambics, except the firft foot, which they allow may be a Trochee. In confequence of this opinion, they have expunged letters from words which were neceffary; and curtailed feet in fuch a manner as to disfigure the beauty of printing, and in many inftances, deftroyed the harmony of our beft poetry.

THE truth is, fo far is our heroic verfe from being confined to the Iambic meafure, that it admits of eight feet, and in fome inftances of nine. I will not perplex my readers with a number of hard names, but proceed to explain the feveral feet, and

T 3 fhow

fhow in what places of the line they are admiffible.

An Iambic foot, which is the ground of Englifh numbers, confifts of two fyllables, the firft *fhort* and the fecond *long*. This foot is admitted into every place of the line. Example, all Iambics.

" Whĕre flāvĕs ŏnce mōre thĕir nātĭve lānd bĕhōld,
Nŏ fiĕnds tŏrmēnt, nŏ chrīftiăns thīrft fŏr gōld."
Pope.

The Trochee is a foot confifting of two fyllables, the firft *long* and the fecond *fhort*. Example.

" *Wārms ĭn* the fun, refrefhes in the breeze,
Glŏws ĭn the ftars, and bloffoms in the trees."
Pope.

The Trochee is not admiffible into the fecond place of the line ; but in the third and fourth it may have beauty, when it creates a correfpondence between the found and fenfe.

" Eve rightly call'd *mŏthĕr* of all mankind."

" And ftaggered by the ftroke, *drŏps thĕ* large ox."

The Spondee is a foot confifting of two long fyllables. This may be ufed in any place of the line.
1. " *Gōōd*

1. "*Good life* be now my tafk, my doubts are done."
Dryden.

2. "As fome *lone mountain*'s monftrous growth he ftood."
Pope.

But it has a greater beauty, when preceded by a Trochee.

"Load the *tall bark* and launch into the main."

3. "The mountain goats *came bound*ing o'er the lawn."

4. "He fpoke, and fpeaking in *proud triumph* fpread,
The long contended honors of her head."
Pope.

5. "Singed are his brows, the fcorching lids *grow black*."
Pope.

The Pyrrhic is a foot of two fhort fyllables; it is graceful in the firft and fourth places, and is admiffible into the fecond and third.

1. "*Nor in* the helplefs orphan dread a foe."
Pope.

2. ————"On they move,
Indiffolubly firm."————Milton.

3. "The two extremes appear like man and wife,
Coupled togeth*er for* the fake of ftrife."
Churchill.

But this foot is moft graceful in the fourth place.

"The dying gales that pant *upon* the trees."
"To

" To fartheft fhores the ambrofial fpirit flies,
Sweet to the world and gratef*ŭl tŏ* the fkies."

THE Amphibrach is a foot of three fyllables, the firft and third fhort, and the
fecond long. It is ufed in heroic verfe only when we take the liberty to add a fhort
fyllable to a line.

" THE piece you fay is incorrect, *whȳ tāke ĭt,*
I'm all fubmiffion, what you'd have *ĭt, māke ĭt.*"

THIS foot is hardly admiffible in the
folemn or fublime ftile. Pope has indeed
admitted it into his Effay on Man :

" WHAT can ennoble fots or flaves ŏr cōwărds,
Alas ! not all the blood of all thĕ Hōwărds."

AGAIN :

" To figh for ribbands, if thou art fŏ fĭllў,
Mark how they grace Lord Umbra or Sĭr Bĭllў."

But thefe lines are of the high burlefque
kind, and in this ftile the Amphibrach
clofes lines with great beauty.

THE Tribrach is a foot of three fyllables,
all fhort ; and it may be ufed in the third
and fourth places.

" AND rolls impet*ŭŏŭs tŏ* the fubject plain."

OR thus :

" AND thunders down impet*ŭŏŭs tŏ* the plain."
                                        THE

The Dactyl, a foot of three fyllables, the firft long and the two laft fhort, is ufed principally in the firft place in the line.

" *Fŭrĭoŭs* he fpoke, the angry chief replied."

"*Mŭrmŭrĭng*, and with him fled the fhades of night."

The Anapæft, a foot confifting of three fyllables, the two firft fhort and the laft long, is admiffible into every place of the line.

> "Căn ă bōfŏm fŏ gēntlĕ rĕmāin,
> Unmoved when her Corydon fighs?
> Will a nymph that is fond of the plains,
> Thefe plains and thefe valleys defpife?
> Dear regions of filence and fhade,
> Soft fcenes of contentment and eafe,
> Where I could have pleafingly ftay'd,
> If ought in her abfence could pleafe."

The triffyllabic feet have fuffered moft by the general ignorance of critics ; moft of them have been mutilated by apoftrophes, in order to reduce them to the Iambic meafure.

Thus in the line before repeated,

"*Murmuring*, and with him fled the fhades of night,"

we find the word in the copy reduced to two fyllables, *murm'ring*, and the beauty of the Dactyl is deftroyed.

Thus

THUS in the following :

"ON every fide with fhadowy fquadrons deep,"

by apoftrophizing *every* and *fhadowy*, the line lofes its harmony. The fame remark applies to the following :

"AND hofts infuriate fhake the fhudd'ring plain."

"BUT fafhion fo directs, and moderns raife
On fafhion's *mould'ring* bafe, their tranfient praife."
                                                  Churchill.

POETIC lines which abound with thefe triffyllabic feet, are the moft flowing and melodious of any in the language ; and yet the poets themfelves, or their printers, murder them with numberlefs unneceffary contractions.

IT requires but little judgement and an ear indifferently accurate, to diftinguifh the contractions which are neceffary, from thofe which are needlefs and injurious to the verfification. In the following paffage we find examples of both.

"SHE went from op'ra, park, affembly, play,
To morning walks and pray'rs three times a day ;
To part her time 'twixt reading and bohea,
To mufe and fpill her folitary tea ;
Or o'er cold coffee trifle with the fpoon,
Count the flow clock, and dine exact at noon ;
Divert her eyes with pictures in the fire,
Hum half a tune, tell ftories to the 'fquire ;
                                                  Up

> Up to her godly garret after fev'n,
> There ftarve and pray, for that's the way to heav'n."
>
> Pope's Epiftles.

HERE *e* in *opera* ought not to be apoftrophized, for fuch a contraction reduces an Amphibrachic foot to an Iambic.   The words *prayers*, *feven* and *heaven* need not the apoftrophe of *e*; for it makes no difference in the pronunciation.   But the contraction of *over* and *betwixt* is neceffary; for without it the meafure would be imperfect.

PAUSES.

HAVING explained the feveral kinds of feet, and fhown in what places of a verfe they may be ufed, I proceed to another important article, the paufes.   Of thefe there are two kinds, the *cefural* paufe, which divides the line into two equal or unequal parts; and the *final* paufe which clofes the verfe.   Thefe paufes are called *mufical*, becaufe their fole end is the melody of verfe.

THE paufes which mark the fenfe, and for this reafon are denominated *fentential*, are the fame in verfe as in profe.   They are marked by the ufual ftops, a comma, a femicolon, a colon, or a period, as the

fenfe

fenfe requires, and need no particular explanation.

THE cefural paufe is not effential to verfe, for the fhorter kinds of meafure are without it; but it improves both the melody and the harmony.

MELODY in mufic is derived from a fucceffion of founds; harmony from different founds in concord. A fingle voice can produce melody; a union of voices is neceffary to form harmony. In this fenfe harmony cannot be applied to verfe, becaufe poetry is recited by a fingle voice. But harmony may be ufed in a figurative fenfe, to exprefs the effect produced by obferving the proportion which the members of verfe bear to each other.*

THE cefural paufe may be placed in any part of the verfe; but has the fineft effect upon the melody, when placed after the fecond or third foot, or in the middle of the third. After the fecond:

> "In what retreat, inglorious and unknown,
> Did genius fleep, when dulnefs feized the throne."

AFTER the third:

> "O SAY

---

*SHERIDAN's Art of Reading.

"O say what ſtranger cauſe, yet unexplored,
  Could make a gentle belle reject a lord ?"

In the middle of the third :

"Great are his perils, in this ſtormy time,
  Who raſhly ventures, on a ſea of rhime."

In theſe examples we find a great degree of melody, but not in all the ſame degree. In comparing the diviſions of verſe, we experience the moſt pleaſure in viewing thoſe which are equal ; hence thoſe verſes which have the pauſe in the middle of the third foot, which is the middle of the verſe, are the moſt melodious.   Such is the third example above.

In lines where the pauſe is placed after the ſecond foot, we perceive a ſmaller degree of melody, for the diviſions are not equal ; one containing four ſyllables, the other ſix, as in the firſt example.

But the melody in this example, is much ſuperior to that of the verſes which have the ceſural pauſe after the third foot ; for this obvious reaſon : When the pauſe bounds the ſecond foot, the latter part of the verſe is the greateſt, and leaves the moſt forcible impreſſion upon the mind ; but when the pauſe is at the end of the third

foot,

foot, the order is reverfed.   We are fond of proceeding from fmall to great, and a climax in found, pleafes the ear in the fame manner as a climax in fenfe delights the mind.   Such is the firft example.

It muft be obferved further, that when the cefural paufe falls after the fecond and third feet, both the final and cefural paufes are on accented fyllables ; whereas when the cefural paufe falls in the middle of the third foot, this is on a weak fyllable, and the final paufe, on an accented fyllable. This variety in the latter, is another caufe of the fuperior pleafure we derive from verfes divided into equal portions.

The paufe may fall in the middle of the fourth foot ; as,

> " Let favor fpcak for others, worth for me ;"

but the melody, in this cafe, is almoft loft. At the clofe of the firft foot, the paufe has a more agreeable effect.

> " That's vile, fhould we a parent's fault adore,
> And err, becaufe our fathers err'd before ?"

In the middle of the fecond foot, the paufe may be ufed, but produces little melody.

" And

> " And who but wifhes to invert the laws
> Of order, fins againft the eternal caufe."

Harmony is produced by a proportion between the members of the fame verfe, or between the members of different verfes. Example.

> " Thy forefts, Windfor, and thy green retreats,
> At once the monarch's, and the mufe's feats,
> Invite my lays.   Be prefent fylvan maids,
> Unlock your fprings, and open all your fhades."

Here we obferve, the paufe in the firft couplet, is in the middle of the third foot ; both verfes are in this refpect fimilar.   In the laft couplet, the paufe falls after the fecond foot.   In each couplet feparately confidered, there is a uniformity ; but when one is compared with the other, there is a diverfity.   This variety produces a pleafing effect.*   The variety is further encreafed, when the firft lines of feveral fucceeding couplets are uniform as to themfelves, and different from the laft lines, which are alfo uniform as to themfelves. Churchill, fpeaking of reafon, lord chief juftice in the court of man, has the following lines.

> " Equally form'd to rule, in age and youth,
> The friend of virtue, and the guide to youth ;

To

---

* Sheridan.

> To *her* I bow, whofe facred power I feel ;
> To *her* decifion, make my laft appeal ;
> Condemn'd by *her*, applauding worlds in vain
> Should tempt me to take up my pen again ;
> By *her* abfolv'd, the courfe I'll ftill purfue ;
> If *Reafon*'s for me, *God* is for me too."

THE firft line of three of thefe couplets, has the paufe after the fecond foot ; in this confifts their fimilarity. The laft line in three of them, has the paufe in the middle of the third foot ; they are uniform as to themfelves, but different from the foregoing lines. This paffage, which on the whole is very beautiful, fuffers much by the fixth line, which is not verfe, but rather hobbling profe.*

THE foregoing remarks are fufficient to illuftrate the ufe and advantages of the cefural paufe.

THE final paufe marks the clofe of a line or verfe, whether there is a paufe in the
fenfe

---

* CHURCHILL has improved Englifh verfification, but was fometimes too incorrect. It is a remark of fome writer, " That the greateft geniufes are feldom correct," and the remark is not without foundation. Homer, Shakefpear, and Milton, were perhaps the greateft geniufes that ever lived, and they were certainly guilty of the greateft faults. Virgil and Pope were much inferior in point of genius, but excelled in accuracy. Churchill had genius, but his contempt of rules made him fometimes indulge a too great latitude of expreffion.

fenfe or not. Sentential paufes fhould be marked by a variation of tone ; but the final paufe, when the clofe of one line is intimately connected with the beginning of the next, fhould be merely a fufpenfion of the voice without elevation or depreffion. Thus :

> "OF man's firft difobedience, and the fruit
> Of that forbidden tree, whofe mortal tafte
> Brought death into the world, and all our woe," &c.

WHEN thefe lines are read without a paufe after the words *fruit* and *tafte*, they degenerate into profe. Indeed in many inftances, particularly in blank verfe, the final paufe is the only circumftance which diftinguifhes verfe from profe.

EXPRESSION.

ONE article more in the conftruction of verfe deferves our obfervation, which is *Expreffion*. Expreffion confifts in fuch a choice and diftribution of poetic feet as are beft adapted to the fubject, and beft calculated to imprefs fentiments upon the mind. Thofe poetic feet, which end in an accented fyllable, are the moft forcible. Hence the Iambic meafure is beft adapted to folemn and fublime fubjects. This is the

U

meafure

meafure of the Epic, of poems on grave moral fubjects, of elegies, &c. The Spondee, a foot of two long fyllables, when admitted into the Iambic meafure, adds much to the folemnity of the movement.

> "WHILE the clear fun, rejoicing ftill to rife,
> In pomp *rolls round* immeafurable fkies."
> Dwight.

THE Dactyl, *rolls round*, expreffes beautifully the majefty of the fun in his courfe.

IT is a general rule, that the more important fyllables there are in a paffage, whether of profe or verfe, the more heavy is the ftile. For example :

> "A PAST, vamp'd, future, old, reviv'd new piece."

> "MEN, bearded, bald, cowl'd, uncowl'd, fhod, unfhod."

SUCH lines are deftitute of melody and are admiffible only when they fuit the found to the fenfe. In the high burlefque ftile, of which kind is Pope's Dunciad, they give the fentiment an ironical air of importance, and from this circumftance derive a beauty. On the other hand, a large proportion of unaccented fyllables or particles, deprives language of energy ; and it is this circumftance principally which in profe conftitutes the difference between the grave hiftorical,

torical, and the familiar ftile.   The greateft number of long fyllables ever admitted
into a heroic verfe, is feven, as in the foregoing; the fmalleft number is three.

> " Or to a fad variety of woe."

The Trochaic meafure, in which every
foot clofes with a weak fyllable, is well
calculated for lively fubjects.

> " Softly fweet in Lydian meafures
> Soon he footh'd his foul to pleafures;
> War he fung is toil and trouble,
> Honor but an empty bubble," &c.

The Anapæftic meafure, in which there
are two fhort fyllables to one long, is beft
adapted to exprefs the impetuofity of paffion or action.   Shenftone has ufed it to
great advantage, in his inimitable paftoral
ballad.   It defcribes beautifully the ftrong
and lively emotions which agitate the lover, and his anxiety to pleafe, which continually hurries him from one object and
one exertion to another.

> " I have found out a gift for my fair,
> I have found where the wood pigeons breed;
> Yet let me that plunder forbear,
> She will fay 'twas a barbarous deed.
> For he ne'er could prove true, fhe averr'd,
> Who could rob a poor bird of her young:
> And I lov'd her the more when I heard
> Such tendernefs fall from her tongue."

U 2

The

The Amphibrachic meafure, in which there is a long fyllable between two fhort ones, is beft adapted to lively comic fubjects ; as in Addifon's Rofamond.

> " Since conjugal paffion
> Has come into fafhion,
> And marriage fo bleft on the throne is,
> Like Venus I'll fhine,
> Be fond and be fine,
> And Sir Trufty fhall be my Adonis."

Such a meafure gives fentiment a ludicrous air, and confequently is ill adapted to ferious fubjects.

Great art may be ufed by a poet in choofing words and feet adapted to his fubject.　Take the following fpecimen.

> " Now here, now there, the warriors fall ; amain
> Groans murmur, armor founds, and fhouts convulfe
> the plain."

The feet in the laft line are happily chofen.　The flow Spondee, in the beginning of the verfe, fixes the mind upon the difmal fcene of woe ; the folemnity is heightened by the paufes in the middle of the fecond and at the end of the third foot : But when the poet comes to fhake the plains, he clofes the line with three forcible Iambics.

Of

OF a fimilar beauty take the following example. ·

" SHE all night long, her amorous defcant fung."

THE poet here defigns to defcribe the length of the night, and the mufic of the Nightingale's fong. The firft he does by two flow Spondees, and the laft by four very rapid fyllables.

THE following lines, from Gray's Elegy, written in a country church yard, are diftinguifhed by a happy choice of words.

" FOR who, to dumb forgetfulnefs a prey,
This pleafing anxious being e'er refign'd ?
Left the warm precincts of the cheerful day,
Nor caft one *longing lingering* look behind ?"

THE words *longing* and *lingering* exprefs moft forcibly the reluctance with which mankind quit this ftate of exiftence.

POPE has many beauties of this kind.

" AND grace and reafon, fenfe and virtue fplit,
With all the rafh dexterity of wit."

THE mute confonants, with which thefe lines end, exprefs the idea of *rending afunder*, with great energy and effect. The words *rafh* and *dexterity* are alfo judicioufly chofen.

In defcribing the delicate fenfations of the moft refined love, he is remarkable for his choice of fmooth flowing words. There are fome paffages in his Eloifa and Abelard, which are extended to confiderable length, without a fingle mute confonant or harfh word.

Of READING VERSE.

WITH refpect to the art of reading verfe, we can lay down but a few fimple rules ; but thefe may perhaps be ufeful.

1. WORDS fhould be pronounced as they are in profe and in converfation ; for reading is but rehearfing another's converfation.

2. THE emphafis fhould be obferved as in profe. The voice fhould bound from accent to accent, and no ftrefs fhould be laid on little unimportant words, nor on weak fyilables.

3. THE fentential paufes fhould be obferved as in profe ; thefe are not affected by the kind of writing, being regulated entirely by the fenfe. But as the cefural and final paufes are defigned to encreafe the melody of verfe, the ftricteft attention muft be paid to them in reading. They mark

a

a fufpenfion of voice without rifing or falling.

To read profe well it is neceffary to underftand what is read; and to read poetry well, it
is further neceffary to underftand the ftructure of verfe.   For want of this knowlege,
moft people read all verfe like the Iambic
meafure.   The following are pure Iambics.

> " Above how high progreffive life may go !
> Around how wide, how deep extend below !"

It is fo eafy to lay an accent on every
fecond fyllable, that any fchool boy can
read this meafure with tolerable propriety.
But the misfortune is, that when a habit
of reading this kind of meter is once formed, perfons do not vary their manner to
fuit other meafures.   Thus in reciting the
following line,

> " Load *the* tall *bark*, and launch in*to* the main,"

many people would lay the accent on every fecond fyllable; and thus read, our
poetry becomes the moft monotonous and
ridiculous of all poetry in the world.

Let the following line be repeated without its paufes, and it lofes its principal
beauty.

> " Bold, as a hero,, as a virgin, mild."

So

So in the following.

"Reason, the card,, but paſſion, is the gale."

"From ſtorms, a ſhelter,, and from heat, a ſhade."

The harmony is, in all theſe inſtances, improved much by the ſemipauſes, and at the ſame time the ſenſe is more clearly underſtood.

Considering the difficulty of reading verſe, I am not ſurpriſed to find but few who are proficients in this art. A knowlege of the ſtructure of verſe, of the ſeveral kinds of feet, of the nature and uſe of the final, the ceſural and the ſemiceſural pauſes, is eſſential to a graceful manner of reading poetry; and even this, without the beſt examples, will hardly effect the purpoſe. It is for this reaſon, that children ſhould not be permitted to read poetry of the more difficult kind, without the beſt examples for them to imitate. They frequently contract, in early life, either a monotony or a ſing ſong cant, which, when grown into a habit, is ſeldom ever eradicated.

NOTES,

NOTES,

HISTORICAL AND CRITICAL.

[A, page 42, Text.]

THE author of the " Specimen of an Etymological Vocabulary," afferts that " the Celtic was
demonftrably the origin of the Greek and Latin ; of
moft, if not all the languages of Europe ; of part of
Africa and the two Tartaries."

MONS. Gebelin, who has, with great induftry, inveftigated the origin of the European languages, is of
opinion that the Celtic was fpoken from the borders of
the Hellefpont to the ocean, and from Troy to Cape
Finifterre and Ireland. " La langue Celtique, dans
fon fens le plus extendu, eft la langue que parlerent les
premiers habitans de l'Europe, depuis les rives de l'-
Hellefpont & de la Mer Egée, jufques a celle de l'O-
cean ; depuis le cap Sigée aux portes de Troie, jufques
au cap de Finifterre in Portugal, ou jufques en Ire-
lande."——Dif. Prelim. art. 2.

FROM this language, he fays, fprung the Greek or
Pelafgic, prior to Hefiod and Homer—the Latin or that
of

of Numa—the Etruſcan, ſpoken in a conſiderable part of Italy—the Thracian, ſpoken on the Danube, from the Euxine to the Adriatic ſea, 'which was the ſame as the Phrygian—the Teutonic or German, ſpoken from the Viſtula to the Rhine—the Gauliſh, ſpoken on the Alps, in Italy, on this ſide the Po, and from the Rhine to the Ocean, including France, the Low Countries, Switzerland, Alemain, and the two Bretagnes—alſo the Cantabrian, or ancient language of Spain—in ſhort, the Runic, ſpoken in the North, Denmark, Sweden, &c.

THE only pure remains of this primitive Celtic, the ſame author ſuppoſes, are found in Wales, Cornwall, and Brittany in France, where the people ſtill ſpeak dialects of a language which is proved to be the ancient Britiſh.

"SEPARES ainſi du reſte de l'univers, ces debris des anciens Celtes ont conſervé leurs anciens uſages, & parlent une lanque qui n'a aucun rapport a celles des peuples qui les ont ſubjugués, & qui s'eſt partagée en trois dialectes, le Gallois, le Cornouaillien, & le Bas Breton.; dialectes qui ont entr'eux le plus grand rapport, & qui ſont inconteſtablement les precieux reſtes de l'ancienne langue des Celtes ou des Gaulois."——Diſ. Prelim.

"SEPARATED from the reſt of the world, theſe remains of the ancient Celts have preſerved their ancient cuſtoms, and ſpeak a language which *has no agreement with thoſe of their conquerors*, and which is divided into three dialects, the Welſh, the Corniſh, and the Armoric—dialects which have a cloſe affinity with each other, and which are, beyond diſpute, the precious remains of the ancient Celtic or Gauliſh language."*

IN this paſſage the author ſeems to contradict what he had juſt before advanced, that the Celtic was the

primitive

---

* IT is ſaid that the Celtic has a great affinity with the oriental languages. "Magnam certe cum linguis orientalibus affinitatem retinet, ut notant Dr. J. Davies paſſim in Dictionario ſuo Cambro Britannico, et Samuel Bochartus in ſua Geographica ſacra."——Wallis, Gram.

primitive language of Europe, from which sprung the Gothic or German. Now the Franks, Normans and Saxons, who subdued Gaul and Britain, spoke dialects of the Gothic; consequently there must have been, upon our author's own hypothesis, some agreement between the ancient Celtic and the more modern languages of the Goths, Saxons, and other northern conquerors of the Celtic nations. This agreement will appear, when I come to collate a number of words in the different languages.

MANY learned men have attempted to prove that the Northern Goths and Teutones, and the Celts who lived in Gaul and Britain, were originally the same people. Monf. Mallet, the celebrated historian, has composed his "Introduction to the History of Denmark" upon this hypothesis. His translator is of a different opinion, and has generally substituted the English word "Gothic" for the "Celtique" of the original. In a preface to his translation, he endeavors to confute the opinion of Monf. Mallet, Cluverius, Pellutier and others, and prove that the Gothic and Celtique nations were *ab origine* two distinct races of men. Great erudition is displayed on both sides of the question, and those who have a taste for enquiries of this kind, will receive much satisfaction and improvement, in reading what these authors have written upon the subject.

AFTER a close examination, I freely declare myself an advocate for the opinion of Monf. Mallet, Lhuyd, and Pellutier, who suppose the Celts and Goths to be descended from the same original stock. The separation however must have been very early, and probably as early as the first age after the flood. To say that the Gothic and Celtique languages have *no affinity*, would be to contradict the most positive proofs; yet the affinity is very small—discoverable only in a few words.

THE modern English, Danish, Swedish and German are all unquestionably derived from the same language;

they have been fpoken by diftinct tribes, probably not
two thoufand years, and almoft one half of that period,
the founds have been in fome meafure fixed by written
characters, yet the languages are become fo different
as to be unintelligible, each to thofe who fpeak the other.   But, fuppofe two languages feparated from the parent tongue, two thoufand years earlier, and to be fpok-
en, thro the whole of that time, by rude nations, unacquainted with writing, and perpetually roving in for-
efts, changing their refidence, and liable to petty conquefts, and it is natural to think their affinity muft become extremely obfcure.   This feems to have been the
fact with refpect to the Gothic and Celtic tongues.
The common parent of both was the Phenician or Hebrew.   This affertion is not made on the fole authority of Mofes ; profane hiftory and etymology furnifh
ftrong arguments to prove the truth of the fcripture account of the manner in which the world was peopled
from one ftock or family.   Of thefe two ancient languages, the Celtic or Britifh comes the neareft to the
Hebrew, for which perhaps fubftantial reafons will be
affigned.   The Gothic bears a greater affinity to the
Greek and Roman, as being derived through the ancient Ionic or Pelafgic, from the Phenician.

LHUYD, a celebrated and profound antiquary, remarks, Arch. Brit. page 35.   "It is a common error
in etymology to endeavor the deriving all the radical
words of our weftern European languages from the
Latin and Greek ; or indeed to derive conftantly the
primitives of any one language from any particular
tongue.   When we do this, we feem to forget that all
have been fubject to alterations ; and that the greater
and more polite any nation is, the more fubject, (partly
for improvement, and partly out of a luxurious wan-
tonnefs) to new model their language.   We muft
therefore neceffarily allow, that whatever nations were
of the neighborhood and of one common origin with
the Greeks and Latins, when they began to diftinguifh
themfelves for politenefs, they muft have preferved their

languages

languages (which could differ from theirs only in dialects) much better than they; and consequently no ab-
surdity to suppose a great many words of the language,
spoken by the old aborigines, the Osci, the Læstrigones,
the Ausonians, Ænotrians, Umbrians and Sabines, out
of which the Latin was composed, to have been better
preserved in the Celtic than in the Roman. "Lingua
Hetrusca, Phrygia, Celtica (says the learned Stiernhelm)
affines sunt omnes; ex uno fonte derivatæ. Nec
Græca longe distat, Japheticæ sunt omnes; ergo et
ipsa Latina. Non igitur mirium est innumera vocab-
ula dictarum Linguarum communia esse cum Latinis."
And that being granted, it must also be allowed that the
Celtic (as well as all other languages) has been best preserved by such of their colonies, as, from the situation
of their country, have been the least subject to foreign
invasions. Whence it proceeds that we always find the
ancient languages are best retained in mountains and
islands."

THE result of this doctrine is, that the primitive Celtic was preserved, in greatest purity, in Britain, before
the Roman and Saxon conquests, and since those periods, in Wales and Cornwall. Hence the affinity between the Hebrew and British, which will afterward
appear.

WALLIS remarks that it is doubtful whether many
words in the English and German languages are derived from the Latin, or the Latin from the Teutonic,
or whether all were derived from the same stock. "Mul-
tas autem voces, quæ nobis cum Germanis fere sunt
communes, dubium est an prisci olim Teutones a Latinis, an hi ab illis, aut denique utrique ab eodem commune fonte, acceperint."——Gram. Cap. 14.

BUT I presume that history, as well as etymology,
will go far in solving the doubt, and incline us to believe that the Teutonic, Greek and Latin were all children of the same parent tongue.

WE firſt hear of men in the mild climate of Aſia Minor, and about the head of the Mediterranean. Soon after the flood, the inhabitants began to migrate into diſtant countries. Some of them went northward and ſettled in Bactriania and Hyrcania, thence extending weſtward along the ſhores of the Caſpian ſea into Armenia. From theſe Aſiatic colonies, ſprung the Scythians and the numerous tribes that afterwards covered the territory of modern Ruſſia, Sweden and Denmark. The different tribes or hords of theſe people were called Cimbri, (perhaps from Gomer) Galli, Umbri, &c. and ſettled the northern parts of Europe as far as the Rhine.

THE northern Greek countries, Thrace and Myſia, were peopled by the deſcendants of Tiras or Thiras, a ſon of Japhet. The whole country from Thrace to Peloponneſus was inhabited by the poſterity of Javan and Cittim ; indeed Ionia, the ancient name of Greece, ſeems to be derived from Javan, *J* or *I* being anciently pronounced as liquid *i*, or *y* conſonant, and as it is ſtill pronounced in the German *ja*, yaw. Theſe ſettlements were made long before the Pelaſgic migrations into Greece, which happened at leaſt 2000 years before Chriſt. The original language of Greece was called *Ionic*, from *Javan* or *Ion*. The Pelaſgi were probably Phenicians ; and ancient hiſtorians relate that they carried letters into Greece ; but theſe muſt have been in a very rude ſtate, ſo early after their invention ;* nor do we find that they were ever much uſed ; at leaſt no records or inſcriptions, in theſe characters, are mentioned by the Greek hiſtorians.

CADMUS introduced the Phenician letters into Greece 1494 years before Chriſt. Theſe letters were introduced with ſome difficulty, and both Cadmus and his followers were obliged to adopt the *Ionic* or original

Japhetic

---

* THE invention of letters is aſcribed to Taaut or Theuth, the ſon of *Mizraim*, ſoon after the flood.

Japhetic language, which was afterwards written in his Phenician characters.

THE Greeks, at different periods, sent colonies into distant parts of the country. These settled in Thrace, Macedon, on the banks of the Euxine, in Asia Minor, in Italy, Sicily and on the southern shore of the Mediterranean. This Ionic or Japhetic language was therefore the root of the Greek and Latin. It was also the root of the Gothic language, spoken in the north of Europe ; and from which, after the revolution of ages, the shocks of war, and the improvements in science, no less than seven or eight different languages are derived.*

PROFANE history therefore warrants us in asserting that the Greek, Roman, and all the modern languages of the north of Europe, and the English, among the rest, had a common stock. But history alone would not silence our objections to this theory, were it not incontestibly proved by a number of radical words, common to all, which are not yet lost in the changes of time. Etymology therefore furnishes a demonstration of what is related in history. When one sees the words γινωσκω and γνοω in Greek, *nosco*, and anciently, *gnosco* in Latin, and *know* in English, conveying the same idea, he is led to suspect that one nation borrowed the word from another. But when did the English borrow this word ? The word was used by the Saxons, long before they could have had any knowlege of Greek or Roman authors. It furnishes therefore a strong presumption that all the streams came from the same fountain. But when we examin further, and find many, perhaps a hundred words or more, common to all these languages, the evidence of their common origin becomes irresistible. This in fact is the case.

THE authors then who have labored to prove the Greek and Latin Languages to be derived from the

Celtic,

* I STRONGLY suspect that the primitive language of the north of Europe was the root of the Sclavonic, still retained in Russia, Poland, Hungary, &c. and that the Gothic was introduced at a later period.

Celtic, miftake the truth.   The *Celtic* was not *prior* to the Greek and Latin, but a branch of the *fame flock* ; that is, cotemporary with thofe languages.

THIS Japhetic language, I take to be coeval with the Phenician or Hebrew ; and there are fome Hebrew words in the Englifh language, which muft have been derived thro the Saxon or Teutonic.   But the old Britifh, as I before remarked, retained the greateft affinity to the Hebrew.   The reafon which appears probable, has been already affigned ;   the Celts and Britons in the weft of Europe, remained, till the times of Julius Cæfar, lefs difturbed by wars and revolutions, than the inhabitants of Afia, Egypt and Greece.

BUT I am inclined to believe further, that the defcent of the Britons from the firft Japhetic tribes that fettled in Greece, was more direct, than thro the Gomerians or Cimbri, who travelled northward along the fhores of the Baltic.   I fufpect that very ancient colonies fettled on the fhores of the Mediterranean, in Italy and Spain, and thence found their way to Gaul and Britain, before the northern tribes arrived thro Germany and Belgium.   This would account for the affinity between the Hebrew language and the Welfh.   The opinion however is not well fupported by hiftorical facts, and the ancient name of the Britifh language, *Cymraeg*, denoting its defcent from the *Cimbric* is a weighty objection.*

IT is certain however that Carthage was fettled by Phenicians, about 900 years before Chrift.   Greek colonies went thither in the following century, and not long after they fettled at Marfeilles in Gaul.   The people therefore on both fhores of the Mediterranean were defcended from the fame flock as the northern nations.
Accordingly

* THIS objection however may be obviated by Lluyd's fuppofition, mentioned in the note, page 50, that the primitive inhabitants of Britain were denominated Guydelians, and the Cymri or Welfh were another branch of the Celtic Cimbri, who came from the North, fettled in Britain and gave name to the language.

Accordingly we are not furprized to find forre radical words nearly the fame in all the exifting languages of Europe. See Jackfon's Chronological Antiquities, vol. 3, with Lhuyd, Geblin, and others.

To illuftrate what I have advanced, refpecting the firft peopling of the world, and the derivation of moft European languages from one mother tongue, I will here infert fome remarks from Rowland's Mona Antiqua Reftaurata, p. 261, with a table of words, evidently of Hebrew original.

" *A* TABLE, *fhewing the Affinity and near Refemblance, both in Sound and Signification, of many Words of the Ancient Languages of Europe with the Original Hebrew Tongue.*

" FOR the better underftanding of the parallels of this following table, it is to be obferved, that letters of one and the fame organ are of common ufe in the pronunciation of words of different languages—as for example, *M, B, V, F, P,* are labials : *T, D, S,* are dentals : *G, Ch, H, K, C,* are gutturals—and therefore if the Hebrew word or found begins with, or is made of, any one of the labials, any of the reft of the fame organ will anfwer it in the derivative languages. The fame is to be obferved in ufing the dental and the guttural letters. For in tracing out the origin of words, we are more to regard the found of them than their literal form and compofition ; wherein we find words very often, by the humors and fancy of people, tranfpofed and altered from their native founds, and yet in their fignification they very well fit their original patterns. I fhall only exemplify in the letters *M, B,* and *V,* which are of one organ, that is, are formed by one inftrument, the lip ; and therefore are promifcuoufly ufed the one for the other, in pronouncing words of one language in another. The Hebrew *B* is generally pronounced as a *V* confonant. And the Irifh alfo, moft commonly in the middle of a word, pronounce *M* as a

W

V ;

V; as we find the ancient Britons to have made use of
V, or rather *F*, which they pronounce as *V*, for *M* and
B in many Latin words ; as,

LATIN.	BRITISH.	LATIN.	BRITISH.
Animal	*Anifail*	*Numerus*	*Nifer*
Turma	*Tyrfa*	*Columna*	*Colofn*
Terminus	*Terfyn*	*Gemelli*	*Gefeill*
Calamus	*Calaf*	*Roma*	*Rhufain*
Primus	*Prif*	*Scribo*	*Scrifenu*
Amnis	*Afon*	*Liber*	*Llyfr*
Arma	*Arfau*	*Remus*	*Rhwyf*
Firmus	*Ffyrf*	*Domo*	*Dofi*
Monumentum	*Menfent*	*Rebello*	*Rhyfela*
Firmomentum	*Ffurfafen*	*Pluma*	*Pluf*
Lamentor	*Llefain*	*Catamanus*	*Cadfan*
Elementum	*Eifen*	*Dimetæ*	*Dyfed*
Memorare	*Myfyrio*	*Lima*	*Llif*
Hyems	*Gauaf*	*Lamina*	*Llafn*, &c.
Clamare	*Llafaru*		

" WE are not to wonder at this analogy of sounds in
the primitive distinction of languages. For before the
use of writing, which has established the correct form
of words, people were only guided by the car in taking
the sound of words, and they pronounced and uttered
them again as the organs of their voice were best fitted
for it ; and it happening that the aptitude and disposi-
tion of those organs, peculiar to some people and countries, were various (as we find to this day some nations
cannot shape their voice to express all the sounds of another's tongue,) it accordingly affected and inclined
some parties of people to speak the same consonants
harder or softer, to utter the same vowels broader or
narrower, longer or shorter, as they found themselves
best disposed to do. And thereupon custom prevailing
with particular sets of people, to continue the use of
such different pronunciation as they affected, the words
so varied came at length to take on them different forms,

and

and to be efteemed and taken as parts of different languages, tho in their origin they were one and the fame.*

Hebrew.	Derivatives.		Englifh.
" AUCH	Awch	Brit.	The edge of a fword
Even	Maen		A ftone
Agam or Leagam	Lagam	Corn.	A pool or lake
Ivah	Deis-yfu	Br.	To defire
Auor	Awyr		Lightned air
Ano	Yno		Then
Achei	Achau		Brethren or kindred
Aedenei	Gwadnau		The foles of the feet
Calal	Cyllell		To wound or pierce
Domen	Tomen		Muck or dung
Gehel	————		Coal
Sâl	Sâl	Br.	Vile or of no account
Kadal	Gadael		To forfake or defift
Aggan	Angeion	Greek	A veffel or earthen pot
Alaph	'Alphō		To find
Bama	Bōmòs		An altar
Hag	Agios		Holy
Hadar	{ Cadair { Katha	Br. Irifh	Honor or reverence
Hia	Y hi	Br.	She
Goph	Corph		A body, corpfe
Deraich	{ Braich { Raich		An arm

Dad

* It is commonly obferved, that different climates, airs and aliments,
do very much diverfify the tone of the parts and mufcles of human bodies ; on fome of which the modulation of the voice much depends. The
peculiar moifture of one country, the drought of another (other caufes
from food, &c. concurring) extend or contract, fwell or attenuate, the
organs of the voice, that the found made thereby is rendered either fhrill
or hoarfe, foft or hard, plain or lifping, in proportion to that contraction
or extenfion. And hence it is, that the Chinefe and Tartars have
fome founds in their language, that Europeans can fcarcely imitate :
And it is well known in Europe itfelf, that an Englifhman is not
able agreeably to converfe with a ftranger, even in one and the fame
Latin ; nay, even in England, it is noted by Mr. Camden and Dr. Full-
er, that the natives of Carleton Curlew in Leicefterfhire, by a certain
peculiarity of the place, have the turn of their voice very different from
thofe of the neighboring villages.

Hebrew.	*Derivatives.*		*English.*
Dad	Diden	*Br.*	The dug or udder
Ager	Aggero	*Lat.*	To heap together
Elah	-Illi, illæ		They, *mafc. & fem.*
Angil	Axilla		The arm pit
Dapfh	Daps		Cheer or dainties
Hen	En! ecce!		Lo! behold!
Phar	Phérō	*Greek*	To bear or carry
Harabon	Arrhabon		A pawn or pledge
Phalat	Phulátto̅		To keep or defend
Pathah	Peíthō		To perfuade
Gab	Gibbus	*Lat.*	Bent or crooked
Dur	Duro		To endure
Laifh	Lis	*Greek*	A lion
Deka	Dekō		To bite
Ephach	Ophis		A ferpent
Dath	Deddf	*Br.*	A law
Denah	Dyna		This, that, there it is
Hiffah	{ Ys taw { Diftaw		Be filent
Cala	Claf		To be fick
Clei	Cleas	*Irifh*	Jewels, ornaments
Devar	Deveirim		To fpeak
Ein	Ynys	*Br.*	Ifland
Hama	{ Aman *Armor.* { Ymenyn *Br.* { Im *Irifh*		Butter
Ivo	Nava		His enemy
Beala	Mealam		To be wafted
Vock	{ Vacuus *Lat.* { Gwâc *Br.*		Empty
Aita	Ydyw		Is, or are
Bar	Bar	*Irifh*	Son
Bareh	Bara	*Br.*	Meat, or victuals
Beram	Verùm	*Lat.*	But, neverthelefs
Beth	Bwth	*Br.*	A houfe, booth
Se	She	*Irifh*	He, or him
Gaha	Iachau	*Br.*	To heal, or cure
Gad	Càd		An army

Boten

Hebrew.	*Derivatives.*		*English.*
Boten	Potten	Br.	The belly
Gever	Gwr		A man
Hada	Edō	*Greek*	To cherifh
Boa	Báō		To come
Aniah	Anía		Sadnefs
Charath	Charâttō		To infculp
Maas	Mifeō		I hate
Semain	Semaínō		I fhew
Aaz	'Aix		A goat
Aleth	Alaeth	*Br.*	A curfe
Elil	Ellylly		Idol
Allun	Llwyn		A grove of oaks
Amunath	Amynedd		Conftancy
Ap	Wep		Face
Itho	Iddo		With him
Atun	Odyn		A furnace
Atha	Aeth		Went, or came
Ifche	Yffu		To burn
Emaeth	Ymaith		From him
Barach	Parch		To efteem, or blefs
Gobah	Coppa		The top
Geven	Cefn		A ridge, or back
Gedad	Gwiwdod		Excellency
Gaiaph	Cau		To fhut, or inclofe
Evil	——		Evil
Beafch	——		Bafe
Babel	——		To babble, cabal ; and hablar in Spanifh, to fpeak ; Lat. fabula ; Fr. fariboles, idle talk
Baroth	——		Broth
Gaah	——		Gay
Dum	——		Dumb
Dufch	——		To dafh
Hebifch	——		To abafh
Hua	——		He, *mafc. gend.*
Haras	——		To harafs

W 3

Chittah

Hebrew.	Derivatives.	English.
Chittah	——	Wheat
Mesurah	——	A measure
Sahap	——	To sweep
Charath	——	To write
Saar	——	A shower
Aanna	——	To annoy
Phæer	——	Fair
Pheret	——	A part, or portion
Phærek	——	Fierce
Eretz	——	Earth; Sax. hertha
Sad	——	Side
Spor	——	A sparrow
Kinneh	——	A cane
Kera	——	To cry
Shekel	——	Skill
Rechus	——	Riches
Kre	——	A crow
Pasa	——	To pass
Halal	——	A hole
Catat	——	To cut
Ragez	——	To rage
Ragal	——	To rail, or detract
Maguur	Magwyr	Habitation
Madhevi	Myddfai	Distempers
Doroth	Toreth	Generations, encrease
Dal	Tal	Tall and high
Havah	Y su	Was, or has been
Mahalac	Malc	A pathway, or a balk
Hilo	Heulo	Shining. *Apollo, Sol.*
Tor	{ Toar *Irish.* { Terfyn *Br.*	A boundary, or limit
Siu	Syw	Resplendent
Achalas	Achles	Defence, Achilles
Machaneh	{ Machno { *and* { Mechain	Places of defence of old in the co. of Montgomery. Penmachno
Chorau	Crau	Holes

Choresh

Hebrew.	Derivatives.		English.
Choresh	Cors	Br.	A place full of small wood or reeds
Nodah	Nodi		To make known, or note
Jadha	{ Addef { 'Oída	Greek	To know
Hathorath	Athrawiaeth	Br.	Discipline
Jch	Eich		Your, or your own
Jared	I wared		Descended
Cha	Chwi		You
Jain	Gwîn		Wine
Toledouth	Tylwyth		Generations
Lus	Llyfu		To go away, or avoid
Caolath	Colled		A lofs
Hounil	Ynnill		Gain
Jefter	Yftyr		Confideration
Jadadh	Gwahodd		To invite
Cafodoth	Cyfoeth		Honours, or wealth
Cis	Cift		A cheft
Bar	{ Far { Bara	Lat. Br.	Bread corn
Shevah	——		Seven
Dakar	——		A dagger
Hinnek	——		To hang
Shelet	——		A fhield
Hever	——		Over, or above
Shibbar	——		To fhiver, or quake
Jiled	——		*A child
Chœbel	——		A cable
Parak	——		To break
Gannaf	——		A knave, or a thief
Coll	——		All
Hannah	——		To annoy, or hurt
Eth	{ Etos { Ætas	Greek Lat.	A year, or age
San	Cœna		A fupper
Nabal	Nebulo		A churl

Mot

* JILD Teka, thou art my fon. Pfalm ii. 7.

Hebrew.	*Derivatives.*		*English.*
Mot	Motus	*Lat.*	Motion
Bath	Batos	*Greek*	A thorn
Eden	Edone		Pleafure
Kolah	Kleiō		To praife
Sas	Ses		A moth
Phac	Phake		Lentil
Skopac	Scopō		To fpeculate
Jounec	Jevange	*Br.*	A fuckling
Hamohad	Ammod		Covenant
Parad	Pared		A partition
Keren	Corn		A horn
Kefel	Cefail		The armpit
Me-Ab	Mâb		Son, or from a father
Luung	Llyngcu		To fwallow
Temutha	Difetha		Deftruction
Ceremluach	Cromlech		A facrificing ftone
Hamule	Aml		Plenty, or ftore
Mah ?	Mae ?		What ? where ? how ?
Magal	Maglu		To betray
Makel	Magl		A ftaff
Meria	Mêr		Fat, or marrow
Mout	Mudo		To remove
Meth	Methu		To die, or fail
Mar	Maer		A lord
Marad	Brad		* Rebellion
Nafe	Nef		Joyful
Taphilu	Taflu		To caft
Hanes	Hanes		To fignify
Nevath	Neuadd		Habitation
Jiffal	Ifel *or* Ifelu		To throw down
Naoaph	Nwyf		Luft
Nadu	Nadu		They moan
Sethar	Sathru		To throw under feet
Heber	Aber		A ford, or paffage
Nucchu	Nychu		Being fmitten
Nuu	Nhwy		They, or thofe
Naodhad	Nodded		To efcape

Gadah

* *MEREDUTH* is the fame with *Merad,* a Britifh name.

Hebrew.	Derivatives.		English.
Gadah	Gadaw	*Br.*	To pafs by
Niued	Niweid		To fpoil
Goloth	Golwyth		Burnt offerings
Mohal	Moel		Top of a hill
Galas	Glwys		Pleafant
Hafem	Afen		A rib, or bone
Garevath	Gwarth		Shame
Taphug	Diffyg		Want, or defect
Phoreth	Ffrwyth		Fruit, or effect
Pach	Bach		A crooked ftick
Pinnouth	Pennaeth		Chief, or uppermoft
Phinnah	Ffynnu		To profper
Path	Peth		A part or portion
Philegefh	Ffiloges		A concubine
Caton	Cwttyn		Short and little
Cir	Caer		A walled town
Reith	Rhîth		Appearance
Tireneh	Trîn		To feed and look after
Ragah	Rhwygo		To tear, rag
Rafah	Râs *and* Rhâd		Grace, or good will
Semen	Saim		Fat, or oil
Saraph	Sarph		A ferpent
Sac	Sâch		A *fack
Phuk	{ Ffûg { Fucus	*Lat.*	Difguife
Phærek	Ferocia		Fiercenefs
Pinnah	Pinna		Battlement
Pigger	Piger fuit		Lazy
Naca	Neco		To flay
Ad	Ad		Unto
Nut	Nuto		To nod
Darag	Trechō	*Greek*	To run to, or come at
Bala	Palai		Some time ago
Hannak	{ 'Agchō { Tagu	*Br.*	To ftrangle
Naar	Nearos	*Greek*	New or lately
Agab	'Agapaō		To love

Pacha

* It has this found in moft of the ancient tongues.

Hebrew.	*Derivatives.*		*English.*
Pacha	Pege	*Greek*	A fountain
Parafh	Phrafō		To declare, phrafe
Kol	Kalèō *G.* Galw *B.*		To call
Mafhal	Bafileuō	*Greek*	To reign
Shareka	Syrinx		A fyringe
Bekarim	Pecora	*Lat.*	Cattle
Ahel	Aula		A hall
Carpas	Carbafus		Fine linen, or lawn
Æfh	Æftes *La.* Tês *Br.*		Heat, or hot weather
Gibar	Guberno	*Lat.*	To govern
Parah	Vireo		To look green
Ki	Quia		Wherefore
Olam	Olim		Of old
Golem	Glomus		A clew of thread
Amam	Ymam		Mother, mamma
Coaphar	Gwobr		Reward
Cala	Caula	*Lat.*	A fheepfold
Sarch	Serch	*Br.*	Luftful
Goliath	Glwth		A bed
Pathehen	Puttain		A whore
Burgad	Bwrgais		A burgefs
Terag	Drwg		Bad, or evil
Dafgar	Dyfgl		A difh
Shiovang	Siongc		Honorable
Anas	Annos		To inftigate
Tam	Dim		Nothing
Pherch	Y ferch		A daughter
Tetuva	Edifar		Penitent
Leamor	Ar lafar		Saying
Cafas	Ceifio		To fearch
Cark	Carchar		To bind ; *Lat.* carcer
Kam	Cammu		To bend
Caffa	Cyff		A beam
Cevel	Ar gyfyl		Near
Dumga	Dammeg		A fimile
Tor *and* Sor	Tarw		A bull ; *Lat.* taurus
Turna	Teyrn		A prince, tyrant
Manos	Myddyn		A mountain

Malas

Hebrew.	Derivatives.		English.
Malas	Melys		Sweet
Palac	Plygu		To fold
Banc	Mainc		A bench
Malal	Malu		To grind
Marak	Marc		A note
Cadif	Gwadu		To tell a lie
Tohum	Eyfn		Depth
Colar	Coler		A neck band, collar
Corontha	Coron		A crown
Berek	Brêg		A breach
Bagad	Bagad		A great many
Arach	Arogli		To fmell
Nagafh	Yn agos		To approach
Ciliah	Ceilliau		Stones
Gevr	Cawr		A giant
Kec	Cêg		A mouth
Kun	Cwyno		To lament
Natfar	Dinyftr		Deftruction, or ruin
Pinnah	Pinagl		Pinnacle
Mahalal	Mawl *or* Moli		To praife
Hedel	Hoedl		Life
Halal	Haul		Sun
Gavel	Gafael		Tenure
Lafhadd	Glafaidd		Blueifh
Gerem	Grym, grymmus		Bony or ftrong
Mafac	Cym-myfcu		To mingle
Gana	Canu		To fing ; Lat. cano
Celimah	Calumnia	*Lat.*	Reproach
Netz	Nifus		Endeavor
Ptfel	Pfileō		To make bear
Shufhan	Soufon		Lilly
Shecan	Sceneō		To dwell in tabernacles
Kalal	Gwael	*Br.*	Vile
Taffi	Diffoddi		To extinguifh
Tfelem	Delw		An image
Hoberi	Obry		Men over againft
Aen-adon	Anudon		Difclaiming God, or perjury."

HERE

HERE are about fifty Englifh words, which, from their near refemblance to the Hebrew, both in found and fignification, muft have been borrowed from the latter in modern ages, or been preferved thro fucceffive generations from Heber to the prefent times. But they could not have been introduced into Englifh in modern ages, for many of them are found in the other branches of the Gothic, the German, Danifh and Swedifh ; and it can be proved that they exifted in the original Gothic or northern language. For example, our word *earth* is found in Hebrew, and in all the dialects of the Gothic. Hebrew, *crt* or *crtz* ; Welfh, *d'aira* ; Greek, *ēra* ; Latin, *terra* ; Gothic, *airthai* ; ancient German, *erth* or *herth* ; Saxon, *eartho* ; Low Dutch, *aerden* ; High Dutch, *erden* ; Swifs, *erden* ; Scotch, *airth* ; Norwegian or Norfe, *iorden* ; Danifh, *iorden* ; Swedifh, *iordenne* ; Irelandic, *iordu*. In the pronunciation of thefe words there is little difference, except fuch as is common to the feveral languages. The ancients afpirated their words more frequently than the moderns ; hence the old Germans pronounced the word with *h*, as appears by a paffage in Tacitus, De Mor. Germ. 40. " Nec quidquam notabile in fingulis, nifi quod in commune *Herthum*, id eft *terram*, matrem colunt."—The modern nations of the north generally write and pronounce *d* where we write *th* ; as *erden* ; and the *i* of the Norwegians anfwers to our *e* or *y*, fo that *iorden* is pronounced *yorden* ; and it is remarkable that many of the common Englifh people ftill pronounce *earth*, *yerth*.

THE Hebrew *turna* is found in the Britifh *teyrn*, fignifying a prince or ruler. This word is the root of the Greek *turannos*, the Latin *tyrannus*, the Britifh *dyrnas*, a kingdom or jurifdiction, which is ftill preferved in the modern Welfh *dcyrnas* ; and we fee the word in the name of the celebrated Britifh commander, *Vortighern*. Our word tyrant is derived from it, but it is always ufed in a bad fenfe.

IN the Hebrew *rechus* or *rekus*, we have the origin of the Englifh *rich*, *riches*, and the termination *rick* in bifhop-*rick*, and anciently, in king-*rick* ; the word originally denoting *landed property*, in which wealth was fuppofed to confift, and afterwards *jurifdiction*. From the fame word are derived the Anglo Saxon *ryc* ; the Franco Theotifc, *rihhi* ; the Cimbric, *rickie* ; the ancient Irifh or Gaedhlig, *riogda* ; the Low Dutch, *rijcke* ; the Frific, *rick* ; the German, *reich* ; the Swifs, *rijch* ; the Danifh, *rige* ; the Norwegian, *riga* ; the Swedifh, *ricke* ; the French, *riche*, and the Spanifh, *riccos*, a general name for nobility, or wealthy proprietors of land.

THE word *Caer* feems to have been a very ancient name for a city or town. We probably fee this word in a great number of Welfh names, *Carmarthen*, *Carnarvon*, *Carlifle*, &c. This word feems alfo to be the origin of *Cairo*, in Egypt ; *Carthage* or town of the horfe ;* the *cirthe* of the Numidians, and the *Caere* of the Etrufcan. " Inde Turnus Rutilique, diffifi rebus, ad florentes Etrufcorum opes Mezentiumque eorum regem, confugiunt ; qui *Caere*, opulento tum oppido imperitans—haud gravatim focia arma Rutulis junxit." —Liv. lib. 1. 2. Here we hear of the word before the foundation of Rome.

BUT the affinity between the Hebrew and Britifh is much more obvious, than that between the Hebrew and Englifh. There are about one hundred and eighty Britifh words in the foregoing table, which are clearly the fame as the Hebrew ; and there is no way to account for the fact, but by fuppofing them to be all derived from the fame primitive tongue.

THE refemblance between the Welfh, Latin and Englifh may be obferved in the following.

Welfh.	*Latin.*	*Englifh.*
Y'fgol	fchola	fchool
Y'fpelio	fpolio	fpoil
		Y'fprid

---

* THE armorial enfign of Carthage was a *horfe*.

Welſh.	*Latin.*	*Engliſh.*
Y'ſprid	ſpiritus	ſpirit
Y'ſtad	ſtatus	ſtate
Y'ſtod	ſtadium	*furlong.*

THE old Britons however might have borrowed theſe words from the Romans, during their government of the Iſland; as the Engliſh did many of theirs at a later period.

THE ſame remark will not apply to the following:

Welſh.	*Latin.*	*Iriſh.*	*Engliſh.*
Guin	vinum	fin	wine
Guyl	vigiliæ	feil	watch
Gur	vir	fearr	man
Guynt	ventus		wind
Gual	vallum		wall
Goſper	veſper	feaſkor	*Armoric.* gueſpor
Guedhar			*Eng.* weather
Guerth	virtus		worth
Guylht			wild

IN this table, we ſee the different nations begin the ſame word with a different conſonant. The ancient Latin *v* was pronounced as our *w*; vinum, *winum*; hence the Engliſh *wine*. So in the following:

Latin.	*Engliſh.*	*Latin.*	*Engliſh.*
Via	way	Veſpa	waſp
Venio, ventum	went	Volvo	wallow
Vellus	wool	Volo	will.*

THAT

---

* IT is remarkable that the Germans pronounce this word *wollen*, and *woll*, like the Roman *volo*, pronounced *wolo*. Many old people in America retain this pronunciation to this day; I *woll*, or *wool*, for *will*.

THE Roman pronunciation of *v* is ſtill preſerved in England and America; *veal*, weal; *veſſel*, weſſel; and *w* is often changed into *v* or *f*; *wine*, vine, or even fine.

THE Romans often pronounced *t* where we uſe *d*; as *trabo*, draw.

THAT the Welſh ſhould pronounce *gu*, where we pronounce *w*, may ſeem ſtrange ; yet ſuch is the faꝗt, and an anatomiſt will readily aſſign the reaſon. The French, in the ſame manner, uſe *g* where we write and pronounce *w*.

Engliſh.	*French.*
War	guerre
Warrant	garrant
Ward	gard
Wiſe	guiſe
Wile	guile
Wage	gage
Wicket	guicket
William	Guillaum
Wales	Gales, Gaul, Gallia.*

A NUMBER at leaſt of the words in the foregoing ta-bles, muſt have exiſted in the ſeveral languages from the earlieſt times ; and therefore muſt have been derived from the ſame ſtock.

IN the following words, we trace the common origin of the Greek and Gothic languages.

Greek.	*Engliſh.*	*Greek.*	*Engliſh.*
Kardia ⎰ Kear ⎱	heart	Pur	fire
		Platus	plate
Kiō	hie	Xeras	ſear
Kaleō	hail, call	Mignuō	mingle
Koilas	hollow	Eileō	heal, hail
Kēdas	heed, care	Kairō	cheer
Kerdas	hire	Gonu	knee
Keras	horn, herald	Knix	gnat
Axine	ax	Zēteō	ſeek
Ophrun	frown		

THE

* IN teaching Engliſh to a Spaniard, I found that in attempting to pronounce words beginning with *w*, he invariably began with the ſound of *gu* ; *well*, he would pronounce *guell*.

THE reader will find no difficulty in believing thefe words to be from the fame root, when he is told that the Greeks and the northern nations of Europe pronounced with a ftrong guttural afpirate; and that *k* among the Greeks was often a mere afpirate, like *h*. Thus the Romans often pronounced *c*; for which reafon that letter is often omitted, and *h* fubftituted in modern Englifh.   *Curro* and *hurry* are the fame word; and fo are *cornu* and *horn*; *Carolus* and *Harold*.

Greek.	*Latin.*	*Englifh.*
'Oinos	vinum	wine
Damaō	domo	tame
Zeugos	jugum	yoke
Upper	fuper,	upper
Gnoō	nofco	know.
Ginofko	cognofco	

SOME old people ftill pronounce the *k* in *know*.

IN the following, the Welfh differ from the Greek in the prepofitives or initial mutes; but they are clearly from the fame root.

Greek.	*Welfh.*	*Englifh.*
Stoma	faman	'mouth
Ikanos	digon	fufficient
Arkē	d'erke	beginning
Airō	d'uyrey	arife
Platun	lhydon	broad
Papyrun	bruyn	rufhes
Trekō	rhedeg	run
Petalon	dalen	loaf.*

IN the following words, the Welfh are nearer the Greek than the Latin; yet all came from one ftock.

Greek.

---

* THIS word is found in moft of the branches of the Gothic.

Greek.	Welsh.	Latin.	English.
Helios	heil	fol	fun
Hypnos	hyn, heppian	fomnus	fleep
Halon	halen	fal	falt
Hamolos	hamal	fimilis	like
Bounos	ban	mons	mountain
Kleas	klad. *Cornifh*, klas	laus	praife
Pepto	pobo	coquo	cook
Hyle	hely	fylva	woods
Krios	kor	aries	ram.

THESE words are inconteftibly the fame, with mere dialectical variations. All are branches of the fame ftock, yet neither can claim the honor of being that ftock.

BUT the moft curious etymological analyfis ever exhibited perhaps in any language, is that found in Gebelin's works. Take the following fpecimens.

IN the primitive language (of Europe) the monofyllable *tar*, *ter*, *tor* or *tro*, for it appeared under thefe forms, fignified *force*. It was compofed of *t* and *ar* or *d'ar*, *roughnefs*, *rapidity*. Hence *tar* expreffed the idea of force, with the collateral ideas of violence, rigor, grandeur, &c. From *tar* are derived, *taurus*, a bull ; *torrent*, *target*, *trunk*, *truncare*, to cut off ; *terror*, *trepan*, *tare*, *detriment*, *trancher*, to cut ; *retrench* ; *tardus*, *tardy*, *retard*, *tergum*, becaufe things heavy, that require force, were carried upon the back ; *intrigue*, for it implies difficulties ; *trop*, too much, *troop*, *ter*, *trois*, which originally fignified a multitude ; for many favage nations have names only for the three firft numbers ; *tierce*, *tres*, very ; *treffes*, a braid or plait of hair in three divifions ; *triangle*, *tribunal*, *tribe*, *attribute*, *contribute*, &c. *trident*, *trillion*, *trio*, *trinity*, *entre*, *enter*, taken from a relation of three objects, *one* between *two*, makes a *third* ; hence *internal*, *external*, *travers*, acrofs ; *tradition*, paffing from one to another ; *traffic*, *trahir*, to draw ; *traitor*, *trepidation*, *intrepid*. From *tra*, between, and *es*, it

X   is, is, came the Celtic, *treh*, a narrow pass, a *strait*, *strict*, Fr. *etroit*, *astringent*, *detroit*, strait ; *distress*, *strength*. The compounds are numerous. *Intrinsic, entrails, introduce, extraneous, extravagant, transcendent, transfer, transform, transgress, transact, translate, transmit, transmigrate, transmutation*, &c.

PALTROON is from *pollex*, a *thumb*, and *truncare*, to cut off ; for cowards use to cut their thumbs to avoid service.

T E M.

TEM signified river, water. Hence *tempero* in Latin signified to *plunge into water*. We to this day say to *temper iron or steel*. *To temper*, is to moderate. From this root come *temperance*, *temperature*, and a numerous catalogue of other words. The river Thames derives its name from the same root.

V A, *to go, radical*.

FROM *vn*, the Celtic root, we find a multitude of branches in Greek, Latin, English and French. It is an *onomatope*, a word borrowed from the sound of our feet in walking. Its derivatives are, *wade, evade, evasion, invade, invasion, venio*, Lat. and *venir*, Fr. to come ; *venia* and *venial*,* *adventure, avenue, convenio, convenience, convention, covenant* perhaps, *contravene, intervene, invent, prevent, province*,† *advance, via, way, voyage, convoy, convey, obviate, vex, invective, vein*, a way for the blood ; *voiture*, Fr. for a load to carry ; *evitare*, Lat. to shun ; *inevitable*.

To these derivatives, I will just add a comparative view of the verbs *have* and *be* in several languages.

English.

* ALLUSIVE to the ancient custom of pardoning by giving permission to depart.

† FRONTIER settlement ; so called, because the Romans *passed thro* this territory, in going to or from Rome.

HAVE.

English.	Latin.	French.	Germ.	Spanish.	Portuguese.
I have	hábeo	ai*	habe	he	éy
Thou haſt	habes	as	haſt	as	has
He has	habet	a	hat	as	ha
We have	habemus	avons	haben	avemos	hamos, ave-mos
You have	habetis	ávez	habet	aveis	éy's, evéy's
They have	habent	ont	haben	an	ham

The Subſtantive Verb B E.

English.	Latin.	French.	Germ.	Spanish.	Portugnese.
I am, be	ſum	ſuis	bin	eſtoy & ſoy	ſou, eſtou
Thou art, beeſt	es	es	biſt	eſtas, eres	es; eſtas
He is, be	eſt	éſt	eſt-es	eſtá, es	he, eſta
We are, be	ſumus	ſommes	ſind	eſtamos, ſo-mos	ſomos, eſta-mos
You are, be	eſtis	êtes	ſeyd	eſtais, ſois	ſoys, eſtoys
They are, be	ſunt	ſont	ſind	eſtan, ſon	ſam, eſtam

It is indiſputable that *have*, in all theſe languages, is
from the ſame root. But there ſeem to have been
anciently two ſubſtantive verbs, or perhaps three, from
which modern nations have borrowed; viz, the Greek
ειναι or ειμι, or the Latin *eſſe*, from which moſt of the
foregoing are derived; the Teutonic *beon*, whence the
Germans have their *bin* and *biſt*, and the Engliſh their
be and *beeſt*; and an old Gothic or Teutonic word, *weorthan*, whence the Danes have derived their *værer*, and
the Engliſh and Germans their *were* and *werden*. In the
old Engliſh phraſe, " woe *worth* the day," we ſee the
ſame verb.

Having ſtated my reaſons and authorities for believing all the European languages deſcended from one
parent tongue, I will here ſubjoin the Lord's Prayer in
ſeveral

---

* The French and Spaniſh rarely or never aſpirate an *h*; and in this
word they have omitted it moſtly in writing.

several languages of Celtic and Gothic origin. The affinity between all the branches of the Gothic is very visible; the affinity likewise between all the branches of the Celtic is very obvious, except the ancient Irish. The Cantabrian and Lapland tongues have little resemblance to either of the stocks or their branches.

Very

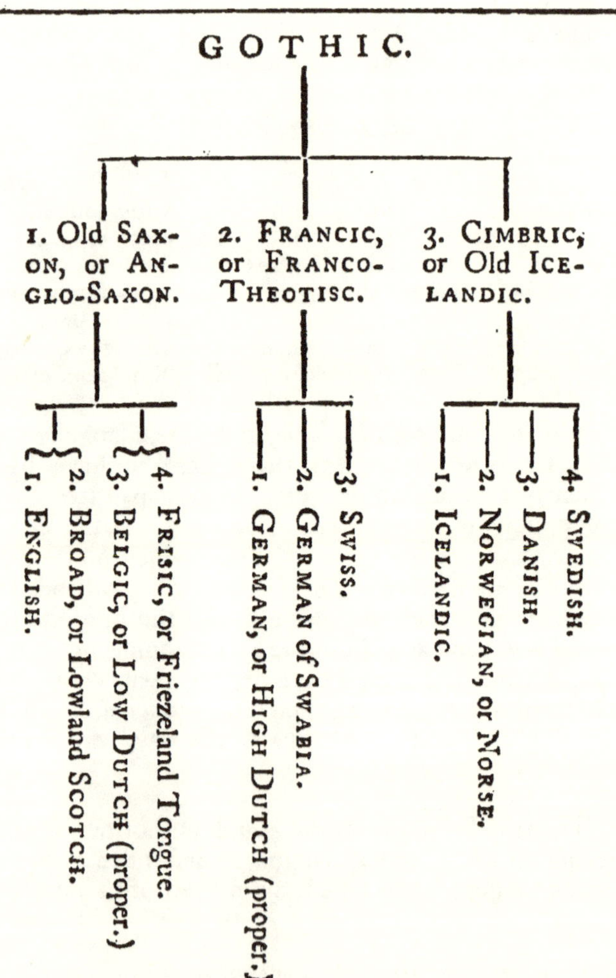

Very little affinity is discoverable between the original Gothic and Celtic or their derivatives; yet this is not a proof that they were *ab origine* distinct languages; for the words in this prayer are few, and it has been proved that there are many words common to both those ancient tongues.

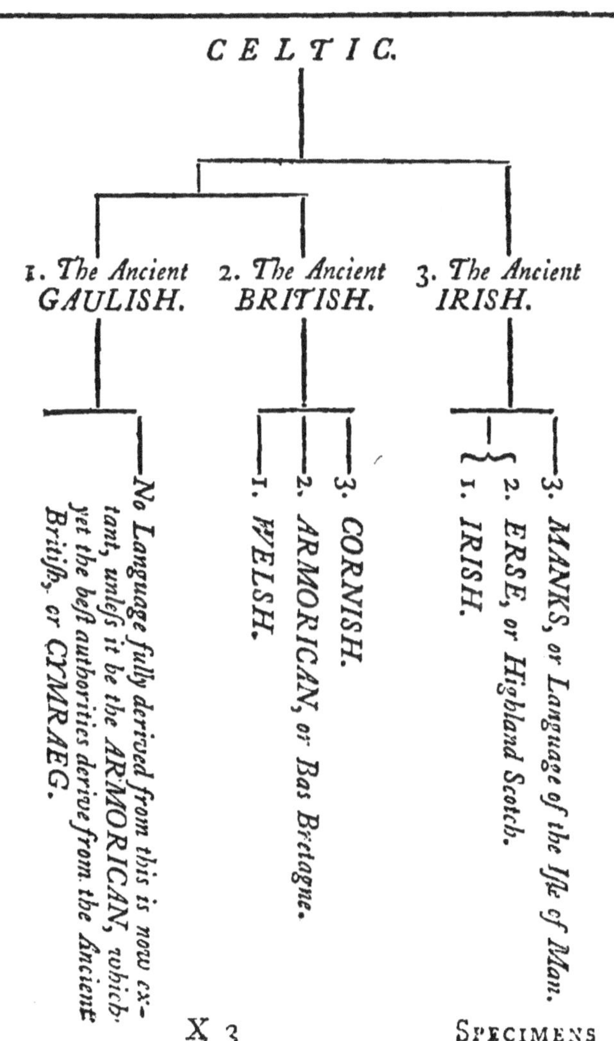

X 3

SPECIMENS *of the* GOTHIC LANGUAGES.

The ancient *Gothic* of *Ulphilas.*

ATTA unfar thu in himmam. 1. Veihnai namo thein.
2. Quimai thiudinaffus theins. 3. Vairthai vilja theins,
fue in himina, jah ana airthai. 4. Hlaif unfarana thana
finteinan gif uns himmadaga. 5. Jah aflet uns thatei
fculans fijaima fua fue jah veis afletam thaim fkulam
unfaraim. 6. Jah ni bringais uns in fraiftubnjai. 7. Ak
laufei uns af thamma ubilin. Amen.

[From Chamberlayn's *Oratio Dominica in diverfas omnium fere Gentium Linguas verfa, &c.*]

The ANCIENT LANGUAGES *derived from the* GOTHIC.

I.	II.	III.
Anglo Saxon.	*Franco Theotifc.*	*Cimbric,* or old *Icelandic.*

I.	II.	III.
UREN Fader, thic arth in heofnas. 1. Sie gehalgud thin noma. 2. To cymeth thin ryc. 3. Sie thin willa fue is in heofnas, and in eortho. 4. Uren hlaf oferwiftlic fel us to daeg. 5. And forgefe us fcylda urna, fue we forgefan fcyldgum urum. 6. And no inlead ufig in cuftnung. 7. Ah gefrig uiich from Ife. Amen.	FATER unfer thu thar bift in himile. 1. Si geheilagot thin namo. 2. Queme thin rihhi. 3. Si thin willo, fo her in himile ift o fi her in erdu. 4. Unfar brot tagalihhaz gib uns huitu. 5. Inti furlaz uns nufara fculdi fo uuir furlazames unfaron fculdigon. 6. Inti ni gileiteft unfih in coftunga. 7. Uzouh arlofi unfi fon ubile. Amen.	FADER uor, fom eft i himlum. 1. Halgad warde thit nama. 2. Tilkomme thitt rikie. 3. Skie thin vilie, fo fom i himmalam, fo och po iordanne. 4. Wort dachlicha brodh gif os i dagh. 5. Ogh forlat os uora fkuldar, fo fom ogh vi forlate them os fkildighe are. 6. Ogh inled os ikkie i fretalfam. 7. Utan frels os ifra ondo. Amen.
[From Chamberlayn, p. 56.]	[From Chamberlayn, p. 61.]	[From Chamberlayn, p. 54.]

SPECIMENS

SPECIMENS *of the* CELTIC LANGUAGES.

☞ I AM not able to produce any specimen of the *Celtic*, at least any version of the Lord's Prayer, which can be opposed in point of antiquity to the *Gothic* specimen from *Ulphilas*, who flourished A. D. 365.—As the *Celts* were settled in these countries long before the *Goths*, and were exposed to various revolutions before their arrival, their language has, as might be expected, undergone greater and earlier changes than the *Gothic*; so that no specimen of the old original *Celtic* is I believe, now to be found.

The ANCIENT LANGUAGES *derived from the* CELTIC.

I.	II.	III.
Anc. Gaulish.	Cambrian, *or* Ancient British.	Ancient Irish, *or* Gaedhlig.
OF this language I cannot find any specimen which can be depended on.	*EYEN Taad rhuvn wyt yn y neofoedodd.* 1. *Santeiddier yr henvu tau.* 2. *Devedy dyrnas dau.* 3. *Guneler dy wollys ar ryddayar megis ag yn y nefi.* 4. *Eyn bara beunyddvul dyro inni heddivu.* 5. *Ammaddcu ynny eyn deledion, megis ag i maddevu in deledvvir ninaw.* 6. *Agna thowys ni in brofedigaeth.* 7. *Namyn gwared ni rhug drug. Amen.* [From Chamberl. p. 47.]	*OUR Narme ata ar neamb.* 1. *Beanich a tainin.* 2. *Go diga de riogda.* 3. *Go denta du hoill air talm in marte ar neamb.* 4. *Tabair deim aniugh ar naran limbali.* 5. *Augus mai duin ar fiach amhail maamhia ar fiacha.* 6. *Naleig fin amaribh.* 7. *Ach faarfa fin o olch. Amen.* [From Dr. Anth. Raymond's Introduction to the History of Ireland, p. 2, 3, &c.][*]

SPECIMENS

[*] THE above specimen of the ancient Irish is judged to be a thousand years old. See O Conner's Dissertation on the History of Ireland. Dublin, 1766, 8vo.

SPECIMENS *of the* GOTHIC LANGUAGES.

I, MODERN LANGUAGES *derived from the*
OLD SAXON.

I.

English.

OUR Father, which art in heaven. 1. Hallowed be thy name. 2. Thy kingdom come. 3. Thy will be done in earth as it is in heaven. 4. Give us this day, our daily bread. 5. And forgive us our debts as we forgive our debtors. 6. And lead us not into temptation. 7. But deliver us from evil. Amen.

[From the English Testament.]

II.

Broad Scotch.

URE Fader, whilk art in hevin. 1. Hallouit be thy naim. 2. Thy kingdum cum. 3. Thy wull be dun in airth, as it is in hevin. 4. Gie ufs this day ure daily breid. 5. And forgive ufs ure debts, afs we forgien ure debtouris. 6. And leid ufs na' into temptation. 7. Bot deliver ufs frae evil. Amen.

[From a Scotch Gentleman.]

III.

Low Dutch, or *Belgic.*

ONSE Vader, die daer zijt in de hemelen. 1. U-wen naem worde ghehey-light. 2. U rijcke kome. 3. Uwen wille ghefchiede op der aerden, gelijck in den hemel. 4. Onfe da-gelijck broodt gheeft ons heden. 5. Ende vergheeft ons onfe fchulden, ghelijck wy oock onfe fchuldenaren vergeven. 6. Ende en leyt ons niet in Verfoeckinge. 7. Maer verloft ons van-den boofen. Amen.

[From the New Teft. in Dutch.]

IV.

Frific, or *Friczeland Tongue.*

Ws Haita duu derftu bifte yne hymil. 1. Dyn name wird heiligt. 2. Dyn rick tokomme.   3. Dyn wille moet fchoen, opt yrt-yck as yne hymile. 4. Ws dielix bræ jov ws jwed. 5. In verjou ws, ws fchyl-den, as vejac ws fchyldnirs. 6. In lied ws naft in ver-fieking.   7. Din fry ws vin it quæd.   Amen.

[From Chamberlayn, p. 68.]

SPECIMENS

SPECIMENS *of the* CELTIC LANGUAGES.

II. MODERN LANGUAGES *derived from the* ANCIENT BRITISH, *or* CYMRAEG.

I.

Welſh, *or* Cymraeg.

EIN Tâd, yr hwn wyt yn y nefoedd.
1. *Sanƈtieddier dy Enw.* 2. *Deved dy
deyrnas.* 3. *Bydaed dy ewyllys ar y
ddaiar megis y mae yn y nefoedd.* 4. *Dy-
ro i ni heddyw.ein bara beunyddiol.* 5.
*A madde ini ein dyledion fel y maddeuwn
ni i'n dyledwyr.* 6. *Ag nag arwain ni
i brofedigaeth.* 7. *Eithr gwared ni
rhag drwg. Amen.*

[Communicated by a Gentleman of Jeſus
College, Oxon.]

II.

Armoric, *or Language of*
Britanny *in* France.

*HON Tad, pehudij ſou en
eſaou.* 1. *Da hanou bezet
ſanƈtifiet.* 2. *Devet aor-
nomp da rouantelaez.* 3.
*Da eol bezet graet en douar,
eual maz con en euf.* 4. *Ró
dimp hyziou hon bara pem-
deziec.* 5. *Pardon dimp
hon pechedou, eual ma par-
donomp da nep pegant ezomp
offanczet.* 6. *Ha na dilaes
quet a hanomp en temptation.*
7. *Hoguen hon diliur diouz
drouc. Amen.*

[From Chamberlayn, p. 51.]

III.

Corniſh.

NY Taz, ez yn neau. 1.
Bonegas yw tha hanaw. 2.
Tha gwlakoth doaz. 3. *Tha
bonagath bogweez en nore
pocoragen neau.* 4. *Roe
thenyen dythma gon dyth bara givians.* 5. *Ny gan
rabn weary cara ry givi-
ans mens.* 6. *O cabin le-
dia ny nara idn tentation.*
7. *Buz dilver ny thart doeg.
Amen.*

[From Chamberlayn, p. 50.]

SPECIMENS

SPECIMENS *of the* GOTHIC LANGUAGES.
II. MODERN LANGUAGES *derived from the* AN-
CIENT GERMAN, *or* FRANCIC, &c.

I.

II.

High Dutch, (proper.)

High Dutch of the *Suevian Dialect.*

UNSER Vater in dem Himmel. 1. Dein name werde geheiliget. 2. Dein reich komme. 3. Dein wille gefchehe auf erden, wie im himmel. 4. Unfer taeglich brodt gib uns heute. 5. Und vergib uns unfere fchulden, wie wir unfern fchuldigern verge-ben. 6. Und fuehre uns nicht in Verfuchung. 7. Sondern erloefe uns von dem vbel. Amen.

[From the common German New Teftament, printed at London. 12mo.]

FATTER aufar dear du bifcht em hemmal. 1. Gehoyleget wearde dain nam. 2. Zuakomme dain reych. 3. Dain will gfchea uff earda as em hemmal. 4. Aufar deglich braud gib as huyt. 5. Und fergiab as aufre fchulda, wia wiar fergeaba aufarn fchuldigearn. 6. Und fuar as net ind ferfuaching. 7. Sondern erlais as fom ibal. Amen.

[From Chamberlayn's Oratio Do-minica, p. 64.]

III.

The *Swifs Language.*

VATTER unfer, der du bift in himlen. 1. Geheyligt werd dyn nam. 2. Rukumm uns dijn rijch. 3. Dyn will gefchahe, wie im him-mel, alfo auch uff erden. 4. Gib uns hut unfer taglich brot. 5. Und vergib uns unfere fchulden, wie anch wir vergaben unfern fchulderen. 6. Und fuhr uns nicht in verfuchnyfs. 7. Sunder erlos uns von dem bofen. Amen.

[From Chamberlayn, p. 65.]

SPECIMENS

SPECIMENS *of the* CELTIC LANGUAGES.

III. MODERN LANGUAGES *derived from the* ANCIENT IRISH.

I.

Irish, *or* Gaidhlig.

*AR nathair atá ar ne-
amh. 1. Naomhthar hainm.
2. Tigeadh do rioghachd. 3.
Deuntar do thoil ar an ttal-
ámh, mar do nithear ar neamh. 4. Ar narùn laéath-
amhail tabhair dhúinn a niu.
5. Agus maith dhúinn ar
bhfiacha, mar mhaithmid-
ne dar bhféitheamhnuibh
fein. 6. Agus na léig sinn
a ccathughadh. 7. Achd
fáor sinn o olc. Amen.*

[From Bishop Bedel's Irish Bible.
Lond. 1690. 8vo.]

II.

Erse, *or* Gaidhlig Alban-naich.

*AR n' Athair ata air ne-
amh. 1. Gu naomhaichear t
tinm. 2. Tigeadh do riog-
hachd. 3. Deanthar do thoil
air an tá amh mar a nithear
air neamh. 4. Tabhair
dhuinn an diu ar n aran
laitheill. 5. Agus maith
dhuinn ar fiacha amhuill mar
mhaithmid d'ar luehd-fiach-
aibh.* 6. Agus na léig am
buaireadh sinn 7. Ach faor
sinn o olc. Amen.*

* Feichneinibh.

[From the New Testament in the
Erse Language.]

III.

Manks, *or Language of the* Isle of Man.

*AYR ain, t'ayns niau. 1. Casherick dy
row dt'ennym. 2. Dy jig dty reeriaught.
3. Dt'aigney dy row jeant er y thalao, myr
te ayns niau. 4. Cur d oin nyn arran
jiu as gaghlaa. 5. As leih dooin nyn logh-
tyn, nyr ta shin leih dauesyn tu jannoo logh-
tyn nyn' oc. 6. As ny leeid shin ayns mio-
lagh. 7. Agh livrey shin veih olk. Amen.*

[From the Liturgy in Manks, printed at London,
1765. 8vo.]

SPECIMENS

SPECIMENS *of the* GOTHIC LANGUAGES.

III. MODERN LANGUAGES, *derived from the* AN-
CIENT SCANDINAVIAN, *or* ICELANDIC, *called*
(*by some writers*) CIMBRIC, *or* CIMBRO GOTHIC.

I.

Icelandic.

FADER vor thu fom ert a himnum. 1. Helgeft thitt nafn. 2. Tilkome thitt ri-ike. 3. Verde thinn vilie, fo a jordu, fem a himne. 4. Gieff thu ofs i dag vort daglegt braud. 5. Og fier-gieff ofs vorar fkulder, fo fem vier fierergiefum vo-rum fkuldinautum. 6. Og inleid ofs ecke i freiftne. 7. Heldr frelfa thu ofs fra illu. Amen.

[From Chamberlayn, p. 70.]

II.

Norwegian, or *Norfe.*

WOR Fader du fom eft y himmelen. 1. Gehailiget woare dit nafn. 2. Tilkom-ma os riga dit. 3. Din wil-ia gefkia paa iorden, fom handt er udi himmelen. 4. Giff ofs y tag wort dagliga brouta. 5. Och forlaet os wort fkioldt, fom wy for-lata wora fkioldon. 6. Och lad os icke homma yoi friftelfe. 7. Man frals oa fra onet. Amen.

[From Chamberlayn, p. 71.]

III.

Danifh.

VOR Fader i himmelen. 1. Helligt vorde dit navn. 2. Tilkomme dit rige. 3. Vorde din villie, paa iorden fom i himmelen. 4. Giff ofs i dag vort daglige bred. 5. Oc forlad ofs vor fkyld, fom wi forlade vore fkyl-dener. 6. Oc leede ofs icke i friftelfe. 7. Men frels os fra ont. Amen.

[From Chamberlayn, p. 70.]

IV.

Swedifh.

FADER war fom aft i himmelen. 3. Helgat war-de titt nampn. 2. Till komme titt ricke. 3. Skei tin willie faa paa lordenne, fom i himmelen. 4. Wart dagliga brod|giff ofs i dagh. 5. Och forlat os wara fkul-der fa fom ock wi forlaten them ofs fkildege aro. 6. Och inleed ofs icke i fref-telfe. 7. Ut an frals ofs i fra ondo. Amen.

[From Chamberlayn, p. 70.]

SPECIMENS

SPECIMENS *of the* FINN *and* LAPLAND TONGUES.

<table>
<tr><td>

I.

The Finn Language.

*IS A meidan joca olet tai-
waſſa.* 1. *Pyhitetty olcon ſi-
num nimes.* 2. *Lahes tulcon
ſinum waldacundas.* 3. *Ol-
con ſinun tahtos niin maaſe
cuin taiwaſa.* 4. *Anna meile
tanapaiwana meidan joca
paiwainen leipam.* 5. *Sa an-
na meille meidan ſyndim an-
dexi nuncuin mekin andex
annam meidan welwottiſtem.*
6. *Ja ala johdata meita kiu-
ſauxen.* 7. *Mutta paaſta
meita pahaſta'. Amen.*

[From Chamberlayn, p. 82.]

</td><td>

II.

The Lapland Tongue.

*ATKA mijam juco lee al-
menſiſne.* 1. *Ailis ziaddai
tu nam.* 2. *Zweigubatta tu
ryki.* 3. *Ziaddus tu willio.
naukuchte almeſne nau ei ed-
na mannal.* 4. *Wadde mi-
jai udni mijan fært pæfwen
laibehm.* 5. *Jah andagaſto-
ite mi jemijan ſuddoid, nau-
kuchte mije andagaſloitebt ku-
di mije welgogas lien.* 6.
Jah ſiſſalaidi mijabni. 7.
*Æle tocko kæckzællebma pa-
haſt. Amen.*

[From Chamberlayn, p. 83.]

</td></tr>
</table>

A SPECIMEN *of the* CANTABRIAN *or* BISCAYAN LANGUAGE, *ſtill preſerved in* SPAIN.

The Baſque.

GURE Aita kerutéan caréna. 1.
Erabilbedi ſainduqui çure jcena. 2. *E-
thorbedi çure ereſſuma.* 3. *Eguinbedi
çure borondatea çerú an becala turre'an
ore.* 4. *Emandieçagucu egun gure eg-
unorozco oguia.* 5. *Eta barkhadietcat-
gutçu gure çorrac gucere gure coidunei
barkhatcendiotçaguten becala.* 6. *Eta
ezgaitçatcu utc tentacionétan erortcerat.*
7. *Aitcitic beguiragaitcatçu gaitc guci-
etaric. Halabiz.*

[From Chamberlayn, p. 44.]

HERE

HERE we find many of the fame words, with fmall variations, in all the languages of Teutonic origin. It is however obfervable that the Englifh have foftened fome words, by omitting the gutturals. Thus *gehalgud* in the Anglo-Saxon; *geheiliget* in the German; *gheheylight* in the Belgic; and *geheyligt* in the Swifs, are foftened into *hallowed* in Englifh; *taeglich* and *dagelijcht* become *daily*. Similar omiffions run thro the language. Thus *nagel, hagel* have become in Englifh *nail* and *hail*. The *gh* in *might, night* are ftill pronounced by the Scotch; but the Englifh fay *mite, nite*.*

THE affinity between the ancient Britifh, the modern Welfh, and the Armoric, is very obvious; but in the latter, we find a few Latin or French words—*pardon, peichdon; deliur*, which we fhould naturally expect from the vicinity of Britanny to the French language.

I HAVE been at the pains to examin a great number of radical words in the Danifh, and find the moft of them, amounting to more than four hundred, very little different from the Englifh. Where the Englifh write *w*, the Danes write *v*; *vind* for *wind*. Where the Englifh write *c* hard, the Danes, with more judgement, write *k*; *klover, kan, kommer*, for *cleave, can, come*. Where the Englifh write *wh*, the Danes, with propriety, write *hv*, *v* having the found of *w*; as *hvad, hvi hval*; *what, why, whole*.

THE words, common to the Danifh and Englifh, are moftly monofyllables.

As a corroborating proof of the Eaftern origin of the Goths, authors produce the refemblance between their religious opinions and the notions of the Magi. The Scandinavian mythology is preferved in the EDDA, written by Snorro Sturlefon, an Icelander, a learned judge and firft magiftrate in the 12th century.

In

* " HUNC fonum (gh) Anglos in vocibus *light, might*, &c. olim protuliffe fentio; at nunc dierum, quamvis fcripturam retineant, fonum tamen fere penitus omittunt. Boreales tamen, prefertim Scoti, fere adhuc retinent feu potius ipfius loco fonum *b* fubftituunt."——Wallis.

In this there are many notions which feem to bear a great analogy to the doctrines revealed in the Bible.

It is reprefented in the Edda, that before creation, " all was one vaft abyfs ;" an idea not unlike the fcripture account of what we ufually call *chaos*.—" That *Surtur*, the black, fhall come at the end of the world, vanquifh the gods and give up the univerfe to the flames"—a crude notion of the conflagration.—" That *Ymer* the firft man or great giant, flept and fell into a fweat, and from the pit of his left arm were born male and female ;" this has fome refemblance to the fcripture account of the creation of the woman—" That the fons of *Bore* flew the giant *Ymer*, and all the giants of the froft were drowned, except Bengelmer, who was faved in his bark ;" in which notion we obferve fome tradition of the deluge.

The opinion that the world will be deftroyed by fire feems to have been univerfal among the Gothic nations. The defcriptions of that cataftrophe refemble thofe of the Stoics and of the ancient Magi and Zoro-after, from whom the idea was probably taken. Thefe defcriptions all agree with the fcripture reprefentation of that event in the material circumftances.

The doctrine of a future ftate, or of a renovation of the world, was part of the Gothic fyftem. It was taught by Zamolxis, the celebrated Druid of the Getæ and Scythians.——Herod. Lib. 4. § 95.

In this fame Edda, we alfo find the origin of fome cuftoms ftill remaining among the defcendants of the northern nations. The drinking of bumpers is not an invention of modern bacchanals ; it is mentioned, fable 25, of the Edda, where it is faid Thor challenged one to a drinking match.

The cuftom of hanging up bufhes on Chriftmas eve is derived probably from the fuperftitious veneration paid to the Miffeltoe by the Scandinavians.

Indeed

INDEED the feftival of Chriftmas was grafted upon an ancient pagan feaft, celebrated at the winter folftice, in honour of the fun and to render the new year propitious. It anfwered to the Roman Saturnalia, and was probably of as high an origin. The night on which it was obferved was called *Mother Night*, as that which produced the reft; and the feaft itfelf was called by the Goths *Iuul.*—See Mallet's North. Antiq. vol. 1. p. 130. Hence the old word *yeul* or *yule* for Chriftmas; a word that is ftill ufed, or at leaft has been ufed till within a century in Scotland and the north of England. "Yule," fays that learned antiquary, Cowel, "in the north parts of England, is ufed by the country people as the name of the feaft of our Lord's nativity, ufually termed *Chriftmas.* The fports ufed at Chriftmas, called Chriftmas Gamboles, they ftile *Yule Games. Yule* is the proper Scotch word for Chriftmas."——Cowel's Law Dictionary, tit. Yule. The Parliament paffed an act for difcharging the *Yule Vacance,* which was repealed after the union by ftat. George I. cap. 8. The feaft was celebrated from time immemorial among the Romans and Goths; the Chriftians changed its object and name; tho fuch is the force of cuftom, that the Gothic name exifted in Scotland till lately, and perhaps ftill exifts among the lower ranks of people.

FROM the northern nations alfo we have the names of the days of the week; or at leaft of fome of them. The ancient Goths devoted particular days to particular deities.

TUESDAY was *Tyrfdag*, from *Tyr* the God of bravery. It is in the Danifh, *Tyrfdag*, and in the Swedifh *Tifdag*.

WEDNESDAY is *Woden'fdag*, from *Woden*, a celebrated warrior deified. In Icelandic, it is *Wonfdag*; in Swedifh, *Odinfdag*; in Dutch, *Woenfdag*; in Anglo Saxon, *Wodenfdag*.

THURSDAY

THURSDAY is from *Thor*, god of the air. In Danish it is *Thorsdag*; in Swedish *Torsdag*.

FRIDAY is from *Frea*, the earth and goddess of love, answering to the Venus of the Greeks. In some languages it is called *Freytag*.——See Mallet's North. Antiquities.

I will just add, it is a weighty argument in favor of the truth of the Scripture history, and of the opinion here advanced of the common origin of languages, that in all the ancient and modern European alphabets, the letters are of a similar figure and power, and arranged nearly in the same order.* The true Greek letters were only the Cadmean letters reversed : This reversal took place early in Greece, when the ancient Phenician and Hebrew order of writing from right to left, was changed for the modern order, which is from left to right. The Hebrew or Phenician Alphabet was clearly the parent of the Greek, Roman and Gothic.

[B, page 52.]

THE reader will please to accept the following specimen, which will convey an idea of the whole.

Punic.	*Irish.*	*English.*
YTH al o nim ua lonuth ! ficorathiffi me com fyth chim lach chunyth mum ys tyal myethi barii im fchi.	IATH all ·o nimh uath lonnaithe ! focruidhfe me com fith chimi lach chuinigh ! muini iftoil miocht beiridh iar mo fcith.	OMNIPOTENT, much dreaded Deity of this country ! affwage my troubled mind ! Thou, the support of feeble captives ! being now exhaufted with fatigue, of thy free will, guide me to my children.

In

---

* THE Runic excepted. The Runic letters were sixteen in number, and introduced very early into the North ; but they went nto difufe about the tenth or eleventh century.

In this example the affinity between the Punic and Irish is striking; and the same runs thro the whole speech.

That Ireland received colonies from Spain or Carthage is probable from other circumstances. The Irish historians say their anceftors received letters from the Phenicians; and the Irish language was called *Bearni Feni*, the Phenician tongue. *Cadiz* in Spain was first settled by Phenicians; and *cadas* in Irish signifies *friendship*.

The Irish seems to be a compound of *Celtic* and *Punic*; and if Ireland was peopled originally from Carthage, and received colonies from thence, the event must have been subsequent to the first Punic war; for this was the period when the Carthaginians adopted the Roman letters, and there is no inscription in Ireland in the Phenician character.

The Hebrew was the root of the Phenician and the Punic. The Maltese is evidently a branch of the Punic; for it approaches nearer to the Hebrew and Chaldaic, than to the Arabic. For this affertion we have the authority of *M. Maius*, profeffor of the Greek and oriental languages in the Ludovician univerfity of Gieffen, who had his accounts from *Ribier*, a miffionary Jefuit and native of Malta. This fact will account for the correfpondence between the Irish and the Maltese, in feveral particulars. In Maltese, *Alla* fignifies *God*; in Irish, *All* is *mighty*. *Baol* in Maltese, and *Bel* or *Bal* in Irish, fignify *Chief Deity* or *Sun*. In Maltese, *ordu* is *end* or *fummit*; in Irish, *ard*, *arda*, are *hill, high*. Thefe words are probably from the fame root as the Latin *arduus*, and the Englifh *hard*, implying labor. *Bandla* in Maltese, is *a cord*; in Irish, *bann* is fufpenfion. In Maltese, *gala* is the fail of a fhip; and in Irish, *gal* is a gale of wind. Thefe Maltese words are taken from a Punica Maltese Dictionary, annexed to a treatife, Della lingua Punica prefentamente ufitate da Maltefe, by G. Pietro Francifco Agius de Solandas.

There

THERE is also a correspondence between the Irish and Punic, in the variation of their nouns, as may be observed in the following example.

Punic.	*Irish.*
Nom. A dar, the house	an dae, the house, &c.
Gen. Mit a dar, of the house	mend na dae
Dat. La dar, with or to the house	la dae
Acc. A dar, the house	an dae
Voc. Ya dar, O house	a dae
Abl. Fa dar, with or by the house	fa dae

IN several particulars the Irish bears a close affinity to the Hebrew and Greek. It was the custom with the Hebrews, and it still remains with them, to face the east in the act of devotion. From this practice it proceeded, that the same word which signified *right hand*, signified also *south* ; the same with *left hand* and *north* ; *before* and *east* ; *behind* and *west*. This is the case also in the Irish language.

Hebrew.	*Irish.*
Jamin,* right hand, south	deas, the same
Smol, left hand, north	thuaidh, the same
Achor, behind, west	tar, the same
Cedem, before, east	oir and oithear, the same, or rising sun. Latin, *oriens.*

THAT the Greeks had an intercourse with the islands of Britain and Ireland, or sent colonies thither, is not impossible ; and Dr. Todd, not many years ago, discovered, at Colchester, in Essex, an altar dedicated to the Tyrian Hercules, with an inscription in Greek capitals,

ΗΡΑΚΛΗΣ ΤΥΡΕΟ ΔΕΙΟ ΔΟΚΑ ΑΡΧΙΕΡΙΑ.

THERE is a place in Ireland called *Airchil*. And it is a remarkable fact, that some fragments of old Irish laws,

* *BENJAMIN* is *son of the right hand.*

Y 2

laws, which, for a long time, puzzled the antiquaries of the nation, are found to be written in a very ancient language, and in the manner which the Greeks called *Bouſtrophedon* ; that is, from right to left, and from left to right, in the manner that oxen plow.   This was ſuppoſed to be an improvement on the Hebrew and Phenician order of writing all the lines from right to left, which Cadmus introduced into Greece.   This manner of writing in Greece was prior to Homer, and if the Iriſh copied from the Greeks, which is not impoſſible, the fact would prove a very early ſettlement of Ireland by Greek colonies or their deſcendants.   See Leland's Hiſt. of Ireland, Prelim. Diſ.

ALL theſe circumſtances corroborate the opinion that the Celts came originally from the eaſt, and formed ſettlements on the ſhores of the Mediterranean and Atlantic.   The affinity between the Phenician, the Punic, the Malteſe, the Iriſh and the Britiſh languages, difcoverable in a great number of words, makes it probable, that after colonies were ſettled at Carthage and at Cadiz, ſome commercial intercourſe was carried on between them and the nations at the head of the Mediterranean, and that an emigration from Spain might people Ireland before any ſettlements had been made there by the Gauls or Britons.   It is however more probable that the Punic words in the Iriſh language might have been introduced into that iſland by ſubſequent colonization.   At any rate, from the Hebrew, Chaldaic, or Phenician, or the common root of theſe languages, proceeded the Punic, the Malteſe, the Iberian or Spaniſh, the Gauliſh, the Britiſh, and the Iriſh. The order I have mentioned is obvious and natural ; and hiſtory furniſhes us with ſome facts to ſtrengthen the ſuppoſition.

[C, page 58.]

BISHOP Hickes, in his Saxon Grammar, which is a vaſt treaſure of valuable learning, has preſerved a ſpecimen

men of the language and of the opinions of the English respecting it, in an extract from a manuscript of one Ranulphus Higdenus, *de Incolarum linguis*, translated by John Trevisa in 1385, and the ninth of Richard II. Trevisa's stile bears some affinity to that of Chaucer, with whom he was cotemporary.

"As it is knowne how meny maner peple beeth in this land: There beeth also so many dyvers longages and tongues. Nathless, Walschemen and Scotts, that hath nought medled with other nations, holdeth wel nyh his firste langage and speeche: But yif the Scottes that were sometime considerat and woned with the Picts draw somewhat after hir 1 speeche: But yif the Flemynges that woneth in the weste side of Wales haveth left her strange speeche and speketh Sexon like now. Also Englishmen, they had from the begynnynge thre maner speeche, northerne, sowtherne, and middel speeche in the middle of the lande, as they come of the maner peple of Germania. Nathless by comyxtion and mellynge 2; first with Danes and afterwards with Normans, in meny the contray langage is apayred 3 and som useth strong wlafferynge, 4 chiterynge, 4 hartynge 4 and gartynge, 4 grisbayting; 4 this apayryng 5 of the burthe of the tunge is because of tweie thinges: oon is for children in scole, agenst the usage and maner of all other nations, beeth compelled for to leve hire owne langage, and for to consture hir lessons and here 6 thinges in Frenche and so they haveth sethe 7 Normans came firste into England. Also gentilmen children beeth taught to speke Frenche from the tyme that they beeth rokked in hire cradle and conneth 8 speke and play with a childes brache and uplandissche men 9 will likne hymself to gentilmen and fondeth 10 with the greet besynesse for to speke Frenche for

to

---

1. THEIR. 2 Mixture; an old French word, now written *melange.* 3 corrupted. 4 These words represent barbarity and roughness in speaking. 5 Corruption of the native tongue. 6 hear 7 since 8 know. The Germans preserve the verb *kænnen*, to be able. The pronouns *hir* and *hire* for *their*, still remain in the German *ibr.* 9 Country-people, so called from their living on the mountains or high lands; hence *outlandish.* 10 attempt

Y 3

to be told of. [Trevifa, the tranflator remarks here—
" This maner was moche ufed to, for firft deth,11 and
is fithe 12 fum del 13 changed. For John Cornwaile,
a maifter of grammer, changed the lore 14 in grammer
fcole and conftruction of Frenche into Englifhe. And
Richard Pencriche lerned the manere techynge of him
as other men, of Penriche. So that now the ycre of
our Lorde a thoufand thre hundred and four fcore and
fyve and of the fecond king Richard after the conqueft,
nyne ; and alle the grammar fcoles of England children lerneth Frenche and conftrueth and lerneth an
Englifhe and haveth thereby advantage in oon fide,
and difadvantage in another fide. Here 15 advantage is
that they lerneth hir grammer in laffe tyme, than children were wonned to doo. Difadvantage is, that now
children of grammer fcole conneth na more Frenche
than can hir *lift heele*,16 and that is harme for hem an
they fchulle 17 paffe the fee and travaille in ftrange
londes and in many other places. Alfo gentilmen haveth now moche left for to teche here children Frenche."]
Ranulphus.—Hit feemeth a great wonder how Englifhe
men and her 18 own longage and tongue is fo dyverfe
of fown in this oon ilande, and the longage of Norman-
die is comlynge 19 of another lande and hath oon maner
foun among all men that fpeketh hit arigt in England.
[Trevifa's remark—" Neverthelefs there is as many
diverfe maner Frenche in the reeme 20 of France, as is
dyvers maner Englifhe in the reeme of England."]
R. Alfo of the aforefaid Saxon tonge that is deled 21
athree and is abide fcarceliche 22 with few uplandifhe
men, is great wonder. For men of the eft with men
of the weft is as it were under the fame partie of hevene
accordeth more in fownynge of fpeeche than men of
the north with men of the fouth. Therefore it is that
Mercii,

---

tempt with eagernefs. 11 time. 12 *fithe* is the origin of *fince.*
13 *Del* fignifies a *part* or divifion ; it is from the verb *dæler* to divide, and
the root of the Englifh word *deal.* *Dæler* is preferved in the Danifh.
14 learning. 15 their. 16 In the original thefe words are obfcure.
17 This is from the verb *follen,* implying obligation, duty. 18 their.
19 foreign ; Lat. *advena.* 20 realm. 21 divided. 22 Scarcely.
23 hardly.

Mercii, that beeth men of myddel England, as it were, parteners of the endes, underſtandeth bettrie the ſide longages than northerne and ſoutherne underſtandeth either other. All the longage of the Northumbers and ſpecialliche at York, is ſo ſcharp, ſlitting and ſrotynge and unſchape that the ſoutherne men may that longage unnethe23 underſtande. I trow that is becauſe that they beeth nyh to ſtrange men and nations, that ſpeketh ſtrongliche, and alſo becauſe the kinges of Englande woneth24 alway fer25 from that contray, for they beeth more turned to the ſouth contray, and yif they goeth to the northe contray, they goeth with great helpe and ſtrengthe. The cauſe why they beeth more in the ſouthe contray than in the northe, for it may be better corn londe, more peple, more noble cities, and more profitable havenes."*

ON this paſſage we may make the following remarks :

1. THAT the third perſon ſingular of the verb is invariably uſed with *plural* as well as ſingular nouns ; *they beeth, haveth.* Whereas in Chaucer and Mandeville the ſame perſon ends generally in *en* ; *they ſeyn* for *they ſay.*

THE ſame third perſon was uſed for the imperative, by the beſt Engliſh writers.

> " AND ſoft take me in your armes twey,
> For love of God, and *hearkeneth* what I ſey."
> Chaucer, Knight's Tale, 2783.

" AND at certyn houres, they ſeyn to certyn offices, *maketh pees* ;" that is, *make peace.*—Mandeville, p. 281.

2. THAT

---

23 hardly. 24 dwelleth. 25 far.

* I FIND in an " Eſſay on the language and verſification of Chaucer" prefixed to Bell's edition of his works, part of this extract copied from a Harlein manuſcript, ſaid to be more correct than the manuſcript from which Dr. Hickes copied it. But on comparing the extracts in both, I find none but verbal differences ; the ſenſe of both is the ſame.

2. THAT *yif* is ufed for *if*; a proof that *if* is a verb, a contraction of *gif* or *yif* (for they were ufed promifcuoufly) the imperative of *gifan*, to give.*

3. THAT the fubjunctive form of verbs was not ufed after *if*; *and yif they goeth to the northe contray.*

4. THAT there were three principal dialects in the Englifh; the *northern*, which was corrupted by the Scots and Picts, and from which the prefent Yorkfhire language is derived; the *middle*, which came from Germany and retained its primitive purity, and is the true parent of modern Englifh; and the *fouthern*, by which is meant, either the language of the fouthern parts which was corrupted by an intercourfe with foreigners; or what is more probable, the language fpoken in Devonfhire, and on the borders of Cornwal, which was mixed with the old Britifh, and is now almoft unintelligible.

5. THAT the conquefts of the Danes and Normans had corrupted the pure language of the Saxons.

6. THAT

* IN a charter of Edward III. dated 1348, *yeven* is ufed for *given.* *Yave* for *gave* is ufed by Chaucer.—Knight's Tale, line 2737. " And *yave* hem giftes after his degree." In a charter of Edward the Confeffor, *gif* is ufed in its Saxon purity. In the fame charter, *Biffop bis land*, is ufed for a genitive. The Scotch wrote *z* for *y*; *zit* for *yet*; *zeres* for *years.*—Douglafs. I do not find, at this period, the true Saxon genitive in ufe: The *Biffop bis land*, is deemed an error. This mode of fpeaking has however prevailed, till within a few years, and ftill has its advocates. But it is certain the Saxons had a proper termination for the genitive or poffeffive, which is preferved in the two firft declenfions of the German.

EXAMPLE of the declenfion of nouns among the Saxons.

A WORD.

	Sing.	Plu.
Nom.	Word	word
Gen.	Wordes	worda
Dat.	Worde	wordum
Acc.	Word	word
Voc.	Eala thu word	eala ge word
Abl.	Worde	wordum

Hickes Sax. Gram.

6. THAT this corruption proceeded principally from the teaching of French in schools.

7. THAT country people, (uplandish men) imitated the practice of the polite, and learnt French, as many do now, *to be told of*.

8. THAT Cornwail and others, in Trevisa's time, had begun to reform this practice.

9. THAT French had almost banished the native Saxon from the polite part of the nation, and that the *uplandish* or western people alone retained it uncorrupted.

10. THAT the kings of England resided principally in the southern parts of the kingdom, where the land was most fertile, best cultivated, most populous, and most advantageous for commerce.

[D, page 59.]

CHAUCER's particular patron was John of Gaunt, Duke of Lancaster. He married Philippa, the sister of Lady Swinford, who before her marriage and after her husband's death, was one of the Duke's family.

> " GRETE well *Chaucer* when you mete—
> Of dittees and of songes glade,
> The which he——made
> The londe fulfilled is over all."
> Gower.

GOWER is said to have been Chaucer's preceptor.

> " MY maister *Chaucer*—chiefe poet of Bretayne
> Whom all this lond should of right preferre,
> Sith of our language he was *the lode starre*,
> That made first to dystylle and rayne
> The gold dew dropys of speche and eloquence
> Into our tungue through his excellence."
> Lydgate.

CHAUCER's merit in improving the English language is celebrated by other poets of his time—Occleve, Douglas

Douglas and Dunbar.   They call him the *fioure of elo-quence*, the *fader in fcience*, and the *firfte fynder of our fayre langage*.

HE died in 1400.

IT muft however be remarked that Chaucer did not import foreign words, fo much as introduce them into books and give them currency in writing.   It muft further be obferved that when I fpeak of the incorporation of Latin words with the Englifh, I would not be underftood to mean that words were taken directly from the Roman tongue and anglicifed.   On the other hand, they moftly came thro the channel of the Norman or Provençal French ; and perhaps we may call them with propriety *French* words ; for they had loft much of their Roman form among the Gauls, Franks and Normans.

THE moft correct account I have feen of the ftate of the language in the 11th, 12th, 13th and 14th centuries, is in the firft volume of Bell's edition of Chaucer.

WE have the authority of Ingulphus, a hiftorian of credit, for alleging that the French began to be fafhionable in England, before the conqueft.   Edward the Confeffor refided many years in Normandy, and imbibed a predilection for the French manners and language.   On his acceffion to the throne of England, in 1043, he promoted many of his Norman favorites to the firft dignities in the kingdom ; under the influence of the king and his friends, the Englifh began to imitate the French fafhions.

BUT the conqueft in 1066, completed the change. The court of William confifted principally of foreigners who could fpeak no language but French.   Moft of the high offices and rich livings in the kingdom were filled with Normans, and the caftles which, by order of the conqueror, were built in different parts of the country,

were

were garrifoned by foreign foldiers, in whom the king
might moft fafely confide.* Public bufinefs was tranf-
acted in the French, and it became difhonorable or a
mark of low breeding, not to underftand that language.
Indeed under the firft reigns after the conqueft, it was
a difgrace to be called an *Englifhman*. In this depreffed
ftate of the Englifh, their language could not fail to be
neglected by the polite part of the nation.

BUT as the body of the nation did not underftand
French, there muft have been a conftant effort to root
it out and eftablifh the Englifh. The latter however
gained ground flowly during the two firft centuries of
the revolution. But in the reign of king John, Normandy, which had been united with England under the
Norman princes, was taken by the French, 1205, and
thus feparated from the Britifh dominions. In the
next reign (Henry III.) fome regulations were made
between the two kingdoms, by which the fubjects of either were rendered incapable of holding lands in the
other. Thefe events muft have reftrained, in fome
degree, the intercourfe between the two kingdoms, and
given the Englifh an opportunity to affume their own
native character and importance. In this reign the
Englifh began to value themfelves upon their birth, and
a knowlege of the Englifh language was a recommend-
ation, tho not a requifite, in a candidate for a benefice.

IT appears alfo by the paffage of Higden before quoted, that the practice of conftruing Latin into French,
in the fchools, had clofed before his time. This, with
the other caufes before affigned, contributed to root out
the French, and make the Englifh reputable ; and in
the reign of Edward III. produced the act, mentioned
in the text, in favor of the Englifh. This act did not
produce a total change of practice at once ; for we find
the proceedings in parliament were publifhed in French
for

* CUSTODES in caftellis ftrenuos viros ex Gallis collocavit, et opu-
lenta beneficia, pro quibus labores et pericula libenter tolera rent, diftri-
buit.——Orderic. Vital. lib. 4.

for sixty years after the pleas in courts were ordered to be in English, and the statutes continued in French about 120 years after the act, till the first of Richard III.

IT may be observed that the royal assent to bills was in some instances given in English during the reign of Henry VI. *Be it ordained as it is asked : Be it as it is axed.** But the royal assent is now declared in French.

[E, page 66 and 34.]

SIR William Temple's stile, tho easy and flowing, is too diffuse : Every page of his abounds with tautologies. Take the following specimen from the first page that presents itself on opening his third volume.

"UPON the survey of these dispositions in mankind and these conditions of government, it seems much more reasonable to pity than to envy the *fortunes* and *dignities* of princes or *great* ministers of *state* ; and to *lessen* and *excuse* their *venial* faults, or at least their misfortunes, rather than to *encrease* and *make them worse* by *ill colors* and *representations.*"——Of Pop. Dif.

FORTUNES and *dignities* might have been better expressed by *elevated rank* or *high stations* ; *great* is superfluous, and so are *lessen* and *make them worse,* and either *colors* or *representations* might have been omitted.

"THE first safety of *princes* and *states* lies in avoiding all *councils* or *designs* of innovation, in *ancient* and *established forms* and *laws,* especially those concerning liberty, property and religion (which are the possessions men will ever have most at heart ;) and thereby leaving the channel of *known* and *common* justice *clear* and *undisturbed.*" Several words might here be retrenched, and yet leave the author's meaning more precise and intelligible. This is the principal fault in Temple's stile.

"BUT

---

* THE word *ax* for *ask* is not a modern corruption. It was an ancient dialect, and not vulgar.

"BUT men, accuftomed to the free and vagrant life of hunters, are incapable of regular application to labor; and confider agriculture as a *fecondary* and *inferior* occupation."——Robertfon's Hift. Amer. book 4.

SUPPOSING *fecondary* and *inferior* not to be exactly fynonimous, in this fentence one would have anfwered the purpofe.

"*AGRICULTURE*, even when the ftrength of man is feconded by that of the animals *which he has fubjeEted to the yoke*, and his power augmented by *the ufe of the various inftruments with which* the difcovery of metals has furnifhed him, is ftill *a work* of great labor."—— The fame.

THIS fentence is very exceptionable. Is *agriculture, a work?* Can fo *definite* a term be applied to fuch a *general* idea? But what a group of ufelefs words follow! It was not fufficient to fay, *the ftrength of man feconded by that of animals*, but the kinds of animals muft be fpecified; viz. fuch as *he has fubjeEted to the yoke*; when every perfon knows that other animals are never ufed; and confequently the author's idea would have been fufficiently explicit without that fpecification. In the fubfequent claufe, the words, *his power augmented by the ufe of the various inftruments of metal*, would have been explicit; for the *difcovery of metals* muft have been implied. Such expletive words load the mind with a chain of particular ideas which are not effential to the difcourfe.

"——AND if any one of thefe prognoftics is deemed unfavorable, they inftantly abandon the purfuit of *thofe* meafures, *on which they are moft eagerly bent*."——The fame.

HERE is an awkward conclufion of the period, and afcribeable to a too nice regard for grammatical rules. *They are moft eagerly bent on*, would perhaps have been

better

better ; but a different conftruction would have been ftill lefs exceptionable. There is however a greater fault in the conftruction. By employing *thofe* and *moft eagerly*, the idea is, that favages, on the appearance of unfavorable omens, would abandon *thofe* meafures *only*, on which they are *moft eagerly* bent, and not others that they might be purfuing with lefs earneftnefs. Why could not the author have faid in plain Englifh— " they inftantly abandon any meafure they are purfu- ing."

THIS writer's ftile likewife abounds with fynonims ; as *ftrengthen* and *confirm, quicken* and *animate* ; when one term would fully exprefs the meaning. " Strong liquors *awake* a favage from his *torpid ftate—give a brifker motion to his fpirits,* and *enliven* him more thor- oughly than either dancing or gaming."——Book 4. What a needlefs repetition of the fame idea ! The au- thor is alfo very liberal in the ufe of *all*—" *all* the *tranfports* and *frenzy* of intoxication."—" War, which between extenfive kingdoms, is carried on with little an- imofity, is profecuted by fmall tribes, with *all* the ran- cor of a private quarrel."

IN fhort, the ftile of Dr. Robertfon, the great, the philofophic hiftorian, is too labored. The mind of the reader is kept conftantly engaged in attending to the ftructure of the periods ; it is fatigued with words and drawn from the chain of events.

THE ftile of Kaims, tho not eafy and flowing, is precife, and generally accurate. The ftile of Blair's Lectures is lefs correct than that of his Sermons ; but at the fame time, lefs formal in the ftructure of the pe- riods.

THESE remarks, the reader will obferve, refpect ftile only ; for the merit of Robertfon, as a judicious and faithful hiftorian ; and of Kaims and Blair, as critics, is above praife or cenfure.

IN

In no particular is the falfe tafte of the Englifh more obvious, than in the promifcuous encomiums they have beftowed on Gibbon, as a hiftorian. His work is not properly a " *Hiftory* of the Decline and Fall of the Roman Empire ;" but a "Poetico-Hiftorical Defcription of certain Perfons and Events, embellifhed with fuitable imagery and epifodes, defigned to fhow the author's talent in felecting words, as well as to delight the ears of his readers." In fhort, his hiftory fhould be entitled, " A Difplay of Words ;" except fome chapters which are excellent commentaries on the hiftory of the Roman Empire.

The general fault of this author is, he takes more pains to form his fentences, than to collect, arrange and exprefs the facts in an eafy and perfpicuous manner. In confequence of attending to ornament, he feems to forget that he is writing for the *information* of his reader, and when he ought to *inftruct* the *mind*, he is only *pleafing* the *ear*. Fully poffeffed of his fubject, he defcribes things and events in general terms or figurative language, which leave upon the mind a faint evanefcent impreffion of fome indeterminate idea ; fo that the reader, not obtaining a clear precife knowlege of the facts, finds it difficult to underftand, and impoffible to recollect, the author's meaning. Let a man read his volumes with the moft laborious attention, and he will find at the clofe that he can give very little account of the " Roman Empire ;" but he will remember perfectly that Gibbon is a moft elegant writer.

History is capable of very little embellifhment ; *tropes* and *figures* are the proper inftruments of *eloquence* and *declamation* ; *facts* only are the fubjects of *hiftory*. Reflections of the author are admitted ; but thefe fhould not be frequent ; for the reader claims a right to his own opinions. The juftnefs of the hiftorian's remarks may be called in queftion—facts only are inconteftible. The plain narative of the Scripture hiftorians, and of Herodotus, with their dialogues and digreffions, is as

far

far fuperior, confidered as pure hiftory, to the affected glaring brilliancy of ftile and manner, which runs thro Gibbon's writings, as truth is to fiction ; or the ver-million blufh of nature and innocence, to the artificial daubings of fafhion. The firft never fails to affect the heart—the laft can only dazzle the fenfes.

ANOTHER fault in Gibbon's manner of writing, is, the ufe of *epithets* or *titles* inftead of *names.* "The Cæfar, the conqueror of the eaft, the protector of the church, the country of the Cæfars, the fon of Leda," and innu-merable fimilar appellations are employed, inftead of the real names of the perfons and places ; and frequently at fuch a diftance from any mention of the name, that the reader is obliged to turn over a leaf and look for an explanation. Many of the epithets are new ; cuftom has not made us familiar with them ; they have never been fubftituted, by common confent, for the true names; the reader is therefore furprized with unexpected ap-pellations, and conftantly interrupted to find the perfons or things to which they belong.

I AM not about to write a lengthy criticifm on this author's hiftory ; a few paffages only will be felected as proofs of what I have advanced. "Decline and Fall of the Roman Empire," vol. 3. oct. chap. 17 : In explaining the motives of the Emperors for removing the feat of government from Rome to the Eaft, the author fays—"*Rome* was infenfibly confounded with the de-pendent kingdoms which had once acknowleged her fupremacy ; and *the country of the Cæfars* was viewed with cold indifference by a martial prince, born in the neighborhood of the Danube, educated in the courts and armies of Afia, and invefted with the *purple* by the legions of Britain." By the author's beginning one part of the fentence with *Rome,* and the other with *the country of the Cæfars,* the reader is led to think two dif-ferent places are intended, for he has not a fufpicion of a tautology ; or at leaft he fuppofes the author ufes *the country of the Cæfars* in a more extenfive fenfe than

Rome.

Rome. He therefore looks back and reads perhaps half a page with a clofer attention, and finds that the writer is fpeaking of the *feat of empire*, and therefore can mean the *city of Rome* only. After this trouble he is difpleafed that the author has employed *five words* to fwell and adorn his period. . This however is not the only difficulty in underftanding the author. Who is the *martial prince?* In the preceding fentence, Diocletian is mentioned, as withdrawing from Rome; and in the fentence following, Conftantine is faid to vifit Rome but feldom. The reader then is left to collect the author's meaning, by the circumftances of the birth, education and election of this martial prince. If he is poffeffed of thefe facts already, he may go on without much trouble.

THE author's affectation of ufing *the purple* for the crown or imperial dignity, is fo obvious by numberlefs repetitions of the word, as to be perfectly ridiculous.

" IN the choice of an advantageous fituation, he preferred the confines of Europe and Afia ; to curb, *with a powerful arm*, the barbarians who dwelt between the Danube and Tanais ; to watch, *with an eye of jealoufy*, the conduct of the Perfian monarch." Here the members of the fentence in Italics, are altogether fuperfluous ; the author wanted to inform his reader, that Dioclefian defigned to curb the barbarians and watch the Perfian monarch ; for which purpofe he chofe a favorable fituation ; but it was wholly immaterial to the fubject to relate in what manner or degree, the emperor meant to exert his arm or his jealoufy. Nay more, thefe are circumftances which are not reduceable to any certainty, and of which the writer and the reader can have no precife idea.

" WITH thefe views, Dioclefian had felected and embellifhed the *refidence of Nicomedia*."—Is Nicomedia a princefs, whofe refidence the emperor felected and embellifhed ? This is the moft obvious meaning of the fentence. But Nicomedia, we learn from other paffages, was a city, the *refidence* itfelf of the emperor.   Yet the author could not tell us this in a few plain words, without fpoiling the harmony of the phrafe ; he chofe therefore to leave it obfcure and ungrammatical.

"—But the memory of Dioclefian was juftly abhor-red by the *Protector of the Church* ; and *Conftantine* was not infenfible to the ambition of founding a city, which might perpetuate the glory of his own name." Who is the *protector of the church ?* By Conftantine's being mentioned immediately after, one would think he can-not be the perfon intended ; yet on examination, this is found to be the cafe.   But why this feparate appel-lation ? It feems the author meant by it to convey this idea ; That Dioclefian was a perfecutor of the church, therefore his memory was abhorred by Conftantine who was its protector ; the *caufe* of *Conftantine's abhorrence* is implied, and meant to be unfolded to the reader, in a fingle epithet.   Is this hiftory ? I muft have the lib-erty to think that fuch *terfenefs* of ftile, notwithftanding the authorities of Tacitus and Gibbon, is a grofs cor-ruption and a capital fault.

In defcription, our author often indulges a figurative poetical manner, highly improper.

" The figure of the imperial city (Conftantinople) may be reprefented under that of an unequal triangle. The obtufe point, which advances towards the eaft, and the fhores of Afia, meets and repels the waves of the Thracian Bofphorus." Here the author foars on poetic wings, and we behold the *obtufe point* of a *triangle*, *marching* eaftward, *attacking* and *repulfing* its *foes*, the *waves* of the Bofphorus ; in the next line, the author finks from the heights of Parnaffus, and creeps on the ' .in of *fimple narrative*—" The northern fide of the city .: bounded by the harbor."

" On thefe banks, tradition long preferved the mem-ory of the fylvan reign of Amycus, who defied the *fon*

of

of Leda to the combat of the Cestus." The author takes it for granted that his reader is acquainted with all the ancient fables of Greece and Rome. Such *allusions* to facts or fables make a wretched figure in *sober history.* [*]

THE author, after the manner of the poets, admits episodes into his descriptions, by way of variety and embellishment. He begins a description of Constantinople ; to do justice to the city, he must describe its situation ; he therefore gives an account of the Thracian Bosphorus, the Propontus and Hellespont, interspersed with ancient fables, and adorned with poetical imagery. When he arrives at the mouth of the Hellespont, his fancy leads him to the feat of ancient Troy, and he cannot pass it, without telling us from Homer, where the Grecian armies were encamped ; where the flanks of the army were guarded by Agamemnon's bravest chiefs ; where Achilles and his myrmidons occupied a promontory ; where Ajax pitched his tent ; and where his tomb was erected after his death. After indulging his fancy on this memorable field of heroic actions, he is *qualified* to describe Constantinople.

BUT it is needless to multiply examples ; for similar faults occur in almost every page. Most men, who have read this history, perceive a difficulty in understanding it ; yet few have attempted to find the reason ; and hardly a man has dared to censure the stile and manner.

To what cause then shall we ascribe the almost unanimous consent of the English and Americans, in lavishing praises upon Gibbon's history ? In some measure

ure

* So Gillies, in his Hist. of Greece, chap. III. talks about the death of the "*friend* of Achilles ;" but leaves the reader to discover the person—not having once mentioned the name of *Patroclus.* I would observe further that such appellations as the *son of Leda* are borrowed from the Greek ; but wholly improper in our language. The Greeks had a distinct ending of the name of the father to signify son or descendants ; as *Heraclidæ.* This form of the noun was known and had a definite meaning in Greece ; but in English the idiom is awkward and embarrassing.

ure doubtlefs to the greatnefs of the attempt, and the want of an Englifh hiftory which fhould unfold the feries of events which connects ancient and modern times. The man who fhould light a lamp, to illuminate the dark period of time from the 5th to the 15th century, would deferve immortal honors. The attempt is great; it is noble ; it is meritorious.   Gibbon appears to have been faithful, laborious, and perhaps impartial.   It is his ftile and manner only I am cenfuring ; for thefe are exceedingly faulty.   For proof of this I appeal to a fingle fact, which I have never heard contradicted ; that a man who would comprehend Gibbon, muft read with painful attention, and after all receive little improvement.

THE encomiums of his countrymen proceed from falfe tafte ; a tafte for fuperfluous ornament.   Men are difpofed to leffen the trouble of reading, and to fpare the labor of examining into the caufes and confequences of events.   They choofe to pleafe their eyes and ears, rather than feed the mind.   Hence the rage for *abridgements*, and a difplay of rhetorical embellifhments. Hence the eclat with which "Millot's Elements of General Hiftory," is received in the world.   This work is no more than an *Index to General Hiftory* ; or a recapitulation of the principal events.   It is calculated for two claffes of people ; for thofe who, having read hiftory in the original writers, want to revife their ftudies, without a repetition of their firft labors ; and for thofe who have but little time to employ in reading, and expect only a general and fuperficial knowlege of hiftory.*   But a man who would know the minute fprings of action ; the remote and collateral, as well as the direct caufes and confequences of events ; and the nice fhades of character which diftinguifh eminent men, with a view to draw rules from living examples ; fuch a man muft pafs by abridgements as trafh ; he muft have recourfe to the original writers, or to collections of authentic papers.   Indeed a collection
of

* READERS of the laft defcription are the moft numerous.

all the material official papers, arranged in the order of time, however dry and unentertaining to moſt readers, is really the *beſt*, and the *only authentic* hiſtory of a country. The philoſopher and ſtateſman, who wiſh to ſubſtitute fact for opinion, will generally ſuſpect human teſtimony; but repoſe full confidence in the evidence of papers, which have been the original inſtruments of public tranſactions, and recorded by public authority.

THESE ſtrictures are contrary to the opinions of moſt men, eſpecially as they regard the ſtile of the authors mentioned. Yet they are written with a full conviction of their being well founded. They proceed from an earneſt deſire of arreſting the progreſs of falſe taſte in writing, and of ſeeing my countrymen called back to nature and truth.

POSTSCRIPT.

THE foregoing remarks were written before I had ſeen the opinions of that judicious and elegant writer, Eaſt Apthorp, M. A. vicar of Croydon, on the ſame hiſtory. The following paſſage is too directly in point to be omitted. It is in his " Second Letter on the Study of Hiſtory."

" I WAS diſappointed in my expectations of inſtruction from this book (Gibbon's Hiſtory) when I diſcerned that the anthor had adopted that entertaining but ſuperficial manner of writing hiſtory, which was firſt introduced by the Abbe de Vertot, whoſe Hiſtory of the Revolutions in the Government of the Roman Republic, is one of thoſe agreeable and ſeducing models which never fail of producing a multitude of imitations. There is, in this way of writing, merit enough to recommend it to ſuch readers, and ſuch writers, as propoſe to themſelves no higher aim, than an elegant literary amuſement : It piques their curioſity, while it gratifies their indolence. The hiſtorian has the advantage, in this way, of paſſing over ſuch events and inſti-

tutions,

tutions as, however effential to the fcience of hiftory, are lefs adapted to fhine in the recital. By fuppreffing facts and violating chronology ; by felecting the moft pleafing incidents and placing them in a firiking point of view, by the coloring and drapery of ftile and com-pofition, the imagination is gratified with a gaudy fpectacle of triumphs and revolutions paffing in review before it ; while the rapid fucceffion of great events affords a tranfient delight, without leaving ufeful and lafting impreffions either on the memory or judge-ment ; or fixing thofe principles which ought to be the refult of hiftoric information.

" Nor is it the werft confequence of this flight and modifh way of compiling hiftory, that it affords to fu-pine and unreflecting readers a barren entertainment, to fill up the vacant hours of indolence and diffipation. The hiftorian who gives himfelf the privilege of muti-lating and felecting, and arranging at difcretion the rec-ords of paft ages, has full fcope to obtrude on his care-lefs readers any fyftem that fuits with his preconceived opinions or particular views in writing."—" The only legitimate ftudy of hiftory is in *original hiftorians.*"

The fame writer complains of a decline of literature in Great Britain, fixing the " fettlement that followed the revolution," as the era of true fcience and great-nefs. He remarks that the " aim of modern writers feems to be to furnifh their readers with fugitive amufe-ment, and that ancient literature is become rather the ornament of our libraries, than the accomplifhment of our minds ; being fupplanted by the modifh produc-tions which are daily read and forgotten."

[F, page 76.]

FOR proof of what I have advanced refpecting the found of *c* in Rome, I would obferve, that the genitive cafe of the firft declenfion in Latin anciently ended in *ai*, which was probably copied from the Greeks ; for

it

it is very evident the Latin *æ* in later writers, was the true reprefentative of the Greek *ai*. Thus *Moufai* in Greek was tranflated into the Roman tongue, *mufæ*. Now *c* before *ai* had the found of *k*; for where the Romans wrote *cæ* the Greeks wrote *kai*. Thus *mufi-ca, muficæ* in the firft declenfion muft have been pronounced *mufika, mufikai*, not *mufifee*, as we now pronounce the *æ*.

As a further proof, we may appeal to the laws of the Roman poetry, by which dipthongs were always long, having the found of two vowels combined.

But a decifive proof that *c* before the vowels *a*, *o*, *u* and the dipthongs, had the power of *k*, is that the Greeks always tranflated the *c* in *kappa*. They wrote Cæfar, *Kaifaros*, &c.

In confirmation of which I may add, that the Germans, among whom the word *Cæfar* became common to all emperors, and now fignifies *empèror*, fpell it *Kaifar*; and in the pronunciation they preferve the true Roman found of *Cæfar*.*

That the Roman *c* before *e* and *i* had the force of *ch* or *tfh*, is probable from the prefent practice of the Italians, who would be the moft likely to retain the pure Roman pronunciation. In modern Italian *ce, ci* are pronounced *che, chi*; as *dolcemente, Cicero*, pronounced *dolchemente, Chichero*.

In this opinion I am fupportrd by Dr. Middleton, who feems to have been thoroughly verfed in Roman literature. It may gratify the learned reader to fee his own words. *De Lat. Liter. pron. differ.*

" Ante vocales *a*, *o*, *v*† eundem olim fonum habuiffe ac hodie habet certiffimum eft : qualem autem ante
reliquas

---

*CZAR, the Ruffian appellation of Emperor, is a contraction of Cæfar. It is pronounced in the Ruffian, *char* or *tfhar*.

† In ancient infcriptions, and the early Roman authors, *c* was written

reliquas *e* et *i*, diphthongofque *æ*, *œ*, *ev* habuerit, hauḍ ita convenit.   Angli illam Gallique etiam, haud ab *s* diftinguunt, in Cœna, Cæfar, Ceres, cinis, &c. at in iifdem Itali, quod Romanos etiam feciffe olim exiftimo, eum huic literæ fonum tribuunt, quo nos *ch* efferimus, in vocibus noftris, *cheek*, *cherry*, *cheap*, &c. itaque pronunciant Cicero, uti nos Chichefter, chicheley, &c. ita tamen ac fi ante *c*, cum in medio vocis fequatur vocalem, litera t leviter admodum et fubobfcuré fonandạ interponeretur ; ut *Citcero*, Chitchefter, quam pronuntiandi rationem expreffiffe plane fculptor quidam videtur, qui in infcriptione veteri contra orthographiæ regulas, *t* ante *c* interpofuit in nomine *Vrbitcius*."

HE obferves however that Lipfius ridicules this opinion, and contends that *c* had in all cafes the force of *k*.   This the Doctor afcribes to his partiality for the pronunciation of his countrymen, the Germans, which, he fays, has often led him into errors.   For altho *k* before *a*, *o*, *u* ufed frequently to be written for *c*, as *Karcer* for *Carcer*, yet it never took the place of *c* before *e* and *i* ; we never find *Karker* for *Carcer*.

BUT that *c* had the found of our *ch*, is probable from another fact : In old infcriptions it is found that *c* was often ufed for *t* before *i* ; *condicio* for *conditio*, *palacium* for
palatium.

ten *u*, and pronounced *oo* or *w*. The following extracts from the laws of Romulus, &c. will give the reader an idea of the early orthography of the Latin tongue :—

1 DEOS patrios colunto : externas fuperftitiones aut fabulas ne admittento.

3 NOCTURNA facrificia peruigiliaque amouentor.

8 VXOR farreatione viro iuncta, in facra et bona eius venito—ius deuortendi ne efto.

13 SI pater filiom ter venumduit, filius a patre liber efto.

A law of Numa.

5 QUI terminum exarafit, ipfus et boues facrei funto.

A law of Tullius Hoftillius.

1 NATI trigemini, donicum puberes efunt, de publico aluntor.

palatium. Now *ch* in Englifh have a compound found, which begins with that of *t*, and hence *ti* and *ci* in Englifh have taken the found of *ch* or *fh*. It is evident therefore that *c* before *i* had a great affinity to *ti*; an affinity which is ftill preferved in the Italian language. Thefe circumftances give us reafon to believe that *ci* and *ti* in *condicio* and *palatium*, were both pronounced *chi, condichio, palachium.* This found of *ci* agrees perfectly well with the Saxon found in *cild*, pronounced *child*; *cele*, now pronounced *chill*, as I have remarked above; text, page 72.

[G, page 82.]

I SHALL not enter into a particular difcuffion of the queftion, whether *h* is a mark of *found* or not. By its convertibility with *k* and *c* in the ancient languages, we have reafon to conclude that it once had a guttural found, and the pronunciation of fome northern nations of Europe confirms the opinion. But it appears in modern Englifh to have no found by itfelf; it however affects, in fome degree, the found of the vowel to which it is prefixed, by previoufly opening the mouth wider than is neceffary to articulate the vowel. Thus in *hand* we hear no found but of *and*; yet in pronouncing *hand* we open the throat wider, and emit the breath with violence before we begin the found, which makes an obvious difference in pronouncing the words *and* and *hand*; and perhaps this diftinction is perceiveable as far as the words can be heard. The fame may be faid of *th* in *think*.

THE inftance of a man who loft a dinner by telling his fervant to *eat* it, when he meant to tell him to *heat* it, affords a ufeful leffon to thofe who are difpofed to treat the letter *h* with too much neglect.

[H, page 85.]

THAT *i* fhort is the fame found as *ee* we have the authority of one of the firft and beft Englifh grammarians.

ans.   "Hunc fonum, (ee) quoties correptus eft, Angli per *i* breve, exprimunt ; quum vero producitur, fcribunt ut plurimum per *ee*, non raro tamen per *ie* ; vel etiam per *ea* ; ut, *fit, fit, feel, fill, fiend, near*," &c.——Wallis, Gram. Sect. 2.

Ash confirms the opinion.   "*Ee* has one found, as in *fee, thee*, and coincides with the narrow *i*."—Gram. Diff. pref. to his Dic.

Kenrick's arrangement of the *long* and *fhort* vowels is exactly fimilar to mine.

Sheridan entertains a different opinion refpecting the fhort *i* and *e*.   He confiders them as diftinct vowels, incapable of prolongation.   Rhet. Gram. pref. to his Dict. page 16.   In this he differs from moft other writers upon the fubject, who have attended to the philofophical diftinctions of founds.   This appears to be an inaccuracy in his diftribution of the vowels ; altho it cannot affect the practice of fpeaking.

The found of the Roman *i*, it is agreed on all hands, was that of the Englifh *ee*.   It retains that found ftill in the Italian, French and Spanifh, which are immediately derived from the Latin.   It had its long and fhort founds in Latin ; as in *vidi, homini* ; the firft pronounced *veedee*, and the laft *homini*, as we now pronounce *i* in *fill*.   The French preferve the long found, and lay it down as a general rule, that *i* is pronounced like the Englifh *ee* : Yet in difcourfe they actually fhorten the found, and in *fentimens, reffentiment*, &c. pronounce *i* as we do in *civil*.   In the French *motif*, *i* is long like *ee* ; in this and all fimilar terminations, we fhorten the found, *motiv*.   Mr. Sheridan, in this particular, is evidently fingular and probably wrong.

That *e* in *let* is but the fhort abrupt found of *a* in *late*, is not fo clear ; but to me is evident.   There is little or no difference in the pofition of the organs with
which

which we pronounce both vowels. The Roman, Italian, Spanish and French *e* is confidered as the reprefentative of the Englifh *a* in *late*, *made* ; and yet in common difcourfe, it is fhortened into the found of *e* in *let*, *men :* Witnefs, *legere*, *avec*, *emmené*, *bueno*, *enten dido :* We obferve the fame in Englifh ; for *faid*, *any*, *many*, which are pronounced *fed*, *enny*, *menny*, exhibit the fame vowel or fhort *a* ; the *e* being the abrupt found of *a:* in *faid*. I muft therefore differ from Mr. Sheridan, and ftill believe that *e* in *let*, and *i* in *fit*, are capable of prolongation. Children, when, inftead of a comparifon, they would exprefs the fuperlative by an emphafis, fay *leetle* inftead of *little* ; which is a mere prolongation of *i* fhort.

MR. Sheridan, in my opinion, is guilty of an error of greater confequence, in marking the two qualities of found in *bard* and *bad* with the fame figure. He diftinguifhes the different qualities of found in *pool* and *full*, and in *not* and *naught* ; and why he fhould omit the diftinction of found in *bard* and *bad*, *afk* and *man*, is to me inconceiveable. The laft diftinction is as obvious as the others which he has marked ; and the defect of his fcheme muft lead a foreigner into miftakes. His fcheme is fingular ; Kenrick, Perry and Burn all make a diftinction in the time of pronouncing *a* in *afk* and *at* ; and even Scott, who copies Sheridan's pronunciation almoft implicitly, ftill makes the fame diftinction.

[I, page 87.]

" NON multum differt hic fonus (*w*) ab Anglorum *oo*, Gallorum *ou*, Germanorum *u* pingui, rapidiffime pronunciatis ; adeoque a quibufdam pro vocali fuit habita, *cum tamen revera confona fit*, quanquam ipfi vocali admodum fit affinis."——Wallis.

" LT is indeed on the celerity of utterance, that all the difference, in many cafes, between confonants and
vowels

vowels depends ; as in *w* and *y*, in Englifh ; which, being difcharged quickly, perform the office of confonants, in giving form only to the fucceeding vowel ; but when protracted or drawled out, acquire a tone and become the vocal *oo* and *ee*."——Kenrick, Rhet. Gram. p. 4.

PERRY has adopted this opinion and contends warmly that *w* is a confonant. If *w* is a vowel, fays he, then *wool*, *wolf*, will be pronounced *oo-ool*, *oo-olf*, or *ool*, *olf*. I am fenfible that in the beginning of words, *w* has not precifely the power of *oo* ; but it is not clear from this fact that it has the properties of a confonant. Place a vowel before *w*, as, *ow*, and there is no compreffion of the lips or other parts of the mouth, to obftruct the found, as there is produced by *b* or *m*, in *cb* and *cm*.

IN oppofition to the authorities mentioned, Sheridan ranks *w* among the vowels, and fuppofes it to form dipthongs with the other vowels, as in *well*, *will*, &c. It appears to me to be a letter rather of an ambiguous nature, of which we have others in the language.

[J, page 88.]

IT has been remarked that by old authors *y* was often ufed for *g* ; *yeve* for *give* ; *foryete* for *forget*.——— Chaucer, Knight's Tale, 1884.

I HAVE obferved that fome foreigners pronounce *year*, in the fame manner nearly as they do *ear* ; and *yeaft* is commonly pronounced *caft*. This pronunciation would cafily lead a man into the fuppofition that *y* is merely *ee* fhort. But the pronunciation is vicious.

. I OBSERVE alfo that Mr. Sheridan fays, "*ye* has the found of *e* long in *ye* ; of *a* long in *yea* ; of *e* long in *year*, *yean* ; and of *e* fhort in *yearn*, *yell*, &c. This confirms my opinion, and is a proof that he does not pronounce *y* at all.

IF

IF *y* has the found of *e* in *year*, then *e* has *no* found, or there are in the word, *two* founds of *e*, which no perfon will undertake to affert. The difpute however is eafily fettled. I have learnt by attending to the converfation of well bred Englifhmen, that they do not pronounce *y* at all in *year* and many other words. They fay *ear*, *e*, for *year*, *ye* ; and the found of *e*, they erroneoufly fuppofe to be that of *y*. In America, *y* has in thefe words, the confonant found it has in *young* ; and the Englifh pronunciation muft in this inftance be faulty.

[K, page 103.]

"NOW the harmony of profe arifes from the fame principle with that which conftitutes the harmony of verfe ; viz. numbers ; or fuch a difpofition of the words as throws them into juft metrical feet, but very different from thofe which conftitute any fpecies of verfe."
—Effay on the Power of Numbers, &c. page 4. Introd.

"A GOOD ftile is both *expreffive* and *harmonious.* The former depends on the happy choice of the words to convey our ideas ; the other on the happy choice of numbers in the difpofition of the words. The language of fome is expreffive, but unharmonious ; that is, the writer's words ftrongly convey his fentiments, but the order in which they are placed creates a found unpleafant to the ear. The ftile of others is harmonious but not expreffive ; where the periods are well turned and the numbers well adapted, but the fenfe obfcure. The former fatisfies the mind, but offends the ear ; the latter gratifies the ear, but difgufts the mind. A good ftile entertains and pleafes both," &c ——Ibm. 2d. Part, page 17.

THE author proceeds to illuftrate his doctrines by fhowing in what the harmony of profe confifts. He remarks that the words fhould in fome degree be an echo to the fenfe, in profe as well as verfe.

Hn

HE proceeds—" Every fentence may be conceived as divifible into diftinct and feparate claufes.; every claufe, where there is an apparent ceffation of the voice, fhould always end with a generous foot ; and all the preceding numbers be fo intermixt, that the fhort ones be duly qualified by the fucceeding long ones ; referving the beft and moft harmonious number for the cadence."

To fhow how much depends on the proper arrangement of words, he quotes the following inftance—" A divine, fpeaking of the Trinity, hath this expreffion—It is a myftery which we firmly believe the truth of, and humbly adore the depth of." Here the language is expreffive, but not harmonious ; not merely becaufe the claufes end with the particle *of*, but becaufe they abound with feeble numbers, *Pyrrhics* and *Trochees*. Let us change the difpofition of the feet—" It is a myftery, the truth of which we firmly believe, and the depths of which we humbly adore." The difference in the melody is very perceiveable. The force and mufic of the laft difpofition is increafed by the Iambics and Anapæfts.

THE moft forceable feet, and thofe beft adapted to fublime and ferious fubjects, are thofe which contain the moft long fyllables, or end in a long fyllable ; as - the Iambic, the Spondee, the Anapæft. The weak feet are thofe which have the moft fhort fyllables or end in a fhort fyllable ; as the Pyrrhic, the Trochee, the Tribrach.

THE want of proper meafures, or a mixture of weak and ftrong fyllables, is very remarkable in a paffage of the Declaration of Independence. " We muft therefore acquiefce in the neceffity, which denounces our feparation, and hold them, as we hold the reft of mankind, *enemies in war, in peace, friends*." The three laft fyllables form, if any thing, a Bacchic ; the firft fyllable, fhort, and the two others, long. But in a juft pronunciation, the foot is neceffarily broken by a paufe af-

ter

ter *peace.* This interruption, and the two long fyllables, render the clofe of the fentence extremely heavy.
The period is concife and expreffive, as it ftands ; but
the arrangement might be much more harmonious—
" Oŭr ēnĕmĭes ĭn wār ; ĭn pēace, oŭr friēnds." Here
the meafure and melody are perfect ; the period clofing
with three Iambics, preceded by a Pyrrhic.

[L, page 111.]

IN a Scotch Ballad, called *Edom o Gordon,* we find
the word *dreips* for *drops.*

> "—AND clear, clear was hir zellow hair
> Whereon the reid bluid *dreips.*"

But it was often fpelt *drap,* agreeable to the pronunciation.   See Edward. Rel. An. Poet. 53.

THE dialect in America is peculiar to the defcendants of the Scotch Irifh.

[M, page 111.]

MOUGHT is the paft time or participle of an old
Saxon verb *mowe* or *mowen, to be able.* It anfwered to
the *poffe* of the Romans, and the *pouvoir* of the French.
This verb occurs frequently in Chaucer.

> " BUT that fcience is fo fer us beforne,
> We *mowen* not, altho we had it fworne,
> It overtake, it flit away fo faft,
> It *wol* us maken beggers at the laft."
> Cant. Tales, l. 16, 148, Bell's edit.

" To *mowen* fuch a knight done live or die."——
Troil and Cref. 2. 1594.   That is, *to be able* to make
fuch a knight live or die.

> " AND *mought* I hope to winne thy love,
> Ne more his tonge could faye."
> Sir Cauline, an old Ballad, l. 163.

" THE

> " Thɛ thought they herd a woman wepe,
> But her they *mought* not fe."
>   Adam Bell, &c. part 3. l. 2. in Rel. of An. Poet.

> " So *mought* thou now in thefe refined lays
> Delight the dainty ears of higher powers.
> And fo *mought* they in their deep fcanning fkill,
> Allow and grace our Collen's flowing quill."
>   - Spenfer, Hobbynall.

THERE feem to have been among our Saxon anceftors two verbs of nearly or exactly the fame fignification, *may* and *might*; and *mowe* and *mought*. There
is fome reafon to think they were not fynonimous;
that *may* was ufed to exprefs *poffibility*, as *I may go next
week*; and *mowe* to exprefs *power*, as *they mowen go*, they
are able to go. But it is not certain that fuch a diftinction ever exifted. The Germans ufe *moegen*, in
the infinitive; *mag*, in the indic. pref. *mæge*, in the
fubj. pref. in the imperfect of the ind. *mochte*; and in
the imp. of the fubj. *mæchte*. The Englifh ufe *may*
and *might* folely in their writings; but *mought* is ftill
pronounced in fome parts of America.

HOLPE or *holp* was not obfolete when the Bible
was laft tranflated, in the reign of king James; for it
occurs in feveral places in that tranflation. It occurs
frequently in old authors.

> "UNKINDLY they flew him, that *holp* them oft at nede."
>   Skelton El. on Earl of Northum. l. 47.

IN Virginia it is pronounced *hope*. "Shall I hope
you, Sir."

BUT we muft look among the New England common people for ancient Englifh phrafes; for they have
been 160 years fequeftered in fome meafure from the
world, and their language has not fuffered material
changes from their firft fettlement to the prefent time.
Hence moft of the phrafes, ufed by Shakefpear, Congreve, and other writers who have defcribed Englifh
manners and recorded the language of all claffes of peo-
                                                        ple,

ple, are ftill heard in the common difcourfe of the New England yeomanry.

THE verb *be*, in the indicative, prefent tenfe, which Lowth obferves is almoft obfolete in England, is ftill ufed after the ancient manner, I *be*, we *be*, you *be*, they *be*. The old plural *houfen* is ftill ufed for houfes. The old verb *wol* for will, and pronounced *wool*, is not yet fallen into difufe. This was the verb principally ufed in Chaucer's time, and it now lives in the pureft branch of the Teutonic, the German.

FOR many years, I had fuppofed the word *dern* in the fenfe of *great* or *fevere*, was local in New England. Perhaps it may not now be ufed any where elfe ; but it was once a common Englifh word. Chaucer ufes it in the fenfe of *fecret*, *earneft*, &c.

> "THIS clerk was cleped Hende Nicholas
> Of *derne* love he could and of folas."
>   Mil. Tale, l. 3200.

> "YE moften be ful *derne* as in this cafe."
>   Ibm. 3297.

THE word is in common ufe in New England and pronounced *darn*. It has not however the fenfe it had formerly ; it is now ufed as an adverb to qualify an adjective, as *darn fweet* ; denoting a great degree of the quality.

THE New England people preferve the ancient ufe of *there* and *here* after a word or fentence, defignating the *place where* ; as *this here, that there.* It is called vulgar in Englifh ; and indeed the addition of *here* or *there* is generally tautological. It is however an ancient practice ; and the French retain it in the pure elegant language of their country ; *ce pays là, celui là, cet homme ici* ; where we obferve this difference only between the French and Englifh idioms, that in French, the adverb follows the noun, *that country there, this man here* ;

A a   whereas

whereas in Englifh, the adverb precedes the noun, *that there country, this here man.* This form of fpeech feems to have been coeval with the primitive Saxon, otherwife it would not have prevailed fo generally among the common people.

It has been before remarked that the word *ax* for *afk* was ufed in England, and even in the royal affent to acts of parliament, down to the reign of Henry VI.

> " And to her hufband bad hire for to fey
> If that he *axed* after Nicholas."——
> Chau. Mil. Tale, 3412.

> " This *axeth* hafte and of an haftif thing
> Men may not preche and maken tarying."
> Ibm. 3545.

This word to *ax* is ftill frequent in New England.

I do not know whether our American fportfmen ufe the word, *ferret,* in the fenfe of driving animals from their lurking places. But the word is ufed in fome parts of New England, and applied figuratively to many tranfactions in life. So in Congreve:

> " Where is this apocryphal elder ? I'll *ferret* him."
> ——Old Bach. act 4, fc. 21.

Sometimes, but rarely, we hear the old imperative of the Saxon *thafian,* now pronounced *thof.* But it is generally pronounced as it is written, *tho.* It is remarked by Horne, that *thof* is ftill frequent among the common people of England.

Gin or *gyn* for *given* is ftill ufed in America ; as Bifhop Wilkins remarks, it is in the North of England.

WITHOUT, in the fenfe of *unlefs,* is as frequent as any word in the language, and even among the learned.

It

It is commonly accounted inelegant, and writers have lately substituted *unless* : But I do not see the propriety of discarding *without*, for its meaning is exactly the same as that of *unless*. It is demonstrated that they are both the imperatives of old verbs. *Without*, is *be out, be a-way* ; and *unless* is *dismiss*, or *be apart*. Instead of the imperative Chaucer generally uses the participle, *withouten, being out*.

THE best writers use *without* in the sense of *unless*.

"—AND if he can't be cured *without* I suck the poison from his wounds, I'm afraid he won't recover his senses, till I lose mine."——Cong. Love for Love, act 4. sc. 3.

"'TWERE better for him, you had not been his confessor in that affair, *without* you could have kept his counsel closer."——Cong. Way of the World, act 3. sc. 7.

THE best speakers use the word in this manner, in common discourse, and I must think, with propriety.

PEEK is also used corruptedly for *peep*. By a similar change of the last consonant, *chirk* is used for *chirp*, *to make a cheerful noise*. This word is wholly lost, except in New England. It is there used for *comfortably, bravely, cheerful* ; as when one enquires about a sick person, it is said, he is *chirk*. *Chirp* is still used to express the singing of birds, but the *chirk* of New England is not understood, and therefore derided. Four hundred years ago it was a polite term.

> " AND kisseth hire swete, and *chirketh* as a sparwe
> With his lippes."——
> Chaucer; Somp. Tale, 7386.

IN the following it is used for a disagreeable noise.

> " ALL full of *chirking* was that sory place."
> Knight's Tale, 2006.

"AND

> " AND al fo ful eke of *chirkings*
> And of many other wirkings."
> Houfe of Fame, 858.

SHET for *fhut* is now become vulgar ; yet this is the true original orthography and pronunciation. It is from the Saxon *fcitten*, and I believe was always fpelt *fhette* or *fhet*, till after Chaucer's time, for he was a correct writer in his age, and always fpelt it in that manner.

> " VOIDETH your man and let him be thereout,
> And *fhet* the dore."——
> Chau. Yem. Tale, 16, 605.

> " AND his maifter *fhette* the dore anon."
> Ibm. 16, 610.

And in a variety of other places. This word is almoft univerfally pronounced *fhet* among all claffes of people, not only in New England, but in Great Britain and the fouthern ftates of America. How the fpelling came to be changed, is not known ; but it was certainly a corruption.

AN for *if* is feen in moft old authors. It remains among the common people, both in England and America. " *An* pleafe your honor;" that is, " *if* your honor pleafe." In New England, the phrafes in which it occurs moft frequently are, " Let him go, *an* he will;" " Go, *an* you will ;" and others of a fimilar kind.

BECAUSE and *becafe* were ufed promifcuoufly by our anceftors. *Becafe* is found in fome ancient writings, tho not fo frequently as *becaufe*. In New England, we frequently hear *becafe* to this day. It is pronounced *becaze*. It is a compound of *be* and *caufe* or *cafe* ; both of thefe words with the verb *be* make good Englifh ; but *becafe* is vulgar.

THE vulgar pronunciation of *fuch* is *fich*. This is but a fmall deviation from the ancient elegant pronunciation, which was *fwich* or *fwiche*, as the word is fpelt

in

in Chaucer. Such is the force of national practice : And altho the country people in New England, sometimes drawl their words in fpeaking, and, like their brethren, often make falfe concord, yet their idiom is purely Saxon or Englifh ; and in a vaft number of inftances, they have adhered to the true phrafes, where people, who defpife their plain manners, have run into error. Thus they fay, "a man is going *by*," and not *going paft*, which is nonfenfe : They fay, "I *purpofe* to go," and not *propofe* to go, which is not good Englifh. They fay, "a fhip *lies* in harbor," not *lays*, which is a modern corruption. They fay, "I *have* done," and never "I *am* done," which is nonfenfe. They fay, "it was *on* Monday evening," not "*of* a Monday evening," which is an error. They never ufe the abfurd phrafes "*expect it was*;" and "the fhip will fail in *all* next week." They never fay "he is home," but always, "at home." They ufe the old phrafe, "it is half *after* fix o'clock," which is more correct than *half paft fix*. They fay, if a perfon is not in health, he is *fick*. The modern Englifh laugh at them, becaufe the Englifh fay a man is *ill*; and confine fick to exprefs the idea of a naufea in the ftomach. The Englifh are wrong, and the New England people ufe the word in its true fenfe, which extends to all bodily diforders, as it is ufed by the pure Englifh writers. *Ill* is a contraction of *evil* ; and denotes a moral diforder. Its application to bodily complaints is a modern practice, and its meaning figurative. So that whatever improprieties may have crept into their practice of fpeaking, they actually preferve more of the genuin idiom of the Englifh tongue, than many of the modern fine fpeakers who fet up for ftandards.

[N, page 120.]

THE letters *ch* in Roman anfwered nearly to the Greek *ki* or *chi* ; for *c* had the found of *k*, at leaft before *a, o, u*. *Ch* or *kh* was therefore the proper combination for the Greek letter ; which had the found of *k* followed

by

by an aspirate. This combination was copied into our language; and perhaps the aspirate was once pronounced, like the Irish guttural in *Cochran*. But when the aspirate was lost, *k* became the proper representative of the sound. It is wished, that in all the derivatives from the ancient languages, where this character occurs, *k* might be substituted for *ch*; that persons unacquainted with etymology, might not mistake and give *ch* its English sound.

A N

E S S A Y

On the NECESSITY, ADVANTAGES *and* PRACTI-
CABILITY *of* REFORMING *the* MODE *of*
SPELLING, *and of* RENDERING *the* OR-
THOGRAPHY *of* WORDS CORRESPONDENT *to*
the PRONUNCIATION.

T' has been obſerved by all writers on the Engliſh language, that the orthography or ſpelling of words is very irregular ; the ſame letters often repreſenting different ſounds, and the ſame ſounds often expreſſ-ed by different letters. For this irregularity, two principal cauſes may be aſſigned :

1. THE changes to which the pronunciation of a language is liable, from the progreſs of ſcience and civ-ilization.

2. THE mixture of different languages, occaſioned by revolutions in England, or by a predilection of the learned, for words of foreign growth and ancient origin,

To

To the firſt cauſe, may be aſcribed the difference between the ſpelling and pronunciation of Saxon words,
The northern nations of Europe originally ſpoke much
in gutturals.   This is evident from the number of aſ-
pirates and guttural letters, which ſtill remain in the
orthography of words derived from thoſe nations ;
and from the modern pronunciation of the collateral
branches of the Teutonic, the Dutch, Scotch and German.   Thus *k* before *n* was once pronounced ; as in
knave, know ; the *gh* in *might, though, daughter*, and other ſimilar words ; the *g* in *reign, feign*, &c.

But as ſavages proceed in forming languages, they
loſe the guttural ſounds, in ſome meaſure, and adopt
the uſe of labials, and the more open vowels.   The
caſe of ſpeaking facilitates this progreſs, and the pronunciation of words is ſoftened, in proportion to a national refinement of manners.   This will account for
the difference between the ancient and modern languages of France, Spain and Italy ; and for the difference between the ſoft pronunciation of the preſent languages of thoſe countries, and the more harſh and guttural pronunciation of the northern inhabitants of Europe.

In this progreſs, the Engliſh have loſt the ſounds of
moſt of the guttural letters.   The *k* before *n* in *know*,
the *g* in *reign*, and in many other words, are become
mute in practice ; and the *gh* is ſoftened into the ſound
of *f*, as in *laugh*, or is ſilent, as in *brought*.

To this practice of ſoftening the ſounds of letters, or
wholly ſuppreſſing thoſe which are harſh and diſagreeable,
may be added a popular tendency to abbreviate words
of common uſe.   Thus *Southwark*, by a habit of quick
pronunciation, is become *Suthark* ; *Worceſter* and *Lei-
ceſter*, are become *Wooſter* and *Leſter* ; *buſineſs, bizneſs* ;
colonel, curnel ; *cannot, will not, cant, wont.** In this
manner

* *WONT* is ſtrictly a contraction of *woll net*, as the word was anciently pronounced.

manner the final *e* is not heard in many modern words, in which it formerly made a fyllable. The words *clothes*, *cares*, and moft others of the fame kind, were formerly pronounced in two fyllables.*

Of the other caufe of irregularity in the fpelling of our language, I have treated fufficiently in the firft Differtation. It is here neceffary only to remark, that when words have been introduced from a foreign language into the Englifh, they have generally retained the orthography of the original, however ill adapted to exprefs the Englifh pronunciation. Thus *fatigue, marine, chaife*, retain their French drefs, while, to reprefent the true pronunciation in Englifh, they fhould be fpelt *fateeg, mareen, fhaze*. Thus thro an ambition to exhibit the etymology of words, the Englifh, in *Philip, phyfic, character, chorus*, and other Greek derivatives, preferve the reprefentatives of the original Φ and X ; yet thefe words are pronounced, and ought ever to have been fpelt, *Fillip, fyzzic* or *fizzic, karacter, korus.*†

But fuch is the ftate of our language. The pronunciation of the words which are ftrictly *Englifh*, has been gradually changing for ages, and fince the revival of fcience in Europe, the language has received a vaft acceffion of words from other languages, many of which retain an orthography very ill fuited to exhibit the true pronunciation.

The queftion now occurs ; ought the Americans to retain thefe faults which produce innumerable inconveniencies

---

* "*TA-KE, ma-ke, o-ne, bo-ne, fto-ne, wil-le*, &c. diffyllaba olim fuerunt, quæ nunc habenter pro monofyllabis."——Wallis.

† The words *number, chamber*, and many others in Englifh are from the French *nombre, chambre*, &c. Why was the fpelling changed ? or rather why is the fpelling of *luftre, metre, theatre, not* changed ? The cafes are precifely fimilar. The Englifhman who firft wrote *number* for *nombre*, had no greater authority to make the change, than any modern writer has to fpell *luftre, metre* in a fimilar manner, *lufter, meter*. The change in the firft inftance was a valuable one ; it conformed the fpelling to the pronunciation, and I have taken the liberty, in all my writings, to purfue the principle in *lufter, meter, miter, theater, fepulcher*, &c.

conveniencies in the acquifition and ufe of the language, or ought they at once to reform thefe abufes,
and introduce order and regularity into the orthography of the AMERICAN TONGUE ?

LET us confider this fubject with fome attention.

SEVERAL attempts were formerly made in England to
rectify the orthography of the language.*   But 1 apprehend their fchemes failed of fuccefs, rather on account of their intrinfic difficulties, than on account of
any neceffary impracticability of a reform.   It was
propofed, in moft of thefe fchemes, not merely to throw
out fuperfluous and filent letters, but to introduce a number of new characters. Any attempt on fuch a plan muft
undoubtedly prove unfuccefsful.   It is not to be expected that an orthography, perfectly regular and fimple,
fuch as would be formed by a " Synod of Grammarians on principles of fcience," will ever be fubftituted
for that confufed mode of fpelling which is now eftablifhed.   But it is apprehended that great improvements
may be made, and an orthography almoft regular, or
fuch as fhall obviate moft of the prefent difficulties
which occur in learning our language, may be introduced and eftablifhed with little trouble and oppofition.

THE principal alterations, neceffary to render our
orthography fufficiently regular and eafy, are thefe :

1. THE omiffion of all fuperfluous or filent letters ;
as *a* in *bread.*   Thus *bread, head, give, breaft, built,
meant, realm, friend,* would be fpelt, *bred, hed, giv, breft,
bilt, ment, relm, frend.* Would this alteration produce any
inconvenience, any embarraffment or expenfe ? By no
means.

<hr>

* THE firft by Sir Thomas Smith, fecretary of ftate to Queen Elizabeth : Another by Dr. Gill, a celebrated mafter of St. Paul's fchool in
London : Another by Mr. Charles Butler, who went fo far as to print his
book in his propofed orthography : Several in the time of Charles the
firft ; and in the prefent age, Mr. Elphinftone has publifhed a treatife
in a very ridiculous orthography.

means. On the other hand, it would leſſen the trouble of writing, and much more, of learning the language; it would reduce the true pronunciation to a certainty; and while it would aſſiſt foreigners and our own children in acquiring the language, it would render the pronunciation uniform, in different parts of the country, and almoſt prevent the poſſibility of changes.

2. A SUBSTITUTION of a character that has a certain definite ſound, for one that is more vague and indeterminate. Thus by putting *ee* inſtead of *ea* or *ie*, the words *mean, near, ſpeak, grieve, zeal,* would become *meen, neer, ſpeek, greev, zeel.* This alteration could not occaſion a moments trouble; at the ſame time it would prevent a doubt reſpecting the pronunciation; whereas the *ea* and *ie* having different ſounds, may give a learner much difficulty. Thus *greef* ſhould be ſubſtituted for *grief*; *kee* for *key*; *beleev* for *believe*; *laf* for *laugh*; *dawter* for *daughter*; *plow* for *plough*; *tuf* for *tough*; *proov* for *prove*; *blud* for *blood*; and *draft* for *draught.* In this manner *ch* in Greek derivatives, ſhould be changed into *k*; for the Engliſh *ch* has a ſoft ſound, as in *cheriſh*; but *k* always a hard ſound. Therefore *character, chorus, cholic, architecture,* ſhould be written *karacter, korus, kolic, arkitecture*; and were they thus written, no perſon could miſtake their true pronunciation.

THUS *ch* in French derivatives ſhould be changed into *ſh*; *machine, chaiſe, chevalier,* ſhould be written *maſheen, ſhaze, ſhevaleer*; and *pique, tour, oblique,* ſhould be written *peek, toor, obleek.*

3. A TRIFLING alteration in a character, or the addition of a point would diſtinguiſh different ſounds, without the ſubſtitution of a new character. Thus a very ſmall ſtroke acroſs *th* would diſtinguiſh its two ſounds. A point over a vowel, in this manner, *ȧ,* or *ȯ,* or *ī,* might anſwer all the purpoſes of different letters. And for the dipthong *ow,* let the two letters be

united

united by a fmall ftroke, or both engraven on the fame piece of metal, with the left hand line of the *w* united to the *o*.

THESE, with a few other inconfiderable alterations, would anfwer every purpofe, and render the orthography fufficiently correct and regular.

THE advantages to be derived from thefe alterations are numerous, great and permanent.

1. THE fimplicity of the orthography would facilitate the learning of the language. It is now the work of years for children to learn to fpell ; and after all, the bufinefs is rarely accomplifhed. A few men, who are bred to fome bufinefs that requires conftant exercife in writing, finally learn to fpell moft words without hefitation ; but moft people remain, all their lives, imperfect mafters of fpelling, and liable to make miftakes, whenever they take up a pen to write a fhort note. Nay, many people, even of education and fafhion, never attempt to write a letter, without frequently confulting a dictionary.

BUT with the propofed orthography, a child would learn to fpell, without trouble, in a very fhort time, and the orthography being very regular, he would ever afterwards find it difficult to make a miftake. It would, in that cafe, be as difficult to fpell *wrong*, as it is now to fpell *right*.

BESIDES this advantage, foreigners would be able to acquire the pronunciation of Englifh, which is now fo difficult and embarraffing, that they are either wholly difcouraged on the firft attempt, or obliged, after many years labor, to reft contented with an imperfect knowlege of the fubject.

2. A CORRECT orthography would render the pronunciation of the language, as uniform as the fpelling

in books.   A general uniformity thro the United States, would be the event of such a reformation as I am here recommending.   All perfons, of every rank, would fpeak with fome degree of precifion and uniformity.*   Such a uniformity in thefe ftates is very defireable ; it would remove prejudice, and conciliate mutual affection and refpect.

3. Such a reform would diminifh the number of letters about one fixteenth or eighteenth.   This would fave a page in eighteen ; and a faving of an eighteenth in the expenfe of books, is an advantage that fhould not be overlooked.

4. But a capital advantage of this reform in thefe ftates would be, that it would make a difference between the Englifh orthography and the American. This will ftartle thofe who have not attended to the fubject ; but I am confident that fuch an event is an object of vaft political confequence.   For,

The alteration, however fmall, would encourage the publication of books in our own country.   It would render it, in fome meafure, neceffary that all books fhould be printed in America.   The Englifh would never copy our orthography for their own ufe ; and confequently the fame impreffions of books would not anfwer for both countries.   The inhabitants of the prefent generation would read the Englifh impreffions ; but pofterity, being taught a different fpelling, would prefer the American orthography.

Besides this, a *national language* is a band of *national union*.   Every engine fhould be employed to render the people of this country *national* ; to call their attachments home to their own country ; and to infpire them with the pride of national character.   However

ever

* I once heard Dr. Franklin remark, " that thofe people fpell beft, who do not know how to fpell ;" that is, they fpell as their ears dictate, without being guided by rules, and thus fall into a regular orthography.

ever they may boaſt of Independence, and the freedom of their government, yet their *opinions* are not ſufficiently independent ; an aſtoniſhing reſpect for the arts and literature of their parent country, and a blind imitation of its manners, are ſtill prevalent among the Americans. Thus an habitual reſpect for another country, deſerved indeed and once laudable, turns their attention from their own intereſts, and prevents their reſpecting themſelves.

OBJECTIONS.

1. " THIS reform of the Alphabet would oblige people to relearn the language, or it could not be introduced."

BUT the alterations propoſed are ſo few and ſo ſimple, that an hour's attention would enable any perſon to read the new orthography with facility ; and a week's practice would render it ſo familiar, that a perſon would write it without heſitation or miſtake. Would this ſmall inconvenience prevent its adoption ? Would not the numerous national and literary advantages, reſulting from the change, induce Americans to make ſo inconſiderable a ſacrifice of time and attention ? I am perſuaded they would.

BUT it would not be neceſſary that men advanced beyond the middle ſtage of life, ſhould be at the pains to learn the propoſed orthography. They would, without inconvenience, continue to uſe the preſent. They would read the *new* orthography, without difficulty ; but they would write in the *old*. To men thus advanced, and even to the preſent generation in general, if they ſhould not wiſh to trouble themſelves with a change, the reformation would be almoſt a matter of indifference. It would be ſufficient that children ſhould be taught the new orthography, and that as faſt as they come upon the ſtage, they ſhould be furniſhed

with

with books in the American fpelling. The progrefs of printing would be proportioned to the demand for books among the rifing generation. This progreffive introduction of the fcheme would be extremely eafy; children would learn the propofed orthography more eafily than they would the old; and the prefent gener- ation would not be troubled with the change; fo that none but the obftinate and capricious could raife ob- jections or make any oppofition. The change would be fo inconfiderable, and made on fuch fimple princi- ples, that a column in each newfpaper, printed in the new fpelling, would in fix months, familiarize moft people to the change, fhow the advantages of it, and imperceptibly remove their objections. The only fteps neceffary to enfure fuccefs in the attempt to introduce this reform, would be, a refolution of Congrefs, order- ing all their acts to be engroffed in the new orthogra- phy, and recommending the plan to the feveral univer- fities in America; and alfo a refolution of the univerfi- ties to encourage and fupport it. The printers would begin the reformation by publifhing fhort paragraphs and fmall tracts in the new orthography; fchool books would firft be publifhed in the fame; curiofity would excite attention to it, and men would be gradually rec- onciled to the plan.

2. "This change would render our prefent books ufelefs."

This objection is, in fome meafure, anfwered under the foregoing head. The truth is, it would not have this effect. — The difference of orthography would not render books printed in one, illegible to perfons ac- quainted only with the other. The difference would not be fo great as between the orthography of Chaucer, and of the prefent age; yet Chaucer's works are ftill read with eafe.

3. "This reformation would injure the language by obfcuring etymology."

This

THIS objection is unfounded.   In general, it is not true that the change would obfcure etymology ; in a few inftances, it might ; but it would rather reftore the etymology of many words ; and if it were true that the change would obfcure it, this would be no objection to the reformation.

IT will perhaps furprize my readers to be told that, in many particular words, the modern fpelling is lefs correct than the ancient.   Yet this is a truth that reflects dishonor on our modern refiners of the language. Chaucer, four hundred years ago, wrote *bilder* for *builder* ; *dedly* for *deadly* ; *erneft* for *earneft* ; *erly* for *early* ; *breft* for *breaft* ; *hed* for *head* ; and certainly his fpelling was the moft agreeable to the pronunciation.*   Sidney wrote *bin, examin, futable*, with perfect propriety.   Dr. Middleton wrote *explane, genuin, revele*, which is the moft eafy and correct orthography of fuch words ; and alfo *lufter, theater*, for *luftre, theatre*.   In thefe and many other inftances, the modern fpelling is a corruption ; fo that allowing many improvements to have been made in orthography, within a century or two, we muft acknowlege alfo that many corruptions have been introduced.

IN anfwer to the objection, that a change of orthography would obfcure etymology, I would remark, that the etymology of moft words is already loft, even to the learned ; and to the unlearned, etymology is never known.   Where is the man that can trace back our Englifh words to the elementary radicals ?   In a few inftances, the ftudent has been able to reach the primitive roots of words ; but I prefume the radicals of one tenth of the words in our language, have never yet been difcovered, even by Junius, Skinner, or any other etymologift.   Any man may look into Johnfon or Afh, and find that *flefh* is derived from the Saxon *floce* ; *child* from *cild* ; *flood* from *flod* ; *lad* from *leode* ; and *loaf*
from

---

* In Chaucer's life, prefixed to the edition of his works 1602, I find *move* and *prove* fpelt almoft correctly, *moove* and *proove*.

from *laf* or *hlaf*. But this difcovery will anfwer no other purpofe, than to fhow, that within a few hundred years, the fpelling of fome words has been a little changed : We fhould ftill be at a vaft diftance from the primitive roots.

In many inftances indeed etymology will affift the learned in underftanding the compofition and true fenfe of a word; and it throws much light upon the progrefs of language. But the true fenfe of a complex term is not always, nor generally, to be learnt from the fenfe of the primitives or elementary words. The current meaning of a word depends on its ufe in a nation. This true fenfe is to be obtained by attending to good authors, to dictionaries and to practice, rather than to derivation. The former *muft* be *right* ; the latter *may* lead us into *error*.

But to prove of how little confequence a knowlege of etymology is to moft people, let me mention a few words. The word *fincere* is derived from the Latin, *fine cera*, without wax ; and thus it came to denote *purity of mind*. I am confident that not a man in a thoufand ever fufpected this to be the origin of the word ; yet all men, that have any knowlege of our language, ufe the word in its true fenfe, and underftand its cuftomary meaning, as well as Junius did, or any other etymologift.

YEA or *yes* is derived from the imperative of a verb, *avoir* to have, as the word is now fpelt. It fignifies therefore *have*, or *poffefs*, or *take* what you afk. But does this explication affift us in ufing the word ? And does not every countryman who labors in the field, underftand and ufe the word with as much precifion as the profoundeft philofophers ?

The word *temper* is derived from an old root, *tem*, which fignified *water*. It was borrowed from the act of *cooling*, or moderating heat. Hence the meaning of

B b

temperate,

temperate, *temperance*, and all the ramifications of the o-
riginal stock. But does this help us to the modern
current sense of these words ? By no means. It leads
us to understand the formation of languages, and in
what manner an idea of a visible action gives rise to a
correspondent abstract idea ; or rather, how a word,
from a literal and direct sense, may be applied to express a variety of figurative and collateral ideas. Yet
the customary sense of the word is known by practice,
and as well understood by an illiterate man of tolerable
capacity, as by men of science.

THE word *always* is compounded of *all* and *ways* ;
it had originally no reference to time ; and the etymology or composition of the word would only lead
us into error. The true meaning of words is that
which a nation in general annex to them. Etymology
therefore is of no use but to the learned ; and for them
it will still be preserved, so far as it is now understood,
in dictionaries and other books that treat of this particular subject.

4. "THE distinction between words of different
meanings and similar sound would be destroyed."

"THAT distinction," to answer in the words of the
great Franklin, " is already destroyed in pronunciation."
Does not every man pronounce *all* and *awl* precisely
alike ? And does the sameness of sound ever lead a
hearer into a mistake ? Does not the construction render the distinction easy and intelligible, the moment
the words of the sentence are heard ? Is the word
knew ever mistaken for *new*, even in the rapidity of
pronouncing an animated oration ? Was *peace* ever
mistaken for *piece* ; *pray* for *prey* ; *flour* for *flower* ?
Never, I presume, is this similarity of sound the occasion of mistakes.

IF therefore an identity of *sound*, even in rapid speaking, produces no inconvenience, how much less would

an

an identity of *spelling*, when the eye would have leisure to survey the construction ? But experience, the criterion of truth, which has removed the objection in the first case, will also assist us in forming our opinion in the last.

THERE are many words in our language which, with the *same orthography*, have *two* or more *distinct meanings*. The word *wind*, whether it signifies *to move round*, or *air in motion*, has the *same spelling* ; it exhibits no distinction to the *eye* of a silent reader ; and yet its meaning is never mistaken. The construction shows at sight in which sense the word is to be understood. *Hail* is used as an expression of joy, or to signify frozen drops of water, falling from the clouds. *Rear* is to raise up, or it signifies the hinder part of an army. *Lot* signifies fortune or destiny ; a plat of ground ; or a certain proportion or share ; and yet does this diversity, this contrariety of meanings ever occasion the least difficulty in the ordinary language of books ? It cannot be maintained. This diversity is found in all languages ;* and altho it may be considered as a defect, and occasion some trouble for foreign learners, yet to natives it produces no sensible inconvenience.

·5. "IT is idle to conform the orthography of words to the pronunciation, because the latter is continually changing."

THIS is one of Dr. Johnson's objections, and it is very unworthy of his judgement. So far is this circumstance from being a real objection, that it is alone a sufficient reason for the change of spelling. On his principle of *fixing the orthography*, while the *pronunciation is changing*, any *spoken language* must, in time, lose all relation to the *written language* ; that is, the sounds of words would have no affinity with the letters that compose

pose

---

* In the Roman language *liber* had four or five different meanings ; it signified *free, the inward bark of a tree, a book,* sometimes *an epistle,* and also *generous.*

B b 2

pofe them.   In fome inftances, this is now the cafe ; and no mortal would fufpect from the fpelling, that *neighbour*, *wrought*, are pronounced *nabur*, *rawt*.   On this principle, Dr. Johnfon ought to have gone back fome centuries, and given us, in his dictionary, the primitive Saxon orthography, *wol* for *will* ; *ydilneffe* for *idlenefs* ; *eyen* for *eyes* ; *eche* for *each*, &c.   Nay, he fhould have gone as far as poffible into antiquity, and, regardlefs of the changes of pronunciation, given us the primitive radical language in its purity.   Happily for the language, that doctrine did not prevail till his time ; the fpelling of words changed with the pronunciation ; to thefe changes we are indebted for numberlefs improvements ; and it is hoped that the progrefs of them, in conformity with the national practice of fpeaking, will not be obftructed by the erroneous opinion, even of Dr. Johnfon.   How much more rational is the opinion of Dr. Franklin, who fays, " the orthography of our language began to be fixed too foon."   If the pronunciation muft vary, from age to age, (and fome trifling changes of language will always be taking place) common fenfe would dictate a correfpondent change of fpelling.   Admit Johnfon's principles ; take his pedantic orthography for the ftandard ; let it be clofely adhered to in future ; and the flow changes in the pronunciation of our national tongue, will in time make as great a difference between our *written* and *fpoken* language, as there is between the pronunciation of the prefent Englifh and German.   The *fpelling* will be no more a guide to the pronunciation, than the orthography of the German or Greek.   This event is actually taking place, in confequence of the ftupid opinion, advanced by Johnfon and other writers, and generally embraced by the nation.

All thefe objections appear to me of very inconfiderable weight, when oppofed to the great, fubftantial and permanent advantages to be derived from a regular national orthography.

Sensible

SENSIBLE I am how much eafier it is to *propofe* improvements, than to *introduce* them. Every thing new ftarts the idea of difficulty; and yet it is often mere novelty that excites the appearance; for on a flight examination of the propofal, the difficulty vanifhes. When we firmly *believe* a fcheme to be practicable, the work is *half* accomplifhed. We are more frequently deterred by fear from making an attack, than repulfed in the encounter.

HABIT alfo is oppofed to changes; for it renders even our errors dear to us. Having furmounted all difficulties in childhood, we forget the labor, the fatigue, and the perplexity we fuffered in the attempt, and imagin the progrefs of our ftudies to have been fmooth and eafy.* What feems intrinfically right, is fo merely thro habit.

INDOLENCE is another obftacle to improvements. The moft arduous talk a reformer has to execute, is to make people *think*; to roufe them from that lethargy, which, like the mantle of fleep, covers them in repofe and contentment.

BUT America is in a fituation the moft favorable for great reformations; and the prefent time is, in a fingular degree, aufpicious. The minds of men in this country have been awakened. New fcenes have been, for many years, prefenting new occafions for exertion; unexpected diftreffes have called forth the powers of invention; and the application of new expedients has demanded every poffible exercife of wifdom and talents. Attention is roufed; the mind expanded; and the intellectual

* THUS moft people fuppofe the prefent mode of fpelling to be really the *eafieft* and *beft*. This opinion is derived from habit; the new mode of fpelling propofed would fave three fourths of the labor now beftowed in learning to write our language. A child would learn to fpell as well in one year, as he can now in four. This is not a fuppofition—it is an affertion capable of proof; and yet people, never knowing, or having forgot the labor of learning, fuppofe the prefent mode to be the eafieft. No perfon, but one who has taught children, has any idea of the difficulty of learning to fpell and pronounce our language in its prefent form.

telletual faculties invigorated.   Here men are prepared
to receive improvements, which would be rejected by
nations, whofe habits have not been fhaken by fimilar
events.

NOW is the time, and *this* the country, in which we
may expect fuccefs, in attempting changes favorable to
language, fcience and government.   Delay, in the plan
here propofed, may be fatal ; under a tranquil general
government, the minds of men may again fink into indolence ; a national acquiefcence in error will follow ;
and pofterity be doomed to ftruggle with difficulties,
which time and accident will perpetually multiply.

LET us then feize the prefent moment, and eftablifh
a *national language*, as well as a national government.
Let us remember that there is a certain refpect due to
the opinions of other nations.   As an independent
people, our reputation abroad demands that, in all
things, we fhould be federal ; be *national* ; for if we
do not refpect *ourfelves*, we may be affured that *other
nations* will not refpect us.   In fhort, let it be impreffed
upon the mind of every American, that to neglect the
means of commanding refpect abroad, is treafon againft
the character and dignity of a brave independent
people.

To excite the more attention to this fubject, I will
here fubjoin what Dr. Franklin has done and written
to effect a reform in our mode of fpelling.   This fage
philofopher has fuffered nothing ufeful to efcape his
notice.   He very early difcovered the difficulties that
attend the learning of our language ; and with his u-
fual ingenuity, invented a plan to obviate them.   If any
objection can be made to his fcheme,* it is the fubftitution of *new* characters, for *th*, *fh*, *ng*, &c. whereas a
fmall ftroke, connecting the letters, would anfwer all
the purpofes of new characters ; as thefe combinations
would thus become fingle letters, with precife definite
founds and fuitable names.

A

* SEE his Mifcellaneous Works. p. 470. Ed. Lond. 1779.

A SPECIMEN of the Doctor's spelling cannot be here given, as I have not the proper types ;* but the arguments in favor of a reformed mode of spelling shall be given in his own words.

COPY of a Letter from Miss S——, to Dr. FRANKLIN, who had sent her his Scheme of a Reformed Alphabet. Dated, Kensington (England) Sept. 26, 1768.

DEAR SIR,

I HAVE transcribed your alphabet, &c. which I think might be of service to those who wish to acquire an accurate pronunciation, if that could be fixed ; but I see many inconveniences, as well as difficulties, that would attend the bringing your letters and orthogrphy into common use. All our etymologies would be lost ; consequently we could not ascertain the meaning of many words ; the distinction too between words of *different meaning* and *similar* found would be useless,† unless we living writers publish new editions. In short, I believe we must let people spell on in their old way, and (as we find it easiest) do the same ourselves.——With ease and with sincerity I can, in the old way, subscribe myself,

Dear Sir,

Your faithful and affectionate Servant,

M. S.

Dr. Franklin.

Dr.

* THIS indefatigable gentleman, amidst all his other employments, public and private, has compiled a Dictionary on his scheme of a Reform, and procured types to be cast for printing it. He thinks himself too old to pursue the plan ; but has honored me with the offer of the manuscript and types, and expressed a strong desire that I should undertake the task. Whether this project, so deeply interesting to this country, will ever be effected ; or whether it will be defeated by indolence and prejudice, remains for my countrymen to determine.

† THIS lady overlooked the other side of the question ; viz. that by a reform of the spelling, words now spelt alike and pronounced differently, would be distinguished by their letters ; for the nouns *abuse* and *use* would be distinguished from the verbs, which would be spelt *abuze, yuze* ; and so in many instances. See the answer below.

Dr. FRANKLIN's *Anfwer to Mifs* S——.

DEAR MADAM,

THE objection you make to rectifying our alphabet, "that it will be attended with inconveniences and difficulties," is a very natural one; for it always occurs when any reformation is propofed, whether in religion, government, laws, and even down as low as roads and wheel carriages. The true queftion then is not, whether there will be no difficulties or inconveniences; but whether the difficulties may not be furmounted; and whether the conveniences will not, on the whole, be greater than the inconveniences. In this cafe, the difficulties are only in the beginning of the practice; when they are once overcome, the advantages are lafting. To either you or me, who fpell well in the prefent mode, I imagin the difficulty of changing that mode for the new, is not fo great, but that we might perfectly get over it in a week's writing. As to thofe who do not fpell well, if the two difficulties are compared, viz. that of teaching them true fpelling in the prefent mode, and that of teaching them the new alphabet and the new fpelling according to it, I am confident that the latter would be by far the leaft. They naturally fall into the new method already, as much as the imperfection of their alphabet will admit of; their prefent *bad* fpelling is only bad, becaufe contrary to the prefent *bad* rules; under the new rules it would be *good*.* The difficulty of learning to fpell well in the old way is fo great, that few attain it; thoufands and thoufands writing on to old age, without ever being able to acquire it. It is befides, a difficulty continually increafing;† as the found gradually varies more and more from the fpelling; and to foreigners it makes the learning to pronounce our language, as written in our books, almoft impoffible.

Now

---

* THIS remark of the Doctor is very juft and obvious. A countryman writes *aker* or *akur* for *acre*; yet the countryman is *right*, as the word *ought* to be fpelt; and we laugh at him only becaufe *we* are accuftomed to be *wrong*.

† THIS is a fact of vaft confequence.

Now as to the inconveniences you mention : The first is, "that all our etymologies would be lost ; consequently we could not ascertain the meaning of many words." Etymologies are at present very uncertain ; but such as they are, the old books still preserve them, and etymologists would there find them. Words in the course of time, change their meaning, as well as their spelling and pronunciation ; and we do not look to etymologies for their present meanings. If I should call a man a *knave* and a *villain*, he would hardly be satisfied with my telling him, that one of the words originally signified a *lad* or *servant*, and the other an under *plowman*, or the inhabitant of a village. It is from present usage only, the meaning of words is to be determined.

Your second inconvenience is, "the distinction between words of different meaning and similar sound would be destroyed." That distinction is already destroyed in pronouncing them ; and we rely on the sense alone of the sentence to ascertain which of the several words, similar in sound, we intend. If this is sufficient in the rapidity of discourse, it will be much more so in written sentences, which may be read leisurely, and attended to more particularly in case of difficulty, than we can attend to a past sentence, while the speaker is hurrying us along with new ones.

Your third inconvenience is, "that all the books already written would be useless." This inconvenience would only come on gradually in a course of ages. I and you and other now living readers would hardly forget the use of them. People would long learn to read the old writing, tho they practised the new. And the inconvenience is not greater than what has actually happened in a similar case in Italy. Formerly its inhabitants all spoke and wrote Latin ; as the language changed, the spelling followed it. It is true that at present, a mere unlearned Italian cannot read the Latin books, tho they are still read and understood by many.

But

But if the ſpelling had never been changed, he would now have found it much more difficult to read and write his own language ;* for written words would have had no relation to ſounds ; they would only have ſtood for things ; ſo that if he would expreſs in writing the idea he has when he ſounds the word *Veſcovo*, he muſt uſe the letters *Epiſcopus*.†

In ſhort, whatever the difficulties and inconveniences now are, they will be more eaſily ſurmounted now, than hereafter ; and ſome time or other it muſt be done, or our writing will become the ſame with the Chineſe, as to the difficulty of learning and uſing it.   And it would already have been ſuch, if we had continued the Saxon ſpelling and writing uſed by our forefathers.

I am, my dear friend,

Your's affectionately,

B. FRANKLIN.

London, Craven Street, Sept. 28, 1768.

* That is, if the language had retained the old *Roman* ſpelling, and been pronounced as the modern *Italian*. This is a fair ſtate of facts, and a complete anſwer to all objections to a reform of ſpelling.

† In the ſame ridiculous manner, as *we* write, *rcugb, ſtill, neighbor, wrong, tongue, true, rhetoric*, &c. and yet pronounce the words, *ruf, ſtil, nabur, rong, tung, tru, retoric.*